What The Hell's Wrong With America

What The Hell's Wrong With America

(Hint: It Ain't Race)
2015-2017 The Evil Years

Dr. Lune A. Teek

CONTENTS

FOREWORD

It wasn't supposed to take this long. It wasn't supposed to take this long and it really didn't have to. But it did. And it's not my fault.

This book took entirely too damn long to write and too damn long to publish. But it's okay now. It's finished. It's now in your hands. You have within your grasp the original, unbiased, unabridged, opinionated ravings of a Class 1, Grade A lunatic. But not just any Class 1, Grade A lunatic. I am the Class 1-iest, Grade A-iest of all Class 1, Grade A lunatics. And this is a part of American life as I see it.

What The Hell's Wrong With America could be viewed as a question and an assertion. When viewed from the context of personal inquiry based on personal observation the answer is and always will remain the sometimes myopic assertion(s) of the observer ("Something *is* wrong with America") until the assertions are proven. Then the assertion(s) cease to be questionable and instead becomes statement(s) of truth; said statement(s) beginning with the demonstrative pronoun and definitive article "THAT" ("That is what's wrong with America"). Everyone got a good example of this back and forth during the 2016 Presidential campaign. Donald Trump's slogan of "Make America Great Again" presupposes that at one time it was but now it's not. Hillary Clinton, in her opposition to his assertion, stated that America *is* great and there is nothing at all wrong with America. Both affirmations, when viewed from the perceptions of each carry certain presumptions that can either be proven as truth or falsehood and the outside observer should carefully note that these assertions are backed by facts as the candidates themselves views them. Note: There are some things however, that empirical observation alone will inform you that either their initial premise holds promise, or it needs to fill unused space in a garbage can. The title of this book is the supposition of its author. Whether or not its contents support the premise of the author (The author is a Class 1, Grade A lunatic), or the title stands as truth (Something is damn wrong with America) will and should be the determination of you, the reader. Be assured of one thing, however. The only way that one can arrive at the truth to the question the title purposes is when one fully acknowledges, understands, then accepts the truth the subtitle imposes. Is America divided, as most commentaries suggest? Is it "race" that is dividing America, as most commentaries suggest? The author's answer to the first question is an emphatic "yes". The author's answer concerning the second question is an emphatic "no". This author's contention is that the citizens of America as well as those who are not citizens of America but think they are have been and still are being psychologically moved by an invented meme called "race". Case in point: Do you, reader, know what factor(s) determines one's race? Do you know how many "races" there are? When, how, and where did this concept called "race" first come into existence? When, how and where did this concept called "race" enter the consciousness of man? What were the plans/objectives of the originators of this concept called "race"? Is a "racist" the same as a "bigot"? If not, what are the differences? If so, what are the similarities? The context of this word is in question.

It never ceases to amaze me how gullible the "American People" can be when something is handed to them by those whom they view as "authority". I used to be that way. Boy, was I dumb.

Who handed you your conception of this word called "race"? How do you know if what you were told was true? Did you at any time after you ingested this information question it? Did you do any independent research/study on the subject? Did you ever stop to consider that EVERYTHING has an origin, including the concepts of social existence and that NOTHING exists without reason as well as a reason? Did you ever consider questioning the reasoning behind why humanity had to be divided into what are now considered by this author as socio/political/legal constructs; namely "black", "white", "Asian", "Indian/Native American", "Hispanic", etc.?

If you don't know the *truth* behind the questions I just literated it means that you can't understand the subject matter ("race"). If you don't know nor understand the subject matter that most commentaries that you've ingested say that is dividing America ("race"), then it will be impossible for you to grasp the author's contention as stated by the subtitle of this book. This is a problem. Why? Because you will be acting on assumptions that you don't have a clue as to if they are real/truth or falsehoods. I liken this behavior to when Stevie Wonder tells you that "if you believe in things that you don't understand you're a sucker." You also have the capacity to be a cause of the very division that you think divides America. There is also something else to consider. Ponder it closely.

When you hear commentators (news people, authors, talk show hosts, etc.) say that "America is divided", what enters your brain? I'll tell you what. Most likely whatever these commentators postulate that is dividing America is what you will either seriously consider or agree to. But what are they re*ally* saying?

"America" is a landmass situated between two bodies of water. America can't do or be anything other than whatever a landmass can do or be. When it is said "America is divided" they are not referring to America the landmass. They are referring to you.

Why are you divided? What are you divided about? When was the last time that you weren't divided? Has it ever been a time when you were not divided?

The same context the above-mentioned commentators spoke/wrote about "America" in is the same context this author is using in the title of this book, to wit:

"What The Hell's Wrong With America?"
"What The Hell's Wrong With *You*?"

What in the hell *is* wrong with you?

I'm asking a lot of questions, aren't I?

You ain't seen nothing yet.

This book is designed to challenge some of your core beliefs, some of which deal with your very existence. You've been told some things. No. You've been told some lies. You have formed some of your core beliefs about your very existence based on these lies. Some of those lies that you have ingested have you seeing boogey men where none exist. One such boogey man is "racism".

Boogey men, such as they are, are the result of a belief in the unknown. Such is the case here. This book, while not telling you what to think or believe, does attempt to do what it can to arouse your interest enough so that you won't be afraid to face said boogey man: race. Your biggest challenge, reader, is to chase that boogey man right back to the recesses of the hell that it came from:

Your mind.

This is not a technical book slammed packed to the gills with technical data nor was it meant to be, I, as the author am letting you, the reader into my mind (the mind of a lunatic mind you) for a look at how I view this issue. I will let you investigate the veracity of what follows. Hopefully, you will do your due diligence here and like any good investigator "let the facts (evidence) take you where they may." Trust me. Of this I am not afraid. Don't you be either.

The chapters of this book appear as they are for a reason. Like any book each chapter's subject matter builds upon the previous chapter even if the chapter's title doesn't look like it.

As this book is a look into my mind as it relates to this subject, I take what is written personally. Right or wrong, correct or incorrect, the issues written about here should be taken personally by everyone. Some of you will enjoy this book immensely. Some of you will think it's garbage. Regardless of which view you take, all I want you to do is to reconsider how we, as a country, are perceiving, thus treating each other. One does proceed from the other, you know. On that note -

Shall we begin?

Dr. Lune A. Teck
October 31, 2017

The First Section

In The Beginning

Chapter One

This Book. Why?

Physician, heal thyself
>> Luke 4:19-23
>> Holy Bible (KJV)

The people of the world are hurting. They are hurting because their souls can find no rest, therefore their bodies and minds are in an agitated state. They have no idea from whence their problems and sorrows come. All they know is that they can find no solutions to their problems, nor can they find solace for their sorrows. It seems to them that they climb one mountain only to find they have to climb another, only bigger. Cross one river only to find they have to cross another, only wider. Why is this? How is it that the people of the world can find no solutions, solace, or peace in the world? Why is it that the only peaceful places on this planet are where modern man is not? Could it be that modern man forgot how to heal himself? Could it be that he is so busy looking for the cure to his sickness outside of himself that he dies trying to find it? If the words "Physician, heal thyself" were either written or spoken then the concept was known. So, what happened?

Everyone is trying to find answers. The problem with this strategy is that it loses sight of the fact that oftentimes an answer is only the first step to a solution. Because most people don't know that an answer and a solution are two different things, they attempt to apply answers to problems that require solutions and when the issues that brought forth the problem(s) resurfaces they become angry, frustrated, and subject themselves to behavior, that is psychotic at best and suicidal at worst. Those who survive the hell where they are attempt one last heroic push in an effort to find heaven elsewhere. All too often that "elsewhere" is a little slice of land called America. If I, you, we could only get to America, everything will be all right. I, you, we will have milk and honey because that's what the land of America is. We'll have a chicken for every pot and a pot for every chicken. We'll all hold hands and sing songs because in America, everything is beautiful and melodic. Or is it?

While it is not remotely debatable in this Authors' mind that America is the greatest piece of real estate to land on in this Monopoly board most people call "the planet", I don't think it's the heaven where you'll find God in a recliner with a glass of Sherry in one hand and a big, fat one in the other. The Author, yes. God, no. But that's just one part of the story.

The subtitle of this book, "Hint: IT AIN'T RACE", is just the author's way of saying that those who cling to this delusion like Linus clinging to his blanket are greatly lending to the issue of "What's The Hell's Wrong W ith America". And a delusion it is and a security blanket it has become for a lot of people who don't have a clue as to what the hell is wrong with America. Racism has become the catch all reason for whatever the ails of society happen to be for that day and if racism is obviously not the cause those who point this out are quickly and vehemently labled as "Racists". There is a reason for this and while the Author may in fact be a Class 1, Grade A lunatic, stupid this Author is not and it would be stupid indeed to postulate that bigotry does not exist in the minds of *some* of the citizenry of America, both "black" and "white" and that these sentiments do not cause damage. In some cases, irreparable damage. However, the quote is "a chicken for every pot", not "a racist in every plot," so one must be able to define situational challenges as carefully, critically, and precisely as possible. That is what the essence of this book is dedicated to. As you read this book hopefully you will begin to understand the Author's rationale. There is something wrong with America because there is something(s) wrong with you. Understand that "America" is a landmass. It's dirt and water. In a profound sense, it is you and me. We are America. However, "we" (No, *you*) aren't acting like it. Why? Because you have been fed and are continuing to be fed a meme that is "fake". As this book unfolds you will see this meme unfold. Hopefully, you'll recognize this meme as the lie that it is. Hopefully, you'll see your continued belief in it as a problem. As such hopefully you will start to provide your own solutions to this problem. The subjects outlined in this book relates to both "black" and "white" people and the issues they face in America. It starts with problem solving and the importance of having good problem-solving skills. *It does not tell you how to solve problems.* It is a book relating to the presented subject matter *as the Author sees it.* Hopefully, if the book (meaning the Author) does its job it will provoke you to THINK. And if I can get you to think you just might save yourself (and America). If I can get you to think you just might heal yourself (and America). Think about it. As Donald Trump told "black" America, "What have you got to lose?"

This book is written in conversational format. It is written as if you and I are having a conversation. And we are. I will guarantee, however, it's not the conversation you're used to having but it is a conversation nonetheless. And the conversation that's been a long time coming.

This is not a "let's hold hands and sing" type of book. There are no songs here. (Well, there is one lullaby). No violins. Just hard facts, reality, and truth.

There are a lot of quotation marks (" ") in this book. This is for the following two reasons:

1. I am placing an emphasis on something in particular;
2. I am pointing out something I don't give a shit about (Therefore neither should you)

There are things in this book that I will tell you to do. There are things in this book that I will tell you to stop doing. There are more things in this book that I will tell you to stop doing than it is of the things that I will tell you to start. I'll let you be the determiner of what that says about you as everything that I'll tell you to stop doing are things that you shouldn't have been doing in the first place and your doing these things on a consistent basis is the reason I had to write this book. And I wrote this book to save you from those who seek to manipulate you.

Manipulate - 2b: to control or play upon by artful, unfair, or insidious means esp. to one's own advantage. 3: to change by artful or unfair means so as to serve one's purpose. (Webster's Dictionary)

Yes, you are being manipulated. Some of you know this. Most of you don't. Some of you know this and you either think you know who's behind it, you know who's behind it, or you want to know who's behind it. Some of you don't give a shit as long as you've got a job, a car, a house, someone who doesn't mind smelling your breath, and $1.62 cents in your pocket. As long as you've got those five things everything and everyone else be damned. And that's okay. It's always been and always will be your choice.

There's an old saying: "Satan is the church's best friend". If you would consider the connotation behind this saying you'll understand why the two need each other. Then gradually you will come to understand the purpose of this book. Once that happens, you'll understand who (or what) Satan is as well as who (or what) the Church is. All Satans don't have horns. All Churches don't have steeples. Both, when it suits them, are all about "the cross". I'm going to unravel some of those little Satans that some of you have deified and deify some of those little Jesus' that some of you have satanized and all the while hint along the border of reality that this same process has been done to you. And that is a problem.

If there is anything I want you to get out of reading this book it is that you and only you can solve your problems. Sure, you can get help but you and you alone must start the process. And yes, problem solving is a process.

The problems of today are your problems. Why are they your problems? Because you created them.

If you believe that the Bible is "the revered word of God", Genesis tells you that you started out in a paradise (Eden). Is it that now? If not, what is it? Who screwed it up? Why? How? Only you can answer these questions because only you have been here. This book is written to remind you of that. Speaking of reminding you of things, let me state this clearer so that there will be no misunderstanding:

1. If you're offended by profanity, don't read this book;
2. If your "sensibilities" are easily hurt, don't read this book;
3. If you don't have a sense of humor; don't read this book;
4. If you don't have a sense of the importance of understanding the truth of things, don't read this book;
5. If you don't have any sense at all, don't read this book

> Let me say for the record that although I have a keen sense of humor, I'm not going to play pansy with you. If you're a spade I'm going to call you that then call you out. Call it your personal lixiviation or in your case a reverse enema. By God somebody's got to do it. Might as well be me.

This book will be written over a time span of two years, from October 31, 2015, to October 31, 2017. It is a narrative based on the events of this period and deals with issues that are said to cause acrimonious divisions between the citizenry of this country. It is also a critique on how you, the citizenry responds to these divisions. I will not highlight every incident of importance during this time frame. This does not, however, take away from the importance of any incident I do not highlight. It will not come as a surprise to me and should not come as a surprise to you at the number of incidents I highlight in this book that will still be occurring after the publication of this book. Whenever that will be. It sort of reminds me of that age old saying:

> "If you keep doing the same thing and expect a
> different result you are a completely hopeless idiot."

Something to think about.

Here's something else to think about. Let's examine a perplexing problem that if you understood it a little (No. A lot.) better than you do now you would see a little more clearly the role that you play in what the hell's wrong with America.

Chapter Two

"The Evil Years" Why?

If it looks like a duck,
Walks like a duck, and
Quacks like a duck -
We're gonna eat good tonight.
    The Author
    2015-2017: The Evil Years. Why call them "evil"?

Because damn it I expect them to be.
You don't believe me, right?
Maybe if I explained a few things you may understand.

Let me first ask you reader, do you know what evil is? Strip away the religious and horror movie aspects of your perception of this word. What is the meaning of evil? What is the understanding behind the knowledge of this word? Is this one more word that you've been using whose meaning was shaped and molded by others whom you viewed as "authorities" and thus you accepted their concept without question? There has been a lot of that going around lately. Stop it. Stop it now. Stop accepting things out of blind trust. As a matter of fact, stop being blind, period.

The meaning that I've found that best defines what was going on during this time period indeed does come from a figure with religious connotations albeit different from what so called "religious scholars" have formulated for us common folk to ingest. This definition comes from an individual most people know as "Jesus" and is referenced in a book called *The Aquarian Gospel Of Jesus Christ*. This book was transcribed by a man named Levi Dowling and according to its content references the eighteen years of Jesus' life that are mysteriously missing from the Bible. Some consider this book to be apocryphal. This is neither here nor there for my intent and purpose. I'll leave that debut to those that make a living from it.

In chapter 39 of my copy of this book, Jesus is in a city called Persepolis. He is attending a feast, as it states in the first verse, to honor the Magian God. When it was time for those who wished to speak to do so, Jesus stood and spoke. After giving salutations and honors, he gave a brief synopsis of what he was taught concerning the creation of the heavens and the earth as well as the seven entities that make up life upon the earth. Then he gets down to business by asking a question. It is as plain to me as the nose on my face that this is a set-up question by the way it's phrased. These people have no idea that Jesus is a past master syllogist. The people assembled at this feast were Magians (Look it up.). While they had heard of Jesus and his history, they still thought he was a lightweight. How do I know this? Read and you'll see. Jesus, true fisherman that he is, baited a hook and threw it in the water. Watch now, how the little fishee fell for the bait. Hook line, and liquor bottle.

We start our fishing expedition at verse 6 of chapter 39:

> "Well say you all. There is one God from whose great being there came forth the seven Spirits that created heaven and earth; and manifested unto the sons of men are these great Spirits in the sun, and moon, and stars."

Verse 7:

> "But in your sacred books we read that two among these seven are of superior strength; that one of these created all the good; the other one created all that evil is."

Verse 8:

> "I pray you, honored masters, tell me how that evil can be born of that which is all good?"

Let's pause here for a minute. Jesus, being a master of all things logic (material) as well as all things of faith (spiritual), understood that the nature of man being what it is, one could not just blurt out; "Hey bud, that mush you're sprouting' ain't kosher!" He wanted to tell these Magians that although their intentions were good, there's an ideology within their belief system that's screwing up the machine. Jesus described this ideology in verse 7. He challenges it in verse 8. And once again, like all great fishermen, he dangles a bait that to an arrogant fish is just too good to pass up. Enter, stage left, an arrogant fish:

Verse 9:

> A magus rose and said, "If you will answer me, your problem will be solved."

Verse 10:

> "We all do recognize the fact that evil is. Whatever is, must have a cause. If God, the One, made not this evil, then, where is the God who did?"

Wait a minute here. Isn't this the perfect example of a politician? Ask them a direct question and instead of giving you a direct answer they'll either give you a sound bite or will answer your question with a question in which in all their smugness and arrogance they believe their answer is the best thing since toilet paper and if you weren't so dumb you'd realize how asinine your question was and as such you should be sorry you asked it.

Jesus recognized this Socratic, sophist reply and decided not to address that aspect of it. He got what he wanted, which was an opening. And in that Jesus way of making an entrance, he produces this explanation:

Verse 11:

> And Jesus said, "Whatever God, the One, has made is good, and like the great first cause, the seven spirits all are good, and everything that comes from the creative hands is good.

Verse 12:

> Now all created things have colors, tones, and forms their own; but certain tones, though good and pure themselves, when mixed, produce inharmonies, discordant tones.

Verse 13:

And certain things though good and pure, when mixed, produce discordant things, yea, poisonous things, that men call evil things.

Verse 14:

So evil is the inharmonious blending of the colors, tones, or forms of good.

Verse 15:

Now man is not all-wise and yet has will his own. He has the power, and he uses it to mix God's good things in a multitude of ways, and every day he makes discordant sounds and evil things.

Verse 16:

And every tone and form, be it good or ill becomes a living thing, a demon, sprite, or spirit of a good or vicious kind.

Verse 17:

Man makes his devil, thus; and then becomes afraid of him and flees; his devil is emboldened, follows him away and casts him into torturing fires.

Verse 18:

The devil and the burning fires and both the works of man, and none can put the fires out and dissipate the evil one, but man who made them both."

Verse 19:

Then Jesus stood aside, and not a magus answered him.

SECTION TWO
WHAT DID WE LEARN?

Good question.
I have a better one.
What would your response have been
if Jesus would have asked you that question?

Hopefully, a lot was learned from that section. Mainly that in order to have evil you don't need a little man in a red suit with horns on his head, a pointed tail and a pitchfork. All you need is a little man. Or a little woman. Or a big man or a big woman. Or a combination of the two. Even kids can get in on the act. In order to have a big or a little dose of evil all it takes is people and the correct situation.

While it is debatable whether the supernaturalistic viewpoint of casualty is correct; one thing is certain and that is the thoughts of man (and woman) play a central role in whether the results of the act(s) of man (and woman) can/are/will be termed as "evil". Conventional wisdom dictates that negative forces from beyond the natural, physical realm influences these thoughts and thus man is in a constant battle in order to keep these influences at bay. In verses 15 thru 18, Jesus dispels "The Devil made me do it" concept. In the first sentence of verse 15 he says:

"Now man is not all wise and yet has will his own.
"He has the power, and he uses it to mix God's good things in a multitude of ways, and every day he makes discordant sounds and evil things."

Remember what I wrote earlier: "people and the correct situation." Better stated, people and opportunity. Still not convinced? O-Kay. Then maybe you have an answer for...

... What makes a 15-year-old kid go to school, walk inside said school, kill 15 of his classmates along with his 51-year-old gym teacher, then shoot himself in the head. And this is after he posts a 501 page manifesto online describing exactly how and why he's going to do this...
... Why a 60-year-old man hears a knock on his door at 6:00 pm, answers said door and greets a man with a 6-year-old boy. The man leaves the 6-year-old boy with the

60-year-old man, who then leads the boy into his bedroom where he has a video recorder aimed at his bed...

... Why a 15-year-old was shooting a 9mm at a 16-year-old boy; missed and shot and killed a 9-year-old girl...

... Why a woman who is covered from her head to her shoes as a symbol of piety and morality go to a shopping center at high noon, stop in the middle of the mall, reach inside her clothing, scream a religious affirmation, then press the button of a detonator connected to 40 pounds of explosives...

... This list can go on.

Understand this if you never understand anything else:

> While it may be fashionable to say things like:
> "I can't believe he/she could do such a thing."
> "I can't understand how he/she could do such a thing."
> "What he/she/they did makes no sense."

Trust me here. It may not "make no sense" to you, but *at the time* of an act it makes damn good sense to them. Evil is not logic. Evil is a *type* of logic. Intentions are created, shaped and bound by this type of logic and acts are executed based on this type of logic.

* People called Charles Manson evil and felt that he was mentally deranged. Charles Manson felt that everyone else was evil and *they* were mentally deranged;

* According to most if not all accounts, Adolph Hitler felt that everything he did was the correct thing to do. And so did quite a few others, including people in the United States;

* The father who kills his 3 children (Ages 6 months, 2 years, and 6 years old, his wife, and his in-laws truly believes that he is ridding himself of a terrible burden. Then, upon further introspection, decides that by killing himself he is ridding the world of a terrible burden.

Dr. Lune A. Teek

To carry a thought from intention to an act involves 3 steps. I call them the 3 C's:

1. Concept
2. Context
3. Construct

Although the context of the thought streams of the above individuals were different the constructs resulting from their actions were the same:

Something that someone, somewhere will/would
define as evil.

SECTION THREE
SOMETHING "THEY" DIDN'T
WANT YOU TO KNOW

Earlier I told you to strip away religious concepts when considering the meaning of this word. I still want you to. Earlier I gave you a look at concepts coming from a religious figure to show even this religious figure utilized a practical concept to explain what some thought was an unexplainable question. I'm going to do it again. This time I'm going to do it in order to show how the figure in the first story (Jesus) came to the conclusion he explained. Follow the story closely.

SECTION FOUR
ONCE UPON A TIME IN A LITTLE
GARDEN CALLED EDEN

It should be evident to you that the subject matter of this section comes from the Genesis chapter of the Bible. The central figures in this story are:

1.   A woman called Eve;
2.   A man named Adam;
3.   A serpent;
4.   An entity named "The LORD God"

For the sake of brevity, as this chapter has gone longer than I initially planned, we'll skip introductions and get to the heart of the matter. At this point, Eve is having a seemingly pleasant conversation with what we are led to believe is a snake.

Chapter 3 - Genesis

Verse 1: Now the serpent was more subtle than any beast of the field which the LORD God had made. And he said unto the woman, Yea, hath God said, Ye shall not eat of every tree of the garden?

Verse 2: And the woman said unto the serpent, We may eat of the fruit of the trees of the garden:

Verse 3: But of the fruit of the tree which is in the midst of the garden, God hath said, Ye shall not eat of it, neither shall ye touch it, lest ye die.

Verse 4: And the serpent said unto the woman, Ye shall not surely die:

Verse 5: For God doth know that in the day ye eat thereof, then your eyes shall be opened, and ye shall be as gods, knowing good and evil.

Verse 6: And when the woman saw that the tree was good for food, and that it was pleasant to the eyes, and a tree to be desired to make one wise, she took of the fruit thereof, and did eat, and gave also unto her husband with her, and he did eat.

Verse 7: And the eyes of them both were opened, and they knew that they were naked, and they sewed fig leaves together, and made themselves aprons.

These 7 verses have been the explanation for everything from sin coming into the world to why a man should never trust a woman. A lot of exploitation went down because of these beliefs. Evil exploitation at that. And then there's the issue of the snake lying to the woman. Or did it? All (well most of them) clergy will say yes to this question. A closer look may reveal something else.

The question the snake asked, first of all, had nothing to with what you have been told that it lied to the woman about, which was death (See verse 1). The question was very simple:

"Yea, hath God said, "Ye shall not eat of every tree of the garden?"

Some may believe it is simplistic to say that if the woman would have given any answer but the one she gave the world would be a totally different place. A few of those answers may have been:

1. Not really;
2. Not necessarily;
3. All except one;
4. What you want to know for;
5. You were there, you heard him;
6. None of our business;
7. Why you asking me;
8. Go pound sand;
9. No

You get the picture?

Actually, and in all honesty the woman has committed a trial lawyer's worst nightmare if they had her for a client. It is the main reason why the best lawyers prepare their clients by asking them questions they know a prosecutor will or may ask. What did the woman do? She offered unsolicited information. What did the snake do? Offer clarification. Now the question becomes was this clarification a lie?

Well, it depends on whose chalice you're drinking from – and what's in it. The woman was correct in her answer for the exception of one thing: she omitted the word "surely" from her answer (see verse 3). Notice the snake did not. Small, irrelevant nonsense you may say. Not so much when you take into consideration that the snake knew the answer to the question before it asked. But in a sense this is small change compared to what comes next, which is the snake's clarification. Look very closely at verses 4 and 5.

Verse 4. And the serpent said unto the woman, Ye shall not surely die.

This statement is not necessarily a lie. Yes, that right I said it. I'll say it again.

This statement is not necessarily a lie. How is this? Read carefully.

In order to understand where the snake (And I) is coming from, you have to go back to Chapter 2 in the Bible where these instructions took place. Read carefully verse 9. I'm not going to print it here. I want you to read it where it is. Note that the "Lord God" caused to grow all the trees in the garden that were "pleasant to the sight and good for food". The bible then references via emphasis two trees:

1. The Tree Of Life;
2. The Tree Of The Knowledge Of Good And Evil

Skip verses 10, 11, 12, 13, 14 and 15. Verses 16 and 17 hold the key to this mystery. Read them carefully. Now read them again. Now let's go back to verse 4 of Chapter 3.

Verse 4. And the serpent said unto the woman, Ye shall not surely die."

Go back to Chapter 2, verses 16 and 17.

What's missing?

In verses 16 and 17 the Lord God gave Adam two commands. They were very explicit. Now I'll include them here.

1st Command:

Verse 16. And the Lord God commanded the man, saying, "Of every tree of the garden thou mayest freely eat"

2nd Command:

Verse 17. But of the tree of the knowledge of good and evil; thou shalt not eat of it, for in the day that thou eatest thereof thou shalt surely die.

Now once again, I ask; What's missing?

Before I give you the answer, once again go back to what the snake said. Now back to the two trees that were highlighted.

1. The Tree of Life.
2. The Tree of the Knowledge of Good and Evil.

Think about the two commands. Have you figured it out yet?

What's missing?

Answer: What's missing is a command not to eat from the Tree of Life.

That's right.

Think about it.

Ask yourself what would have happened if these two would have eaten from the Tree of Life instead of the Tree Of The Knowledge of Good and Evil.

Are you unsure of the answer? Let's examine that for a minute. Let's leave this scene for a moment. Don't worry, we'll be back.

Cut to the "Lord God". At the moment, the Lord God is either talking or thinking. If the Lord God is talking, we don't know to whom or who. Religious figures will attempt to tell you they know or that the LORD God was speaking in second or third person plural. This is not relevant. What is, however, is what the LORD God said; well, decreed would be more like it. If you want to know the answer to the question of what would have happened if Adam and "the woman" had they eaten from the Tree Of Life, it is found in the 22nd verse of the 3rd chapter:

> Verse 22. And the LORD God said, Behold, *the man is become one of us*, to know good and evil; lest he put forth his hand, and t*ake also of the tree of life, and eat, and live forever*: (Emphasis mine)

Now do you understand?

Not only did the snake tell the truth by saying "...For God doth know in the day ye eat thereof, then your eyes shall be opened, *and ye shall be as gods, knowing good and evil...*" (Emphasis mine), the snake left open the chance for the woman to inquire about its first assertion:

> Verse 4. And the serpent said unto the woman, Ye shall not surely die;

She just didn't follow up and because of that we're left to try to figure out what type of "die" the LORD God was referring to, which should be apparent when one reads verse 22.

Or is it?

I'll let you ponder whither this reference of the word "die" was in the physical or innocence sense or both. Besides, you've got to have something else to do.

SECTION FIVE
THE TIE THAT BINDS

Those who preach and/or teach that this story is about man being disobedient to the LORD God are not wrong. However, if this is *all* they preach and/or teach, they are, like the snake, giving you only half the story. As a matter of fact, like the snake, they're leaving out the most important part, which, if you knew, you'd probably exercise better options. The key to this story, as I've stated, is not so much about disobedience as it is about *making the decision to disobey, the thought process involved in making the decision, the follow through (execution), and the consequence.* This story is about power. The power of choice. It is also about decision making based on proper information *or the lack of it.* Observe verse 6:

> And when the woman saw that the tree was good for food, and that it was pleasant to the eyes, *and a tree to be desired to make one wise,* she took of the fruit thereof, and did eat, and gave also to her husband with her, and he did eat.

Compare this to what Jesus explained to the mage:

> Verse 15. Now man is not all-wise and yet has will his own. He has the power, and he uses it...

The woman exercised power when she "ate" from this tree even though she was told not to. Notice that the woman is considering. This is the process of thought that I referred to earlier. Notice that she has either discarded considering the commands placed upon her or she has weighed them and found them lacking real consequence. She and the man are about to experience the second part of the snake's statement:

> Verse 5. For God doth know that in the day ye eat thereof, then your eyes shall be opened, and ye shall be as gods, knowing good and evil.

What was it about having the knowledge of good and evil that made them become as gods?

Is not knowledge power?
Sure, but can it make you a god?

Be careful of what you wish.

SECTION SIX
THE TIE THAT BINDS
(Part 2)

It's time to tell you what all this has to do with the subtitle of the book. Let me review:

> "Now man is not all wise, *and yet has will his own*. He has the power, and he uses it to mix God's good things in a multitude of ways, and every day he makes discordant sounds and evil things."

Know this and know it well. Everything that you have ever seen or will see, in particularly in the years 2015 through 2017 is a result of the execution of choices made by individuals. Whether good or evil, someone exercised the power of decision making. This book is designed to keep that truth in your face. A lot of evil happened since I started this book. A lot of evil will happen while I'm writing this book. And I am as certain as Ms. Piggy's love for a green frog that it will continue after I'm done. Why? Because now "man has become one of us, to know good and evil...".

From suicide bombing; to child abductions and killings; to church and school shootings and killings; to police/civilian - civilian/police shootings and killings; all these things will take place from 2015-2017. And they are all the result of individuals practicing their "godhood". Because of increased media coverage (If it bleeds, it leads.), all of this will be dumped squarely in our laps. The same way that it is impossible to not slow down to look at a wreck is the same way we will slow down to look at the evil that will be thrust into our living/bedrooms via television and radio. And the media, in doing this in the manner that they will, must and will choose to become an institution outside of its original intent. That is, instead of giving you a view of this evil, they've begun to mold/shape your view of this evil. It is here that those who suspect media bias exists will get their suspicions confirmed. Mostly up to this point, media bias was implicit. Now the media stopped caring. Now instead of reporting the news, mainstream media is/will be shaping it. The slogan, "All the news that fit to print" suddenly becomes "All the news that fits a particular narrative". And if it initially didn't fit that narrative, they either improvised so it would, or they didn't run the story at all. Which in itself is evil.

However, you can only put but so much blame on the media. If men (and women) would not do the evil that men (and women) do, the media could not report/improvise the evil that men (and women) do.

There are a lot of people that believe in the/a devil. There are a lot of people that believe in occult sciences. Believe what you will. It's your choice. Just know that in order to work magic you don't need to believe in a devil, nor do rituals. All you need to do is to conceive an intent, choose from a list of options that will solidify that intent, then act on the option you chose. After all, when you take away the hocus-pocus, isn't that what you're doing when you're performing a ritual? The difference is you are the power source. In order for you to become the king (or queen) of your castle you must first make the intent to be a king (or queen). Then you must choose the vehicle (options) that will get you there. Finally, you must execute the option(s) that you've chosen. In short, in order to become the king of your castle, you must decide to not be a pauper. Speaking of kings, pauper, and the like...

SECTION SEVEN
THE EVILIEST THING EVER
CREATED

Class-n.2. Any division of people or objects by quality, rank grade. 3. A social stratum whose members share similar economic, political, and cultural characteristics. 4. a. The division of society into relative strata or ranks. b. Social rank or caste, especially high rank. (Webster's Dictionary)

Caste-n.2. Any social class separated from others by distinctions of heredity, rank, profession, or the line. 3. A social system, or the principle of grading society, based on these distinctions. 4. The social position or status conferred on such a system... Of or characterized by caste... (Webster's Dictionary)–

An evil people it is that would create a system that would identify themselves as superior to their fellow humans. Yet this is the type of system that is in place in several countries including North and South America. What system am I referring to? The system that identifies people with melanin as "Black" and people with trace amounts as "White". These purveyors of evil have created a system that by its very nature forces people to identify themselves as opposites of each other. It, by way of classification, guarantees divisions based on subjective prejudices and in and of itself creates the atmosphere necessary for stereotypical thought.

In language, word definitions and context are an imperative when it comes to conveying thought. Review the definitions of "Black" and "White". With this in mind, ask yourself the following:

1. Who were the originators of this scheme?
2. What were they considering when they created this?
3. What were their objectives?
4. Why was this necessary?

To make matters worse, this insidious construct that started as social engineering somehow became a legal construct. This particular concept called "race"", which would normally be used to denote one's biological origins is now being used to determine social, political, economic, and legal status. This is being done through subliminal means and the effects can be easily seen and have been noted throughout history (Black Codes, Jim Crow, Apartheid, etc.). How did this happen? Who/Whom authorized this? What law(s) authorized this? How was/is this enforceable? How can a system such as this be set up, right under the people's noses that makes "Black" people think they're black just because their skin tone is dark and "White" people think they're "White" because they're supposed to be? We as a nation of people must have had a really bad case of diarrhea on the day they pulled this off. The sad, sad truth, of all this is that many people on this planet believe that this is the way it is supposed to be. They have no idea that it is this evil, maniacal, psychotic perception of reality that is keeping harmony, peace, and tranquility from being achieved throughout the world. Don't believe me? Ask the kids who are happily playing in the sandbox. Race, however, is just one type of classification (class) that is destructive to humanity. Here is another.

SECTION EIGHT
POLITICIANS:
MINIONS OF EVIL

A politician, like a cemetery plot, is a necessary evil. You may not want them, but because of how the government, and life are set up you've got to have them. Most politicians think of themselves as scientists and like all scientist they are firm believers that they are problem solvers. Know that when a politician solves a problem they stop being a politician. Sadly, most politicians, either through ineptitude or through unscrupulous behavior create more problems than they solve. One such problem is class division and class warfare.

Have you ever heard a politician's stump speech? In particular, a presidential stump speech? What's one of the things that they constantly promote?

"I'm going to make sure that the 'middle class' gets a tax cut."
"Too much of the burden of government has fallen on the 'middle class'."
"Healthcare for all is going help millions of 'middle class' Americans."

This constant drumbeat of "middle class" has become a mainstay in the American political lexicon. Initially meant to fool the average American listener that the politician is speaking personally to the "working man and woman", it has now become nothing more than an exercise in pandering and condescension. From "Read my lips. No new taxes"; to "You can keep your doctor...", these pledges were designed to appeal to what political strategist have perceived as the largest swath of the voting population. This should tell people in the "lower class" something. Hopefully they'll hear it. Only a devil of the worst kind would tell you, "I'm going to cut your throat. Vote for me." What was it that P.T. Barnum said?

Class warfare is far eviler and more deceitful than having the flu with a double case of pneumonia and has been in full display in very recent presidential elections. Recent Democratic candidates have raised this insidious evil to an art form. To those like me who know what is happening when watching this being done it is both hilarious and sickening. I won't quote the things said to promote this malicious strategy against the America population of voters. It's too many. And too asinine. And yes, it is a strategy against the voter. Why? Because it's done in order to con you into thinking that the "Evil Rich" are making your vote null and void by "buying" the politician. Guess what? They're right. They just want you to think that they're Jesus and Mother Mary and they're going to rebuke those rich devils right back to the gold-plated mansions they came from. And all the while behind the scenes the bastards are making deals like Judas and Jezebel.

Answer this question reader:

> Why would anyone who is striving to have wealth vote
> for someone who is demonizing wealth?

In many ways wealth means independence and independence means security. Who in their right mind doesn't want to be secure, whether financially or in their person? Wealth also allows one to have the most powerful weapon in the world beside a guaranteed ticket to heaven:

> The Abundance Of Options.

> This is the difference between the "haves and the have
> nots".
> Politicians know this. They know this because they
> understand power.
> They know something else too.

They know they want power. They're going to do everything in their power to keep you believing that they don't. Here's how they're going to do it:

As long as they can get you to hate what they want to become they know that through osmosis you will believe that they hate what they want to become. When this happens they now know they can get you to vote against anything that would be in your best interest. Including the freedom of choice.

> What is the difference between a master and a slave?
> The Abundance Of Options.
> What is it impossible to have without wealth?
> The Abundance Of Options.
> If your interest is to be totally financially secure, why
> would you want to vote for someone who wants to tax a
> certain amount of income 70% and have a "wealth tax"?

What really makes this type of politician evil is that they are aware of all the above and their lifelong mission is to get you to hate anything or anyone that would seek to move you beyond your present income level. A poor and hungry constituency is a constant constituency because they will always want something. All a happy and prosperous constituency wants is for the good times to roll. One gives these types of politicians power. The other gives these types of politicians constipation. Regardless of which constituency you happen to be, remember one thing:

> You can have economics without politics; but you can't have politics without economics.

No matter what they tell you.

SECTION NINE
WHAT DID WE LEARN?

This chapter is about the power of choice and the sin that comes from executing options without considering the consequences. In a general sense it is about evil and most people's perception of it. I used the term "evil" in my subtitle because I know that this is how an exceptionally large percentage of the population is describing the events that they are seeing or experiencing. My objective in writing this chapter is to get the world to know that evil, whatever event one may describe as this, begins in the hearts and minds of man. For it to end, it must end there also.

While vast amounts of evil have occurred in other epochs of time, we have a media that seems hell bent on showing us every scintilla of evil occurring now. A heavy enough dose of this and one will have what I believe are very asinine thoughts. Asinine acts follow:

> "I don't want to raise a child in this type of world";
>
> "I hate cops";
>
> "You're not gonna cheat on me and get away with it";
>
> "Kids today don't have enough respect for law enforcement;
>
> As a school resource officer, those kids better "do what I say, or else.";
>
> "Boy, I brought you into this world, I'll take your ass out!";
>
> Etcetera, etcetera, etcetera.

All the above thoughts and corresponding actions happened as of the writing of this chapter. It is my hope that by considering what is in this chapter you will conclude that you create your own heaven and your own hell. The "Butterfly Effect" is the rule here. Know that while creating what you may consider as your heaven you may be also creating a hell for someone else. Don't be that guy/gal. Life is short. Don't waste it being evil. Believe me, I know from that which I speak. Execute the options you choose wisely and choose options that upon careful consideration are for the betterment of all concerned. And even those who are not.

CHAPTER THREE

Problem Solving

"What You Don't Know Won't Hurt You"
Old Saying

"What You Don't Know Could Kill You"
The Author

I've heard this and other "truisms" my whole life. For a large part of that life, I never questioned these so-called wise sayings because everyone I've ever known counted them as gospel. It wasn't until I understood one thing that my view of people, places, and things began to change:

"General opinion is no proof of truth for the generality
of men are ignorant"

Those of us who understand certain aspects of life understand that power is an illusion. Who or what is powerful today may not be powerful tomorrow because power changes as the ethers change. Its existence is not fixed therefore it is not a constant of life. It's here today, gone tomorrow. Be that as it may, we also know that this illusion called power is an absolute necessity for one to ascend to the throne of the ultimate absolute: Force. When one becomes a force one ceases to be a power because it is force that directs the power. Therefore, the one power that is essential for a person to have and master in order to become that force is the power of effective problem solving.

This book is about problems. It is also about problem solving. Notice I didn't say answers. If I would have said "it is also about answers" you may assume that it is in the same model as the "problem-answer" construct that often appears as a "self-help" book. That concept, if you think about it, is oxymoronic. How can a book that gives you answers to your problems be a *self-help* book? The other thing about answers you need to know is just because you have an answer to a problem doesn't mean that you've solved the problem. For example, is there a cure for the common cold? How much money does the common person spend for medications to fight the common cold? Billions of dollars are spent by consumers and made by drug companies annually in an attempt to provide solutions to a problem that the drug companies and any competent doctor themselves will tell you there is no cure (At least one "they" will allow the public access to). As a matter of fact, in all the medical research done in the last 50 years, what medication has been developed that has cured any disease? Makes one wonder, doesn't it? And don't get me started on "side effects".

The world is full of what I call "answer therapists" and they do a very brisk business from those who don't or can't do the work themselves. People have spent billions of dollars on self-help books, tapes, records, CDs, seminars, etc. and will continue to do so until they learn to become proficient if not master the skills involved in effective problem solving. In order to do this, it is going to require something from you. Something many of you have only taken halfhearted stabs at. You are going to have to think. And while I am aware that it literally hurts some of you to do this activity, I can only suggest that you try to grit and bear with it. Let's start with the basics.

SECTION TWO
UNCOMMON CORE

I've often been told that the "Common Core" curriculum that has educational systems across the country in a panic "world is coming to an end right dammit now so grab your bible and load your gun" mentality simply is an attempt to have one standard curriculum that applies to all children and that the teacher teaches according to that standard only. If this is true, anyone, including and especially teachers can see why this is getting the type of push back that it has and will continue to get. Let me explain.

Teachers are a lot like lawyers (I know I'm getting cursed out by teachers but please, bear with me). Both must have a general knowledge of their occupation (education and law). However, they may branch off into a specialty field. They both apply a set of standards in what they do (Teachers apply a set curriculum. Lawyers apply the law according to constitutions, legislation, and stare decisis). They both represent clients. (A teacher's clients are children. They are judged based on what their clients know at the end of a year and at the end of 12 years. Lawyers represent their clients to judges, juries, etc.). The worth of both are judged upon the presentation of the final product: the client. However, the most important aspects that both shares are the following:

1. A lawyer tells you to give no statements not only because you don't know the tricks and tactics coming at you, but more importantly, because your statement(s) *locks him or her into a particular strategy.*
2. A teacher's primary focus is to *infuse* knowledge. A good teacher doesn't have to have a degree in psychology to understand that there are a myriad of factors that could hinder the infusion of that knowledge. No good teacher wants to be *locked into a particular methodology of teaching by way of teaching a particular method of learning.* (Teaching to the test, etc.) only.

A trait that defines a good teacher is the same that defines a good lawyer and that is the ability to apply techniques that I have come to refer to as "the elasticity of thought" in order to impart knowledge. This is why Common Core math problems are at the center of this controversy. They defy common sense rationale (of course, this is my humble opinion). The lack of this elasticity of thought means that the teacher has been stymied from using his' or her's range of options in order to reach a child who might can't readily grasp fundamental concepts. And attempting to apply Common Core concepts are anything but fun let alone fundamental.

Now what does anything I just explained have to do with problem solving? Everything and nothing. It all depends on how far you can see.

There's a saying that goes "if common sense was so common everybody would have it." This saying infers that everyone doesn't have "common sense". For someone to come up with this saying and for others to believe it lets me know that there are people who don't have a clue as to what common sense is. I can tell you now without doubt or contradiction that everyone (maybe for the exception of the mentally challenged) has common sense. The problem is not that people don't have it. The problem is people don't use it. It is here that I'll start my explanation of problem solving.

SECTION THREE
MAKING SENSE OF IT ALL

I started this foray into problem solving by telling people they are going to have to think. I started the last section of this chapter by highlighting a critical change taking place within the educational system within this country. It is an attempt, not to change the overall curriculum being taught, but to change the way the overall curriculum is going to be presented and on top of it all, to lock the teacher into a "standard" in which instructors with doctorates in education can't understand. You'll begin to understand why this is important when you answer this question:

Where did most people learn the fundamentals necessary to process thought? Answer: In school.

School is where you first learned (in a formal setting) the protocols involved in the process of thought. You didn't know your faculties of reasoning were being shaped and honed. You didn't know you were being taught discernment and logic. You had no idea you were being taught to discriminate between this and/or that. You were taught mathematics but the thin line between mathematics and logic was only hinted at. You were never taught that everything you learn in school is in one way or another connected to the skills you need in order to actuate effective problem solving. Let me show you by example what this looks like. The bell has rang (not "rung"). School is now in session.

> You: Ms. Smith, you took a half a point away from each one of my math problems. Why you do that?
> Ms. Smith: You didn't follow my instructions.
> You: What instructions?
> Ms. Smith: I said, "Show Your Work".
> You: I thought you were saying you wanted to see our homework.

It's very easy to say (or write) $(12{\times}2){\div}2{-}1{=}11$, but would your teacher know what steps you took to get that answer? You don't think it's important? Watch this:

$$12{\times}2{\div}(2{-}1)=$$

Is the answer still "11"?

You could have used a calculator, copied someone's answers, or maybe paid someone to do your work. So, in order for your teacher to know that you know how to solve this problem he or she told you to go to the board and "work out" the problem. Show your work. It also showed something else:

Your Brain At Work (Wow! When's the last time you've seen that?).

If you got this problem wrong, barring the fact that you know how to add, subtract, multiply and divide, the teacher would have known you either didn't know or didn't understand the specific formula being applied. This formula is giving you a specific set of instructions on how to solve this problem. This equation involves a formula called "Order Of Operations". The equation itself lists three things to do: Multiply, divide, and subtract.

Order of operations demands that you do whatever operation is in parenthesis first. Sounds easy right? Trust me. I know some mathematicians that can take this one concept and turn your brain to water. But now, lest we forget why we're here, let's return to where we started.

$$(12 \times 2) \div 2 - 1 = 11$$

This time let's substitute the numbers for problem situations. It would look like this:

Car Payment × Mortgage ÷ Student Loan - Layoff Notice =

Where would you put the parenthesis?

Now before you've had a chance to think "is this idiot a lunatic?", let me ask you this: Have you ever asked yourself why mathematical equations are called problems? Could it be that in order to get the correct answer you first have to identify what you must do, then know the correct formula to apply to what can only be described as a vacuum? Even if you know what to do, if you apply the wrong formula or if you apply the right formula the wrong way you're going to get the wrong answer. Such is the mathematics involved in solving the problems of life.

If this hypothesis is correct (and it is), then there is a specific methodology (science) involved in problem solving. If you expedite life affected problem solving the way you would solve a math equation you might begin to unravel this mystery. The only thing here, and this is important, is that the math problem as it is presented to you on paper is fixed. If you've been presented with $(12 \times 2) \div 2 - 1 = 11$, then barring some kind of high magic that is what the equation is. Life is different. Right in the middle of solving the problems of life a variable changes and you must change either the process you've committed to in order to solve the problem or you must change the order of operations. Depending on what the variable change is and how it occurs you might have to change both the process and the order simultaneously. You may even have to change the formula.

Problems, almost always, will not hit you one at a time. Even as you solve them often others arise that are a consequence of enacting the solution to the initial one. There are a host of materials out there that deal with this issue. Some of them are pretty good. Some of them not so good. This book is not meant to be one. It is designed to make you realize the importance of good, sound problem solving *ONLY* and that you as a people have been doing a piss poor job of it. Don't agree? Answer this question. It goes to black people:

> Why is it that black people as an aggregate are at or near the bottom of every "good" list and at or near the top of every "bad" list?

This phenomenon holds true whether the list deals with economics, education, life expectancy, health, employment, social standing, incarceration, crime, average family income, savings, investments, business, wealth, etc. There is a segment of black people who say that "racism", be it institutional or otherwise, is the problem. For the sake of argument, let's say that racism is the problem. *Now solve the problem.* Oh no. Don't look to white people. Don't look to government. Don't look to aliens from Planet X. As a matter of fact, don't even look for God to solve these problems. These are your problems. That being the case only you can solve them and only you should solve them. So, solve them. Of course, if racism is the problem, and I can tell you truthfully that it is not, then it is an easy fix. If you can't see how this is something easy to fix it may be due to your inability to understand the mathematics of life.

Dr. Lune A. Teek

SECTION FOUR
THE ONE PARTICULAR

The particulars of problem solving are legion. However, the most critical aspect of problem solving is the ability to effectively communicate and the most important facet of the skills that make up effective communication is the communication with oneself. In school this was called critical thinking. Here it's called self-talk.

It's been said that if you talk to yourself you're nuts and if you start answering yourself you're crazy. I say if you don't talk to yourself you're dead and if you don't answer yourself you're in hell. EVERYBODY talks to themselves. People with sense call it thought and the fact that the world is in the state it's in is a pretty good indicator that either people aren't answering themselves but letting others do the answering for them or the answers they're giving themselves are of extremely poor quality and here lies the issue. Your ability to process your thoughts clearly and logically is paramount to your growth and survival. Your success or failure depends totally upon the quality of your thought process. It all starts and ends in your head.

The conversations you have in your head are called thoughts. Your thoughts are the amalgamation of the perceptions of your subconscious brought to the conscious level. You can only achieve what you can conceive and what most people don't understand is that *true* perceptions and conceptions begin at the subconscious level. The process of thought is a very fast one. You can't understand something you have no conceptual knowledge of. Therefore, the one thing that will be the death of you as it relates to problem solving and life in general is ignorance. And let me say this: As long as you stay ignorant as you are about certain issues concerning the world around you instead of affecting change you will be affected by change and you will find yourself unable to deal with the consequences of said changes. And that is a problem. Now solve it. First, let's understand the mechanics of our mathematics example as we would in deciding how to deal with a problem. These three things must be noted. Keep in mind the process of thought is fast. And so is life.

1. The answer you get is going to depend on where you put the parenthesis (which problem variable do you/should you give priority to?);
2. Once your decision moves to an act it is irreversible (regrets are pointless and irrelevant);
3. The equational size is unlimited (problems never come one at a time)

Once you decide and act on it the decision and act are irreversible. What does this have to do with the type of person you are? Let's explore that for a minute.

If the worth (value) of a person is the sum of the decisions he/she makes what was the purpose of being made in "the image and likeness of God," which is the best of molds. Man/Woman are not the sum of their decisions. Man/Woman are Man/Woman because of their *power to make decisions* and with this power they can make or mar their fortune. It is because of this power that man becomes the master of his destiny, the captain of his ship, the king of his castle. The fact that a man does evil makes him no less of a man than the man who decides to do good. In fact, the same two acts (good and evil) can and do often come from the same man. And in some cases it happens minutes apart. Of this I am reminded of a very wise saying:

> "... So blended is weakness in thy nature, O man, that thou hast not the strength either to be good nor evil, *entirely*. Rejoice that thou canst not excel in evil and let the good that is within thy reach contend thee. The virtues are allotted to various stations. Seek not after impossibilities, nor grieve that thou canst not possess them all ..." (Emphasis mine)

Can a dog, a cat, a lizard, a monkey, or a snake choose to do evil? Can they choose to do good? Do they have a conscious concept of what good and evil is? These are very good questions to ask when you're trying to find out what separates man from beast. Especially when at times man displays such a beastly nature in thought, word, and deed that you can hardly tell the two apart. And that is a problem. Let's look at a list of some of the skills you're going to need in order to deal with life's problems as seen through the eyes of those who are experts on the subject of problem solving:

1. Effective Listening
2. Effective Questioning
3. Giving Effective Feedback
4. Knowing Your Feelings
5. Understanding That Thinking Controls Behavior
6. Paying Attention To Your Thoughts
7. Recognizing Risky Thoughts And Behavior
8. How To Channel New Thoughts
9. Understanding And Utilizing Empathy
10. Making An Assertive And Effective Complaint

11. How To Apologize
12. How To Respond To Anger
13. How To Effectively Negotiate
14. Stopping To Think
15. How To State A Problem
16. How To Set Goals
17. How To Handle Consequences
18. How To Plan And Evaluate
19. How To Apply Problem Solving Skills
20. Effective Time Management
21. Effective Social Skills
22. Defenses Against Manipulation
23. How To Forgive And Not Forget

These are just twenty-three aspects of this scientific concept called problem solving. Each one has sub facets. There are more and you will learn them as you continue to live. If your plan is to live as stress free as possible then slighting any one of these is not an option. This is about one aspect of a successful life and just like anything else in life you get out of it what you put into it.

SECTION FIVE
FORGET ME NOT

Throughout my adult life and as a child I've heard that I should "forgive and forget" and for a large part of that life I've wondered why it was so difficult to do. Now I know, and although I don't see the phrase as a total oxymoron, I do see those who believe this is what is actually happening as oxen who are morons.

Unless something extreme happens to your brain you don't "forget" anything. You may not be able to readily recall past events and it takes a particular thing, event, or person to trigger that memory but it's there. This fact is the rationale behind the sayings "First impressions last forever", and "The first impression is the most important". Although both are correct it is the conduct of the unenlightened to place emphasis here. *Every* impression, whether it's first, second, third, etc. is a lasting one and is of importance and no greater emphasis should be placed on one versus the others. This is a key fact to learn because it is the misunderstanding of this truth that is the vital element necessary in the art of con (manipulation). The smoothest, slickest, shystiest con men (and women) rely on you to believe this myth because they know that your first impression of them will get you to open your door, your wallet, your accounts, your heart, your mind, your body, etc. All you have to do is believe. Don't. You'll run into problems. And out of the above.

I could go on with lightning storms of insight concerning this subject, but I don't want to get too far off course. I included it in this segment for this important reason. You need to understand this so that you can survive *yourself* after you've been conned, hurt, deceived, or any of the other negative things that living around people can make you susceptible to. What I am referring to is the high science of forgiveness.

I am almost 100% sure that there is someone reading this book who has embarked on the most (well, at least one of the most) misunderstood strategies of living ever placed on the doorstep of the consciousness of man and woman, and as such because of its impossible implementation has witnessed it as a great source of frustration because they haven't yet figured out it's impossible to implement. I can't count the times I've heard people say, "I can forgive but I can't forget". Wow! No shit Ruby! Here's the problem. When they say this it's not in the context of knowing that they'll never forget an event, particularly if it was traumatic. They're saying it in the context of the belief that they can do this thing, but they won't because of their own reasoning and willpower. This type of thinking leads to severe cases of frustration as expressed by what is experienced by the forgiver. Even if this individual says they forgive, the fact that they can't (won't) forget what the person did to warrant their forgiveness in the first place brings back all the feelings of pain, hurt, resentment, embarrassment, anger, distrust, etc. every time they see, hear, or think about that person. Therefore, the process of forgiveness never unfolds to fruition within the forgiver. There is an amazingly simple reason for all this foolishness.

Some very simpleminded person felt that it would be a clever idea to put the words "forgive" and "forget" in the same contextual phrase. It wasn't. As a matter of fact, it was a rotten idea and whoever did it should have had their feet cut off and stuck in their rear end. Heel first. They are responsible for a great bit of psychotic behavior among well-meaning but seriously naïve people.

Those who understand their mental faculties know that painful impressions are locked in impressions and thus are unforgettable. Those who understand their spiritual faculties understand that forgiveness is a spiritual act that transcends the boundaries of one's physical faculties and is done not in an act to compliment an impossibility but in spite of it. Forgiveness is not easy nor was it meant to be. It is a spiritual principle and as with all things spiritual it can't be understood nor practiced correctly when viewed through the myopic lens of a tightly compacted mind.

I can honestly say that *one* of the main causes of depression, feelings of worthlessness, even suicide is due directly or peripherally to the inability to forgive and to forgive totally without reservation or regret. Mind you, here, I'm not talking about the forgiveness of others. I'm referring to the forgiveness of *self.* Mother, father, sister, brother, wife, husband, children, friends, strangers, even God Almighty can forgive you but until you forgive yourself you will never be whole, and you will be subject to all the abuses and mistreatments that you care to bestow upon yourself and believe you me no one, I mean no one can abuse and mistreat you as worse as you can abuse and mistreat yourself. Especially if guilt and shame are the driving forces behind the abuse and mistreatment. And that is a problem.

I stated earlier that I wouldn't get too deep into any of the aspects of problem solving. And I'm not. You need to seek this information out for yourself. However, I had to briefly broach this subject because it effects so many people. Also, because it is such a crucial aspect of problem solving insomuch as so many problems people have stem from conflictive situations with others and these problems will never be fully "solved" unless the concept of forgiveness, correctly applied, becomes a part of the healing process. And it starts with the healing (forgiveness) of oneself. When your mind and your spirit become one, the next paragraph will make sense.

It is a particularly useful practice to remember that everything in existence yesterday, today, and tomorrow began with a thought. Which means everything in your world begins and ends in your head. Forgiveness is no exception. Forgiveness starts with the belief that one is worth forgiving. This applies to you as well as to others. Ironic as it may seem, whether you believe someone else is worth forgiving is secondary to whether you believe you are. The second you decide not to forgive someone is the beginning of the torment you start to put yourself through. If your wish is to move on you first must move. The type of person you are and hope to become is guided by your thoughts as is the type of life you wish to live. The quality of the conversations you have with yourself will determine the success you have with this process. The success you have with this process will determine the success you have with (and in) life. I will revisit this later.

SECTION SIX
WHAT DID YOU LEARN?

Good question. I can't answer it for you. I can tell you that I wrote this chapter with as many twists as I could. I did this so you can consider the twists as well as the topic and also to consider the twists as an aspect of the topic. For example:

The Common Core curriculum is (at least as of the writing of this book) an extremely hot topic and one that has received a lot of press. And while I didn't want to over emphasize Common Core, the curriculum, I did want to emphasize Common Core, the curriculum as what more than a small number of people view as a very disturbing problem and this chapter centers on problem solving. My interest of this issue is a more in depth reading of what's at stake. The question I have is one I know that's not being openly discussed:

Is the Common Core curriculum putting children
inside "a box"* or teaching them to think "outside the box"?

As I stated earlier, school is where a child's faculties of reasoning are shaped, honed, and tested. This is done by the infusion (look up the word 'infuse') of a curriculum that is designed as a matrix (look up the word), constructed for the express purpose of your child receiving it as the mechanism by which he or she is to process into thought the world around them. By the way, it is crucial that you review the words I suggested that you research the definitions of. Knowing what they specifically mean gives you an insight as to the concepts I am referring to as being crafted for your children. And to what purpose? Listen. If you can't process your thoughts on the basis of reason and logic applicable to the situation it is impossible for you to begin let alone excel at the skills involved in effective problem solving. So since so much of one's thought process begins to be formally initiated at this institution called "school" and reformatted in another institution called "college", I found it necessary to examine this issue in this chapter dealing with problem solving. With this fact in mind, the question above is the only place one should start in seeking to understand just what these unknown, unnamed, shadowy type entities (human or otherwise) are attempting to do with your children's brains. As I said, it's not the curriculum that is alien. It's the format that the curriculum is presented to the teacher for him or her to propagate. It is not the concepts that are alien to you, it is the context that is alien to your sensibility as to what the

---

* The "box" is what the author refers to as a casket.

constructs of reading, writing, and 'rithmatic are really like. And then, of course, there's the business of implanting an agenda that looks nothing like education. I'm not here to discuss that although it does add dimensions to a problem in which those who are tasked to solve this problem must give very grave consideration to and if they move ahead without taking these grave considerations into account then that will be a problem also. I hope they (and you) learned that.

SECTION SEVEN
WHY MATHEMATICS?

This is a very simple question and as such the answer is simple. I said earlier in the chapter that mathematical equations are called problems because you must first identify what you have to do to get the correct answer as well as know the correct formula to apply otherwise you have a vacuum. And that's correct. Let me explain.

1. Identify what you must do - All math equations (problems) have "symbols". These symbols tell you what to do. A plus symbol "+" tells you to add something to something else. A minus "-" symbol tells you to take something away from something else. A "times" sign "×" tells you to multiply something by something else, and then you have division "÷" signs which tells you to divide, etc. One must know and be able to incorporate these directions wherever one sees them. If one is ignorant of these operations one will have a void. One can't follow instructions.

2. Know The Correct Formula - An equation, depending on how long it is, (and I've seen some pretty long ones) can contain as many as five different formulas. One must be able not only to know what formula he or she needs in order to get the answer that will "prove" the equation, but also which ones won't fit. Sometimes trial and error is a must. One will have a void until the correct formulas are applied (Show your work).

3. Equal - Every equation has an "equal" sign. And while this word is synonymous with the word *same*, mathematicians don't quite see it that way (and neither should you). Mathematicians see equations as the variables that form different relationships that when "worked" or "proven" the end results in a *symmetry* of relationship more than a sameness. And here lies the power of a master problem solver.

    The master problem solver, once he or she has "worked" and/or "proven" a problem through to its essence via application of the correct formula will result in a symmetry that cannot be denied. And as I stated at the beginning of the chapter, force is the ultimate absolute. It and only it is the only thing that cannot be denied.

Before I close this chapter let me reiterate one thing of great importance. Various aspects of the problem-solving model can be utilized in connection with others. The aspect of reference called forgiveness is at its most powerful level when the aspect of empathy is utilized in conjunction. Empathy is a powerful tool because it places you in another's dynamic. Once in that dynamic it is impossible for you to say, "I don't know why he did that.", or "I don't understand why she'd say that.". Empathy makes you not only see the person, but it also makes you see the person's situation. Once you do this, you're able to see everything in a holistic manner and that person's reasoning become clearer. If empathy is not employed, then you'll be attempting to move a mountain without understanding the mountain's nature. There is a reason why a mountain is a mountain. Those who understand this reason make the best mountain movers. Sometimes forgiveness is like moving a mountain. Sometimes living life is like moving a mountain. You are now going to witness four groups of people and the mountains they have been trying to move. I can tell you that neither will be successful until they deal with an obstacle that is bigger, wider, and stronger than the mountains they have been trying to move. That would be an inability to think outside of the casket that some incredibly devious minded morticians have put them in.

Chapter Four

The "Black" Section

There is such a thing you know. Even after Jim Crow. The difference here is that Jim Crow was a socio-governmentally created, influenced, and perpetuated construct. The black section in this era is self-imposed and even though its existence is influenced by deeper, sinister forces for deeper, sinister reasons than the deeper sinister forces that crafted Jim Crow; all the target group has to do is realize this:

1.   Who those "deeper, sinister forces are
2.   What those "deeper, sinister forces use
3.   Accept the truth about 1 and 2
4.   Act accordingly

...in order to rid themselves of the consequences set upon them by these deeper, sinister forces.

And now, I introduce you to,

The "Black" Section.

By the way, there is a "White" section too. But don't you worry about that right now.

SECTION ONE
MAMA DON'T LET YOUR "BLACK" BOYS GROW
UP TO BE "BLACK" MEN

There is a famous country and western song that was sung by a famous country and western singer in which the artist tells his listeners not to let their babies grow up to be cowboys. Well, in this incarnation of that sentiment I'm telling "black" mothers not to let their "black" boys grow up to be "black" men. If you listen to the song you'll see that the reasons for not growing up to be cowboys are far, far different from not growing up to be "black" men. Do I agree with this premise? Absolutely. After all, I wrote it (not the song) and after exhaustive study I've found it to be irrefutable.

In the first chapter I stated that my use of quotation marks within these pages are for two reasons. The fact that I have placed quotation marks around the word "black" in this sense denotes my disdain for the word as it is used in the context of referring to people. Therefore, it falls into the second category; that being bringing attention to things that I don't give a shit about (and therefore neither should you).

I put quotation marks around the word "black" not because I don't give a shit about you, but because I don't give a shit about the context of this word as it applies to you. I don't give a shit about the fact that you have embraced this word without knowing and understanding its origin and purpose. I don't give a shit about those who branded you with that word because I know their true origin and purpose. Will I tell you this in this book? Absolutely not. Suffice it to say that "black" is not what you are, not what you were, and not what you could ever be. So, the premise of not letting your boys grow up "black" let alone to be "black" is rooted in quite a bit of truth. And not necessarily just because I said so. Let me give you something to think about:

The biggest sin one can commit before God and man is the sin of not knowing oneself. The second biggest sin one can commit before God and man is the sin of not being oneself. The third biggest sin one can commit before the eyes of God and man is the sin of not caring to know nor be oneself. The practice of all three makes one a devil before the eyes of God and man and one's day of reckoning shall forever be at the pleasure of a fool.

Dr. Lune A. Teek

Think about this also:

> If you don't know who you are,
> You have to be what they call you.

"Mama Don't Let Your Black Boys Grow Up To Be Black Men" is a composition that's geared toward five aspects:

1. If you don't know who you are you have to be what they call you;
2. What they call you and what you call yourself is based on a paradigm that is not of your making nor choosing and is a paradox to your true way of life;
3. You as parents don't know what much of what you say to and/or teach your children is garbage;
4. Much of what a child is supposed to learn is supposed to be drawn from you as the subject matter. You have abdicated your position as subject matter and the television by of VHI and BET, etc., has taken your place, therefore you have abdicated your position of superior and moral authority as parents;
5. You must go back to the basics (if it's not too late)

Let's take a closer look at these five aspects.

The First And Second Aspects
If You Don't Know Who You Are You've
Got To Be What They Call You;
You Are Not What They (nor you) Call You

Look up the word "Black" in any dictionary.

Now I know what you're thinking - "Here's another smartass who wants to tell us about the negative definitions of the word "black" and that these definitions apply to us in a negative manner. We've heard that before so we ain't buyin' it."

Okay. You've got me. Can't pull the wool over your eyes can I? All right. So I am one of those smartasses who's going to tell you just that. And no Mr. and Mrs. (or Ms.) black America, I'm not asking you to "buy it." However, consider this: Have you ever considered how Webster's and other dictionaries come up with the words and definitions in their dictionaries? If you haven't then you should, seeing that every word you use, whether you're awake or dreaming is defined by way of dictionary recording. Of course, the exception is words you make up. However, if they're used enough by enough people the word and its definition will eventually find its way into a dictionary near you.

Dictionaries are components of publishing companies. The Webster's in front of me is a component of the G&C Merriam Company. Within this component is a group of people whose function is to scour society and social media in order to find trends and terms that have the capacity to become encapsulated into society. Once these trends/terms achieve that status, a committee chooses which ones make the cut. Keep in mind for the purpose of this topic that there is no such thing as a trend/term not predicated upon an act or a construct that was not first a concept. Such is the way of all things whether they're recorded in a dictionary or not.

A second way entries find their way into dictionaries is if a social, economic, political, psychological, medical, moral, or legal concept is applied to a specific person or persons or to a particular thing. When this happens the concept then is converted into a specific context. Once this takes place a construct is created. This created construct is then used to reference a particular person or persons, a particular thing or a particular group of things. These entries once they've been accepted into the dictionary then become the definition. The concept, which is now a construct becomes the word entry. The words (concepts) Negro, Black, and Colored fall into this category. Now I'm going to ask you something you may not have thought about. If you have and you're still calling yourself black you didn't think about it long:

WHO TOLD YOU YOU WERE BLACK?

If you have an answer then who told them? And who told who told them? And who told who told who told them?

Please take this question seriously. It is not a joke. Don't screw around with this question. And don't be an assclown with the "nobody had to tell me I was black. I always knew I was black" nonsense. To a person who truly knows who you are those words sound stupid because you're attempting to play on someone's intelligence. If you don't know say you don't know. Then find out. Trust me. By the time, all these people ask at the people who told them, they're not going to get past the third or fourth person before the words "I don't know." come into play. Especially when on most birth certificates from the early 1960's either the words "Negro" or "Colored" appear in the box or on the line marked "Race". So which one is it? Is it black, negro, or colored? Is it all three or neither? Remember:

If You Don't Know Who You Are
You've Got To Be What They Call You.

Dr. Lune A. Teek

Saying things like "It ain't what they call you it's what you answer to", and "you have the power to decide" are disingenuous ways of trying to fool yourself into thinking that this issue is not important as well as to make yourself feel good about what in truth is your unnecessary ignorance.

What if I told you that according to all true and divine records of the human race there is no negro, black, or colored race attached to the human family. Would you believe me? If I told you that there is only one race – the human race, subdivided into two groups: Asiatic and European; would you believe me? What if I told you that the terms Negro, Black, Colored, Afro-American, African-American, White, etc. are social and political status categories. Would you believe me? If not, why? It is evident that you believed someone when they told you these terms were you without giving you a shred of evidence other than the bill of sale for slaves and a birth certificate which in truth is a certification of the birth of livestock and the receipt of transfer of said stock to the state. But that's another story. I've got a million of 'em.

There was a time when it was a widely known fact that the only entity that could be classified as a citizen of the United States was an entity known in law as "Free White People" (look it up). If you research this entity, you will find a list of nations. From these nations came those "Free white men" in which the citizenship of the United States rested. This is not racism or bigotry coming from the author. It is what it is and can be researched and referenced. What this means is that "free white people" in this context is definitely not referring to skin complexion or racial identity. It is referring to a socio-political category known as "First Class Citizen". And while it is not necessarily easy to see the inner workings of the socio-political undesirable category called "Black", its outward manifestations are very clear (black codes, poll taxes, Jim Crow, "Civil" rights instead of "Unalienable" rights). I will state that there is a difference between civil rights and unalienable rights regardless to what you think or have been told. Civil rights are manifestations of the state and are issued to manifestations of the State (citizens) and as such are given and taken via legislative fiat and at best can only be described as privileges. Unalienable rights (or "inalienable" as it is sometimes called), on the other hand, as referenced by civilian and legal authorities/sources are rights bestowed upon man in accordance with nature by nature's God, and as such are non-negotiable. It also should be noted that it is a "civil" imperative within any society that those who have been classed as undesirable be subjected to all the abuses and mistreatments that the citizens care to bestow upon them and since the citizenship status of "black" people, "colored folks", and yes, "African Americans", regardless of the 14th Amendment's so called "citizenship clause" is still a questionable issue, then they, *as a people,* will still be held in second class status and as second class citizens will be continued to be treated as such. Notice I stated the term," as a people; lest you think that because you see a few black sport stars, entertainment, celebrities, business leaders, doctors, lawyers, etc., all the way up to a mulatto president I am running you amuck, leading you astray, throwing you a curve... Nothing could be further from the truth, 14th Amendment notwithstanding. Just because a clock has two hands and is going to have the correct time twice a day doesn't mean that the clock works. Trust me on this. I know what I'm talking about. If black people knew what they should know about the 14th Amendment they would know it put them in a worse bind than they already were in. If they knew the truth behind how the 14th Amendment was finally "ratified" they wouldn't believe it. However, the truth is there if one wishes to search for it. But we're getting sidetracked. Let's get back to the main issue.

You, as "black" men and "black" women hold on to this term like a boa constrictor gripping his meal after a ten-day involuntary fast because in all truthfulness it's all you know. And because of this you have built an entire life around something that was given to you for your own detriment. You don't think so? Okay, let's stack you up against other "peoples" of the world. Consider these questions:

> With the exception of slang, have you ever heard anyone from China called anything else but Chinese?
> With the exception of slang, have you ever heard anyone from Germany called anything else but German?
> With the exception of slang, have you ever heard anyone from Italy called anything else but Italian?
> With the exception of slang, have you ever heard anyone from Canada called anything else but Canadian?
> With the exception of slang, have you ever heard anyone from Russia called anything else but Russian?
> I could go on.

If your answer to the above is "no", then why is it that you are the only people topside planet spit and dirt whose "racial", "ethnic", or nationalistic identity changes every forty years or so or whenever a trend shapes public opinion of what you should be known as? Ask yourself this question; in particular if you're over the age of 55:

Did "they" ask me if I wanted to be called "African-American"?

Okay, maybe you're still being called black. Well, who asked you if you wanted to be called that? You were born "Negro" (look at your birth certificate). Did you give them the thumbs up to be called a river in west Africa? (research the etymology of Negro), But don't feel neither bad nor sad. You're not the only one this happens to. You're just the only one it happens to that has no knowledge (power) to straighten it out. Ponder this closely.

People, whether they're children or adults who come from either Mexico or any other country in South America are nationals of that country. They're either Mexican Nationals; Argentinian Nationals; Brazilian Nationals; etc. Why is it that when these people get "legal" documents here in the United States, all of a sudden, regardless of the country they're from, they all get classified as "Hispanic." What the hell is that? I mean really. What the hell is a Hispanic? Where did this name come from and who's bright idea was it to name every man, woman, child, dog, or cat that comes north of the boarder this name? And to add insult to injury depending on said man, woman, or child's skin complexion and said dog or cat's fur color they will be listed as either Hispanic "Black" or Hispanic "White". This process is called "denationalization" (look it up in a law dictionary) and it is a human rights violation for a government to practice it in any form. I'm surprised this practice hasn't been attacked by attorneys representing these people. The same thing happens to men, women, and children who come from China, Japan, Vietnam, Korea (North or South), etc. By some strange magic they become "Asians." Okay. Maybe someone can tell me what an "Asian" is. Let me get the straight. Everyone with light brownish (Not "yellow". That sounds like someone with jaundice) skin tone, straight black hair, and a slanted to slightly slanted shaped eye lid structure and descended from lands west of California are Asians? And this is what is specified as "race". Now how and what does this have to do with you, Mr. and Mrs. (or Ms.) black America? Why did I ask you to ponder this? I asked you to ponder it because the same process happened to you for far more insidious reasons and be that as it is these people are in far better shape than you. At least they:

1. Have a knowledge of their *specific* ancient ancestors;
2. Have a knowledge of their *specific* ancient ancestor's geographical location;
3. Have a knowledge of their *specific* ancient ancestor's culture (eventhough they may embrace and/or practice others);
4. Have a knowledge of their *specific* ancestor's language

Aside from the tragedy of losing this specific information about your ancient ancestors and therefore not being able to teach it to your young, an extremely important thing happened to you. At the exact time your intermediate ancestors accepted the cowbells Negro, Black, and Colored two things were taken away from them and as a result you:

1. Status
2. Self Image

Status - "A person's *legal condition* as far as it is *imposed by law without the person's consent* as opposed to a condition that the person has acquired by agreement. (Black's Law Dictionary - 7th Ed. - Emphasis mine.)

As I've related to you, the marks of Black, Negro, and Colored (and yes, African-American) as it applies to you are socio-political concepts that places you, as a people, into a socio-political construct (second class citizen), regardless of the arguments to the contrary. The term "Asian" does the same thing to the people who are given that title but ask anyone of them what they are seen as in the socio-political realm and every one of them that is aware of this will tell you they are seen as "white". Now what pure blooded "Asian" looks "white"? Now that we've dealt with the socio-politic, let's look at the legal context and construct you've been placed in. Remember, this is not, nor has it ever been about race. This is about *Class.*

First, review your definition of status. The first four words deserve your attention: "A person's legal condition...". Doesn't tell you much, does it? At least not until you know what the definition of the word "condition" is and the correct context:

Condition - 4a: a state of being. b: social status: RANK (Webster's Dictionary)

Remember, we're talking about a person's "legal" condition. Keeping the reference on legal, one can take any one of the three above definitions, replace the word "condition", and term the first part of your status definition as

1. A person's legal *state of being* (a)
2. A person's legal *social status* (b)
3. A person's legal rank (c)

Dr. Lune A. Teek

Have you found your friendly neighborhood "Asian" yet? Have you asked them what are they referred to in a social status sense? Trust me on this. They may tell you anything or any color in the rainbow, but they won't tell you "black". And if that doesn't tell you anything, ask yourself this: Are they socially and legally treated like you? A better question is this: Is any nationality of people inhabiting this soil called America treated like you?

There was a time when people from China, Canada, Philippines, Korea, were horribly discriminated against in this country by bone headed "white" males. The well-known truth that Japanese men and women were rounded up and placed in internment camps should tell you something. The truth that the law provided that the act of lynching you and placing said photographed act on a United States Mail post card and said card be mailed to any place in the country should really tell you something. You may say that was then, this is now. Let me remind you that "lynching" is more than the act of putting a rope around your neck. The "rope" around your neck can and does come in many forms and in all forms of lynching a "stabilizer" is used. This stabilizer is then moved and the body falls, the downward pressure tightens the rope around the neck, and the combination of the force of the downward pressure and the tightening of the rope breaks the neck and/or causes strangulation. Your nationality is the stabilizer that was moved from under you. Its absence caused you to be in a lower class. Therefore your...

1.   legal state of being-black;
2.   legal social status-black;
3.   legal rank-black

...is the rope that has been placed around your neck. Let's now examine how and why it got there. Let's go to the next part of the definition of status.

> "... insofar as it is imposed by law without the person's consent..."

Most people, particularly "black" people, have never seen this definition nor seen the word "status" referred to them in this context. And they definitely haven't viewed the term "black" as a legal status term. So, without further ado, let me show you how it's been and is still being done. Let me begin with these questions:

1.   On what document did you first see yourself referred to as "black"?
2.   Did you create these documents?

3. What were the documents referring to?
4. What was the specific reference point (field) that referred to you as "Black"?
5. Was the reference point already filled in? If so, who gave them the information?
6. What was the agency or commercial entity that this (these) document(s) originated from?

Again, review the definition.

> "...insofar as it is *imposed by law without the person's consent*."

The word "impose" comes from the medieval French word *imposer*, which is transferred to the Latin word *imponere*, which literally means "to put upon".

> Impose - 1a: To establish or apply as compulsory. b: To establish or make prevail by force (there's that word again - force).

Keep these definitions in mind when I tell you that the first place that this cowbell termed as "black" was recorded was on your birth certificate and that came about through one of two ways!

1. Your parent's credentials (status identifiers)
2. Hospital administrators took one look of your parents and assumed that they were "black" and therefore assumed you would be too.

And guess what? Based on what your parents have been determined to be it wouldn't have mattered if you were white as the driven snow, you still would have "black" on your birth certificate. What is a birth certificate? Well, the original is a hospital generated document which is filled out according to the set perimeters of the document. It is then sent by law to the Secretary Of State of that state and a registration number is assigned. The document is then sent to the State Bureau of Vital Statistics. The finished product is then sent to the county recorder. It goes other places but that's unimportant for the purpose of this prose at this time. Let's get back to, other than your acquiescence, what made you what you think you are.

Other than the concept of citizenship there is one other means by which "THE STATE" recognizes its members: Nationality.

Dr. Lune A. Teek

Nationality - In law, membership in a nation or sovereign state. It is
to be distinguished from citizenship (q.v.), a somewhat
narrower term that is sometimes used to denote the status
of those nationals who have full political privileges. Before
an act of the U.S. Congress made them citizens in the full
sense of the word, for example, American Indians were
sometimes referred to as "non-citizen nationals".

Individuals, companies (corporations), ships, and aircraft
all have nationality for legal purposes. *It is in reference
to natural persons*, however, that this term finds most
frequent use. Nationality is, in fact commonly regarded
as an *inalienable right of every human being*. Thus, the U.N.
Universal Declaration Of Human Rights (1948) states
that "*everyone has a right to a nationality*" and that "*no one
shall be arbitrarily deprived of his nationality*". Nationality
is of cardinal importance to every person because it is
*mainly through nationality that the individual comes within
the scope of international law and has access to the political and
economic rights and privileges conferred by modern states on their
nationals...*" (Encyclopedia Britanica - Emphasis mine)

Before I go too deep into what status black, negro, colored, or African
American really puts you in, let's dig a little into the work of semantics –
legal style.

Under the term "Nationality" as defined by Encyclopedia Britanica,
the first two words are "*in law*". You may be familiar with the term "*at law*".
In certain legal concerns, both terms are used. You need to know the
difference. Let me explain it to you as it was explained to me. You can be

1.   *at* the pond

or

2.   *in* the pond

You'd get wet in which? This distinction becomes important when you
start dealing with things in the legal vs lawful realm. Now, back to status.
As you can see from both definitions, nationality is synonymous with
a particular type of status. Without a "recognized" nationality (not "race")
one will be known as a "stateless" person. Without a *recognized* nationality one

cannot be included within the "human family". Nationality denotes people having a common origin, tradition, and language and having the ability to form or at least constitute a nation-state. Therefore, it is determined by the land (nation) from which one's ancestors derived and/or you were born.

You must notice that I placed an emphasis on the word "recognized." When I emphasizes this word, I am referring to the recognition one must have from already recognized nation-states. In other words, you came from your ancestors. Your ancestors came from somewhere. Your nationality links you back to your ancestors and identifies you as such. Said identity becomes a political and, within the confines of international law, a legal status and without the legal status of nationality you have no legal standing in the international community. You're either classified as "stateless" or a refugee. In the best of these situations, the most that one can hope for is the status of "legal resident alien", which in truth, although untold, is the status of "black" people. They are told they are "citizens" but are not told that the context that this concept called "citizen" is being referenced is the Old English feudal sense, which classes a citizen as a subject. One would only have to look at the under classed status of black people, as a constant, in order to recognize that this is an apt description of their state – past and present. Once again, the definition of status:

> "A person's legal condition insofar as it is imposed by law, without the persons' consent as opposed to a condition that the person has acquired by agreement."

This question is for parents. "Black" parents.

> When you were asked to sign your child's birth certificate and you saw that the race box or line stated that your child was "black", "negro", or "African-American" did you dispute that? If you didn't (which is the case of about 95% of you), why?

Remember:

> If you don't know who you are
> You have to be what they call you.

The above question relates to the last part of the status definition:

> "... as opposed to a condition that the person has acquired by *agreement*."

Dr. Lune A. Teek

I emphasized the words "did you dispute that" because it obviously denotes that you didn't agree with something. The fact that you didn't dispute that denotes either you didn't think you could, you didn't think it mattered, or you didn't know how, therefore you would not have known what to replace these handcuffs of political, social, and legal slavery with. And yes, they are handcuffs. When you did not dispute that one box or line with that designation either checked or listed you gave this government an admission that you didn't have the key (knowledge) to this set of cuffs and that it is just fine (agreement) to place them on your child for the rest of their natural lives. Or until they come to a realization of who they are and take the necessary steps to correct and proclaim that. Your child, however, should not have to bear that burden but they will unless your knowledge of this issue increases. Only then can you think of yourself as guardians of your children in the truest sense. Once you find out who you really are as well as what you really are and you place that knowledge at the core of your being, that awareness alone will exhort you to stop perpetuating the manufactured myth of "blackness" as your racial and/or cultural make-up and identity. Somehow it must occur to you that if you fancy yourself as deriving from "Africa" and indeed answer to the title of "African-American" you must know that nowhere in the history of that majestic land and its people has there been a tribe consisting of people aboriginal to that land that was named "black people", "Negro", or "Colored folks. I am aware of tribal language translations that allude to various descriptive concepts; however, none approach the context of European colonialist slave construction that these titles have. And you, as a people have accepted and embraced them. As a matter of truth, you, as a people, have a very nasty habit of accepting whatever is given to you by whoever gives it as long as it sounds right and fits an agenda that you have been programmed to intake and process. You do this without knowing nor understanding its origins or whether it's toxic to your overall thinking and being. This happens and will continue to happen only by your continued ignorance of the subject. Stop that! Now! You're sinking into the cesspit of the irrelevance of obliviance. In short, you're "in the way" and your decadent lifestyle and overall lack of awareness is making it extremely easy for those who are set and ready to induce and initiate mechanisms of "clearance" to move you "out of the way".

> Now, let's go on to the second thing that
> was taken from you: Self Image

According to Webster's, self-image means "one's conception of oneself or one's role." This really doesn't tell us much until we investigate the definition of the definition.

Conception - 2d: The sum of a person's ideas or beliefs concerning something. (Webster's)

We're getting warm.

Self-concept- The mental image one has of oneself. (Webster's)

Almost there.

Image - 52: A mental conception held in common by members of a group and symbolic of a basic attitude and orientation. (Webster's)

BINGO!!! Slap Me Off The Toilet *Before* I Get The Toilet Paper!!!

Let me start off by stating the obvious. Everybody that is eating, drinking, sitting, riding, or walking has a mental image of themselves. Some people like this mental image. Some don't. This type of concern is easy to deal with because you gave this mental overlay to yourself, therefore, you can change it at will. However, what happens when someone (or something) else has given you an image, and because you either don't know someone (or something) gave you that image or you don't know the image you are supposed to be portraying and you take that image as your own and start perpetuating that image? Depending upon the attributes of that image you become someone's Frankenstein. Someone's created idea of a sick, twisted joke gone seriously awry. And this is the plight of "black" people; a population of entities designed mentally to be followers of trends subliminally implanted within targeted segments for the express purpose of consumer activity. In short, a commercial transmitting utility. And if there is no other greater truth in this existence be assured that as long as your priority in life is to be a consumer you will never be a producer. Those who gave you your identity/image are aware of this. They're banking on the fact (and the proceeds) that not enough of you realize it. And trust me, they can do that. After all, they own the bank (and the proceeds) and whether you know it or believe it or not, they own you too. But that's another topic I may or may not discuss in another essay.

The issue of self-image is a very powerful one. Joined at the hip with self-esteem, it is the single most important variable necessary to have a complete existence. It is also the single most important variable that will determine the quality of that existence. A powerful self-image equals a powerful existence. A weak self-image equals a weak existence. At first glance this seems elementary, however black people, for some strange reason, can't make it past first grade on this. And in the time-honored tradition of cause and effect there is a reason why black people are on what I call "the Farris wheel of life". Contrary to popular belief, what you don't know *will* hurt you. The amount and severity of pain you will receive will be exponentially proportional to the amount of your ignorance. Therefore, you cannot afford to be ignorant of anything where your sense of self is concerned. Yet this is an arena that black people don't even know how to get to let alone enter. But get there you must. Enter you must. Why? Let me remind you again:

> If you don't know who you are
> You've got to be what they call you.

So, let's examine some of the well-known foibles and fallacies that you have subjected yourselves to in the name of self-image. First up:

#1. Light, Bright, and Damn Near White (aka)
Ms. "High Yella" and Mr. "Light Skinned"

If black people are just becoming concerned about "white privilege" it is because they always had concerns about the privileges connected with and given to lighter hued "black" people. Unless they've lived under a rock at the South Pole somewhere, almost all black people over 45 are aware of this issue. A lot of them have had firsthand experience with it. Black women in particular. Oh my have black women had to deal with this. And the darker their skin, the deeper the knife wound in their back. Believe it or not, if you really think about it, one entity is responsible for all the pain, self-doubt, and self-esteem issues that dark skinned women suffered because of this issue. That one entity of course, is men.

Yes. Men. Think about it.

I knew you'd see things my way. Go with the flow. It's easier.

The concept of light skinned over dark skinned has caused many a conflict that has stretched and even broken bonds from best friends to families and it all stems from one cause: rejection. And most often, darker skinned women were at the receiving end of this rejection, which often came at the hands of men. Oh, of course there were the malicious and hurtful remarks from other women and girls who perceived dark skinned women and girls as not as "pretty". This, however, is social rejection. The rejection from men was different as it spanned from the social realm to the professional circuit. From secretaries to cinema, when a black woman was needed a lighter skinned black woman was often chosen. One of the most famous rejection lines, so famous that in some instances it's still used is "she's too ethnic," which means she's either too dark or too "thick" (curvy). And who's at the giving end of these rejections? Men most often. I'm not going to get into the issue of relationship rejection other than to say that darker skinned men, if they understood the nature of this issue, reacted differently to this type of rejection. Why? If they were rejected they knew that it was always a light skinned or white woman somewhere that they could hold hands and skip through a field of daisies with. Is this a case of opposites attract? No, this is about people with an acute case of the dumbass. Oftentimes black men dealt with lighter skinned women because they felt they were "prettier" than dark skinned women. I've heard black men brag about their "redbones" (This is not correct. Light skinned people are not "red"). I've met light skinned women who've said everything from "I like the contrast"; to "I'm rejecting the 'white' part of me"; to "I don't want nothing to do with a "red" nigger."

This psychotic stir fried rice type of thinking has been written about in books and depicted in movies. Personally, I'm still trying to figure out what the hell "good hair" is. Luckily, a lot of this behavior has died down somewhat. The problem is, other than being able to say, "I'm pretty too", or "Our dark-skinned sisters need us brothers", none of this tear 'em down, push 'em out behavior brought black men and black women closer to the truth about who they really are and therefore the image they should be propagating. And since this mental disorder has never fully been addressed, black people, *as a whole*, cannot and will not make the transition from being a beggar nation of people to a people who are "upright, independent, and fearless." It is impossible for me to wrap my mind around the fact that in 2016 black people are still singing (with tears in their eyes, mind you) "We Shall Overcome." Now before you think I've gotten sidetracked, everything I've described earlier leads to something that you've had and still have and that something you have that under no circumstances can you afford to have is separation. If you've read the writings of Mr. William Lynch, master slave psychologist, you will see that the "pit one nigger against the other nigger" strategy is alive and kicking in 2016 albeit there are those in the black community that are striving to combat this type of thinking. By the way, here's an interesting thing about good 'ole "Willie" Lynch. If some of you have read the "Willie Lynch Letter" (Not a letter. A set of instructions), and some of you have; and if you paid close attention to it, and some of you have; you will notice that Mr. Lynch put a date on the effectiveness of his methods. I believe the date is 300 years. If you count the year this letter was written and add 300 years you will find a very recent date. I know for a fact that I'm not the first to notice this. It is very interesting, nevertheless. One other thing that should be taken into consideration. Read these instructions carefully. It should not escape your notice that the strategy of the Willie Lynch Letter was and is geared specifically toward the black woman. Every black woman should have a copy of this letter. Every "gang" member should be made to memorize it. Every black child should be taught its significance. Especially black girls. It should not be watered down nor should its effects. And make no mistake about it, its objective is based solely on cause and effect. And it has already been witnessed by the world just how effective those causes are. Another important note before I let this go in which you need to take notice of is the atavistic character of these instructions.

> Atavisim - (From the Latin *atavus*, meaning *ancestor*) - recurrence in an organism or in any of its parts of a form typical of ancestors more remote than the parents; usually due to genetic recombination. (Webster's Dictionary - Emphasis mine)

There is an entire section of breeding instructions in this essay as well as objectives and strategies of said breeding instructions. There was a method involved with crossbreeding that you may never have thought about and although the aftermath of this practice is crudely mentioned I am about to present it to you in its purest, rawest form. Please take note. The offspring of the white slave owner and his slave was and still is referred to as "Mulatto". I will now present to you, courtesy of Webster's Dictionary, the etymology of the word "mulatto".

> Mulatto - (Spanish *mulato*, from *mula* mule. From Latin *mulus*)

So, the Spanish form of this word means "mule". Now read the definition. Go back to the section of Mr. Lynch's instructions that detail this issue. Eventhough Mr. Lynch is as much detailed about the specifics of the crossbreeding as this (for obvious reasons), it is evident that it was designed to weaken the gene pool of a specific group. What did you, as a people, allow this issue to become? A wedge to be used to drive you literally insane is what you did. But then again, isn't that what Mr. Lynch said you would do? Please take note and understand, this is not the musings of a bigoted Author.[*] If you "do the knowledge" of what I am reminding you of it should become very apparent that you've wasted a lot of time, energy, and life fulfilling

---

[*] The Author is not a book. The Author is, however, a Class I, Grande A lunatic.

someone else's agenda and you have absolutely nothing at all to show for it. You, in the 21st century are falling for the same sado-masochistic nonsense your ancestors fell for in the 12th thru the 15th century and it has gotten you the same results: rot from the inside out. Now for the next bit of nonsense you have stumbled into on the way to the land of self-delusion:

2. Hard Boiled Eggheads

The first thing I need to do before I get deep into this section is to point out a very simple truth. This truth has been witnessed by many people therefore it is a known fact. Known as it may be, few people if any will openly state it. This may be because of fear or political correctness. I assure you; this Author is neither, therefore let me state for the record that there is a segment of "black" males between the ages of 15-35 that

1. have not been taught how to think for themselves; or
2. have lost the knowledge of how to think for themselves; or
3. will not think for themselves

Either one of these conditions constitutes different degrees of retardation and will most assuredly lead to at least two of the three paths an addict learns he or she is most likely to tread: jail or death. There is a reason for this lack of mental prowess among this group. Before we go there let's go here:

1. retard - 1. To slow up, especially by preventing or hindering advance or accomplishment. (Webster's Dictionary).

    retardation 4a - an abnormal slowness of thought or action...
    b. slowness in development or progress. (Webster's Dictionary)

Keep in mind that this discussion centers on self-image which is necessary in one's development. Whether or not this development manifests itself into a positive individual exemplified through positive examples of thoughts, words, and actions depends much on what this individual has mentally ingested. In short, "garbage in, garbage out". Because of the garbage mentally ingested within the psyche of black males between 15 and 35 an onerous existence has taken root within the black community and it is due to the very thing that makes genocide/fratricide fashionable. That "very thing" being an inability of far too many Black males within this age group to understand that they have been molded into weapons to be used against their own people. How did this happen?

"... if thy right eye offendth thee pluck it out..." (Matt. 5:29 KJV)

I doubt very seriously that the black males I am referring to have read this passage but strangely enough it seems as though they are taking this verse literally when it comes to other black males between the same ages as them. There is a rationale to this behavior and it revolves around the aspect of being "retarded" as it relates to their self-image development. Why is this? To understand this phenomenon, first review the definitions of retarded. Now that you've done this, you can begin to see that something is at work that is "preventing or hindering" their accomplishing a positive self-image. Let us examine this phenomenon I call "the 'Hard' black male", also known as "Hard Boiled Eggheads".

In speaking to a series of black males between 15 and 35 concerning different issues of life as well as lifestyle I asked them thirteen questions. Here are the questions:

1. Are you Hard? What does being Hard mean?
2. Who told you this? Who told them?
3. Who told you that you need to be this?
4. Why are you trying to be this?
5. How are you viewed by your peers if you can't or don't want to be this?
6. What does being "Hard" look like?
7. What does being "Hard" sound like?
8. What happens if you used to be "Hard" and now you want to stop?
9. Will someone "pick" on you? Who? Why?

I 've asked several black males in this age group the first question before I developed the others. I developed the others because I've yet to get a cohesive, uniform response to the first. What I've found in my research which is based on these questions and empirical observation is that America has hatched a generation of black boys and black men who are acting within the parameters of a mentality that has been fed to them from whence they know not and at best can only be described as "psychosomatic niggeristic stress syndrome"; or the stress and fear one gets when they are faced with the decision of whether they want to be a nigger or a man and realizing that they can't be both. Black males across the country are succumbing to this mental disorder which robs them of their fundamental faculties of common sense. By themselves they have no hope of understanding it nor how they developed it. To them, this idea of being "Hard" means the same as standing up for themselves, or, in their eyes, having power. This disorder began as a shield young black males used to hide their insecurities and fears, from academic failure to their place in the pecking order among their peers. Rappers later brought these characteristics to the fore on a nationwide level. Suddenly lyrics that were meant to educate you (which in truth is what Hip-Hop was/is about) became "soft" and "whack" while lyrics about "mo money, mo power, mo respect" became the "in" thing. Rappers throwing money at strippers, driving sport cars, etc., etc. was thrust into the mindsets of young black males. A cottage industry called "video vixens" sprang up. Just for kicks, ask your average black male who told them that wearing their pants below their asscheeks makes them look cool? When did letting the world know that you've got drawers on become the in thing to do? In my day sagging was something you did when you were either pissy drunk or got the piss beat out of you. How does all of this lend itself to what you have now as it relates to what we've gone over? Plenty. Let's start at what's necessary to be "hard".

In order to be "hard" one must be able to enforce their hardness. In street culture, which a vast majority of black males in this age group see themselves as representing, this means having a gun. Why? Because "the street" is not where you will find the CEO of a billion-dollar Fortune 500 corporation. The educational level just isn't there. Neither is the caviar. In order to function (survive) in this environment (survival of course means being able to make money, aka "getting money") one cannot, if one can help it, find themselves on the defensive. Now normal, sane people mostly understand that defensive reaction is a normal part of life, therefore they use offensive strategies such as long-term planning in order to be able to move into a defensive posture. For the "hard" guy in the street, however, being on the defense means someone got the drop and depending on the business at hand, getting the drop on someone has some very nasty consequences associated with it. Just as they are equalizers in the hands of law-abiding citizens, guns are equalizers in the hands of the "Hard" black male of the street. After all, the streets are hard so he has to be "hard" and having a weapon along with the willingness to use it are his means of enforcement. He doesn't (and most often won't) have to have the knowledge of his weapon nor the mental aptitude necessary to know when, where, or who to use this deliverer of death and carnage against. All he needs to perceive is that this weapon gives him power. And it does. And he is still retarded. And still hard.

Another thing one must have in order to be hard is the lingo. Language plays an important role here. Correct cadence is a must. Idiomatic phrases such as "I don't give a fuck"; "Shit on that nigga"; and "Fuck them 'ho's" have to be stated in a certain tone in order for the full meaning to be conveyed and regardless to whether the speaker is from Miami, Maine, Alaska, or Compton the same holds true. Some black women in this environment have adopted this element and have elevated it to an art form. These black women have taken one word "bitch", and this one word can have five different connotations depending on the cadence and the pitch of her voice. And again these things are understood regardless of locale. And lest we forget, one cannot be hard without being "real". The idea of the "real nigga" is the embodiment of everything a hard, black male strives to be. To be sure, there is a criterion to being a "real nigga". Yes, there's being a "nigga"; "my" nigga", "a 'bitch-ass' nigga", and any other "nigga" under the sun and atop of the moon. And then there's a "real nigga". A class of nigga all to itself. Every nigga who is a nigga either wants to be a "real nigga" or is jealous of one. An honor it is to be a "real nigga" as well as a responsibility. He has to hold up the bloodstained banner of the nation of "real nigga". He has to show all other niggas and niggarettes what it is to be a "real nigga". He is the realest nigga of all niggadom. And he is still retarded. And hard. Real retarded. Real hard. A real niggah.

A blueprint is someone's mental conception of how something is supposed to look or work placed on paper. Who created the blueprint for the negro, black and colored (NBC) person? Who created the blueprint for the African -American? Who drew up the blueprint for the "real nigga"? Have you ever given these questions any thought? Probably not. Why would you when you think that who you think you are is who you really are? Why would you when you think that how you are acting is how you're supposed to act? And yet you admit and realize that as a people your lot in life sucks. You can admit and realize that practically every nation of people can come to this nation and thrive while you were born here and are at the bottom of every list that deals with anything pointing toward a positive track. What was that definition of insanity? If I looked up this word in the dictionary, would I see the words "black people" given as an example?

Listen. Words are symbols that define specific (or abstract) concepts. Self-image is about a concept: You. Specifically, what you think about you. If what you think about you is muddled by what others have told you you either should or have to be things normally get very confusing for you. Take this example.

You say you are "African-American". What does it mean to be African-American? What does it mean to be African? What does it mean to be American? Have you ever been to Africa? Can you speak the language? This is impossible because there is no such thing as an "African" language. Do you even know anyone from Africa? Do you know how that name came about and who it really belongs to? Have you gone through a tribal rite of passage?

Do not scarf at these questions. Do not say they don't matter. They do. You are attempting to identify with a group of people as to say that you are a part and partial (parcel) of these people. While it is true that what your ancient forefathers were you are today without doubt or contradiction there is more to this than that. Trust and believe, if you knew who and what you really were and are you would not be calling yourselves every name someone gives you. And you definitely wouldn't be a "real nigga", therefore you wouldn't be retarded. And hard. Have "White" people been called anything but "White"? Think about it.

The Third And Fourth Aspects
"Parents Just Don't Understand"

If you take a good read of aspect #3, you'll most likely will think that I'm nuts for writing it. Until you consider this:

Eventhough you may think that what you're saying makes sense what do you think your kid(s) think about it? If you're saying, "It's not supposed to make sense. They're kids."; then why say it? Once upon a time in a lot of black neighborhoods when parents said "Do as I say and not as I do" the children understood that was the law. This is a new era of time now. Not only do you as parents just don't understand, but your designation as parents has been stripped. By whom or what, you might ask? By social media and videos of course. And then, there's that "real nigga" lurking in the corner.

What are you teaching your children and how are you teaching them? These are extremely important questions because as I stated you are supposed to be the focal point (subject matter) of your child's education. You are (or should be) their first teacher, therefore you should be their primary influence. If I were to ask your daughter who influences her the most and she tells me anyone (or anything) other than you we've got a problem. If I asked your son who influences him the most and he tells me the name of some guy you nor I've never heard of, then when I ask who is this guy and he tells me; "He's a 'real nigga'", we've got a problem. I say "we" to remind you that regardless of whether you realize it or not, believe it or not, or accept it or not your child, like the wings of that proverbial butterfly, will have a direct or indirect influence in the lives of a great number of people, in which I may be one. If your daughter grows up and marries my son and her biggest influence is Lizzie Borden, trust me, we'll be going to a lot of funerals. If your son can say with a straight face, "I don't love dem 'ho's"; someone's life is about to be ruined. In particular if he's trying to date my daughter.

Influence is the result of connecting with someone. People, places, or things that you can connect with have a big influence in your life. When you connect with others you have an influence in their lives. This doesn't limit itself to people to people contact. You have an influence in the life of your pet and vice versa. The issue here is that these influences oftentimes act as conduits for learning. Sometimes the transmissions of learned patterns of behavior happens without one being consciously aware of it. Take "hoodies" for example. Zip up or pull over jackets have been in existence since the dinosaurs were chasing a meal called Adam and Eve through the woods. They had hoods then and they have hoods now. Why is it that now every wardrobe must have at least ten? I've seen grown men wear a pair of Chuck Taylor Converse basketball shoes with a $5,000.00 suit, and glory to Jesus, Joesph, and Mary I've seen men proudly wear pants so tight they'd make Jezebel blush. How did these things become the "in" thing to do? Influence, whether through different forms of media or through peer centered conformity is often the culprit and it is here where when you take a serious, unbiased look at the behavior of your children there is no other explanation you can come up with except that, as I've stated, you've abdicated your position as subject matter and other nouns have taken your place. It is because of this fact a very large portion of black boys and black men between the ages of 15-35 are in prison and not college and although either one can be viewed as an institute of learning the consequence of continued matriculation of the former is not as advantageous as the latter.

Esoterically speaking, a child's mind is extremely developed at birth and is already anchored in certain aspects of life lessons. The mind, being the intangible that it is, must manifest itself through the limitations of the physical functions of the brain. The brain, through its various functions is responsible for the receiving, storing, and transmitting outside stimuli that some of us call either experiences or information/data. When these are stored in a specific area of the brain they are called memories. If past life regressionists are to be believed, these experiences and/or information/data which when stored in the brain are called memories are somehow uploaded to the mind and as the ancient sages say, "mind never forgets". One must understand that if what a past life regressionist's client is seeing under hypnosis really is them in another time (past) they did not have the same brain then that they have now. Hey, go figure!

The importance of this is so you can understand why your children, especially black males between the ages of 15-35 are acting in the manner that they are. Anytime someone or something else other than you looms larger than you in your child's life one of two things are happening:

1. You are not in your child's life enough, or
2. Your child, for whatever reason, is rejecting your presence and influence in their life.

Number 1 is easy enough to understand and is a definite problem. Number 2 however, denotes problems within problems and until the blanket is lifted and the dirty sheets are changed you don't have nor will have any credible influence in your child's life and whatever you try to teach your child will be met with skeptism at best and outright rejection at worst. And whether you as "black" parents want to accept it or not, this is an outright rejection of you. Let me explain.

Let's go back to past life regression, which is a roundabout way of referring to reincarnation. If this phenomenon is true (which in my "humble" opinion it is), have you given thought to the fact that the being you have produced in the "flesh" in this era of time may have been born, lived, and died in another era of time? This is something that can only be understood by viewing it from a metaphysical/esoteric point of reference basically because it is an esoteric metaphysical concept, or what some would call "spiritual".

The reason why this question is important is because if this is true it is a possibility that within your teaching you are forgetting that your children are spirits, fully formed spiritually, that are inserting themselves into physical bodies. Because much of what they see in their environment is not spiritual in nature they are outright rejecting it and if "it" means your position as parents so be it. Don't believe it? Follow me for a minute.

Let's start off with the birth of your child.

Now I'm not going to get into the harsh conditions that is your child's first encounter with beings called humans and all that goes with that. Let's start before that. What did you teach your child before you had (given birth to) your child? Seriously.

I asked you earlier about your knowledge of Africa. This is the importance of that question. In your ancient ancestor's culture, the preparation of a child begins in the mother's womb. A child's education begins in the mother's womb. The education of the mother, in order for her to able to educate her child in the womb, began during her education as a child by the elder mothers of the tribe. She, as a daughter, is taught by the mothers everything she needs to know in order to be a wife, a mother, and her place in the tribe. Likewise with the father. He is prepared as a child by the men of the tribe. He is taught how to be a husband, a father, a provider, and a protector not only for himself and his family, but also for the tribe. While not all tribes do this the ones that do are doing it for a reason. This pattern of instruction is called a rite of passage and can also be seen within the tribes of indigenous Americans (Indians).

The inclusion of this here is for a specific reason that most black people have not considered as a rationale for the patterns of behavior being displayed within the community. Rites of passage have a specific purpose and that purpose is to teach girls and boys how to be women and men. There are specific things that are taught and they are taught in a specific sequence. These are not overnight lessons. In some tribes preparations take years of instruction. For the child, mastering these lessons are of the utmost importance. There is a reason for this. Listen closely black people.

In case you glossed over what I stated earlier, rites of passages have a specific purpose and that is to teach girls and boys to be women and men.

Here is why understanding this is important to you. In order to do this, you must understand the nature of the rite of passage. The rite of passage has four important aspects:

1. Girls are taught by women, separate of boys. Boys are taught by men, separate from girls;
2. The nature of the rite of passage demands a strong communal (tribal) construct to support it;
3. Mastery of the instructions of the rite will be determined by individual or group testing;
4. Mastery of the rites is the gateway to manhood and womanhood. Passage of the rites determine placement in the society. Failure may range from lower communal placement to banishment depending on the rite and the tribe and the reason for the failure.

Regardless to what one may think or say, a woman cannot teach a man how to be a man. Nor should she attempt to. Likewise, a man cannot teach a woman how to be a woman. Nor should he attempt to. Because of the scatterbrained thinking within the black community in this country, a new phenomenon called "single parenting" has become somewhat of the norm. I use the word "scatterbrained" because of some of the reasons behind why black families find themselves in this predicament. At any rate, none of the four things listed above are being done within the black community as a whole. There are consequences to this lack of conscious structure. Notice the first sentence of number 4

"Mastery of the rites is the gateway to manhood and womanhood"

What this means is that a boy doesn't become a man until the elders say he is a man. And this means the passing of tests to prove he has learned what he needs to know. He either passes his tests and passes into manhood or he fails them and is classed as an undesirable. This is very much unlike the culture here wherein one's manhood is given as one reaches a certain age. One does not have to learn anything. A part of your true ancestral custom, "black" man and "black" woman, dictates that boys and girls must *prove* themselves worthy of the status of "man" and "woman". A very interesting concept indeed. In particular when many black males and black females between the ages of 15-35 who live in "urban" centers have never caught, killed, nor plucked a chicken. You may not understand how that fits here but if you think about it for a moment, you will. You never forget what you learn. In this life or the next.

Dr. Lune A. Teek

I had to reference rites of passage to let you know what you as a people are lacking in order for you to have something to relate to so you can understand just how far off track you are by not having them. Because you have gotten so far away from the marks your ancestors set for you to achieve you cannot conceive of what it was to be them and believe it or not you may be the only people on earth who have this problem.

> To "black" parents:
> Men: What standards and protocols do you use to teach your son(s) to be men? Where did they come from? Who gave them to you?
> Women: What standards and protocols do you use to teach your daughter(s) to be women? Where did they come from? Who gave them to you?

Have either of you ever stopped to think that the standards and protocols you are teaching your son(s) and daughter(s) were meant to be taught to someone else's son(s) and daughter(s) and not yours. In short, the primary instruction of a god involves what it takes to be a god. Not a king and certainly not a pauper. What am I saying to you? Simple:

> Render to Ceasar what is Ceasars'
> And render to god what is gods'.
> You are not Ceasar. Stop being a pauper.
> Give Ceasar back "their" instructions.

If you Dad, didn't teach your son that wearing his pants below his asscheeks was cool and he's wearing his pants below his asscheeks, someone or something did. If you Mom, didn't teach your daughter that wearing a skirt so short that it shows her asscheeks was cool and she's wearing a skirt so short that it shows her asscheeks, someone or something did.

Listen. Parenting is the most important job in life. Why are you delegating the responsibility of this sacred duty to someone or something else? It might not look like you are, and you might not think that you are, but you are. All these black males between the ages of 16-23 who have either shot, stabbed, beat, robbed, or murdered other black males between the ages of 16-23 didn't spring up from a tomatoe patch last night. These are your sons. If they didn't see you shoot, stab, beat, rob, or murder someone then where did they get the idea that this is the "in" thing to do? Where did they get their concept of "hard"? Where did they get the perception that being a "real nigga" was something that they should aspire to be? When did going to prison become a badge of honor? If your son is not a cop, why would he rather have a gun in his pants than a belt to hold them around his waist? I'm going to give you the benefit of the doubt and assert that they didn't get these ideas from you, nor did they learn them in school, although you nor school haven't really taught a certain segment of black males between the ages of 15-35 anything that moves them from their current mindset in which they are bent on barreling down a course of self-destruction and genocide through self-destructive and genocidal behavior. How do you stop and reverse that pattern? A few things are in order. It all starts with you. It always starts with you. And because this truth became obsolete with you with you is where your existence as a somewhat "free" people is subject to end. Why? Because you are feeding your children the same garbage that you were fed and you're feeding them from the same garbage can. And when you're not busy feeding them garbage you're allowing garbage men and garbage women to fed them the garbage they've been recycling for centuries. It's okay now. I'm here. You have this book. Now let's review *some* things just to let you know how much garbage you've ingested. Afterward I'll tell you how imparting other things to your sons might have kept them out of the "streets", prison, or a grave.

Dr. Lune A. Teek

Tightening Up

To be sure, it is a sad and damning phenomenon when the life expectancy of black men and women is higher than that of black boys and black girls. It is a sad and damning phenomenon when the most dangerous things to black boys and black girls are black boys and police. It is a sad and damning phenomenon when the most dangerous thing to black babies are black women who seem to have a love affair with abortion clinics and black men who seem to have a love affair with themselves. Not long ago in New York the rate of black abortions were higher than that of black births. Mrs. (or Ms.) black America, you really need to do some honest to damn God research on Margret Sanger. She is the founder of Planned Parenthood. If you can go to Planned Parenthood or any other abortion facility after that then you need help. Serious help. And speaking of New York...

... I read an article in New York Times by noted author Roxanne Gay entitled "Where Are Black Children Safe?". A very apt question considering. This piece starts off by relating the story of the black girl who was enrolled at certain high school in South Carolina and who was literally manhandled (actually a nice way of putting it) from her chair while in class because she refused to leave the classroom for being "disruptive". This of course was caught on camera, placed on the internet, went viral, became the highlight of the 6:00 am, 12noon, 6:00pm and 6:30 newscasts, and set off a firestorm among liberal and conservative talk show hosts and political pundits. My view on this, to put it mildly is as follows: It could not have been my daughter. I'll leave it at that.

With that said, as I read Ms. Gay's article a thought occurred to me that coincides with, as I read it, her frustrations.

In the article Ms. Gay highlighted a philosopher who wrote about a phenomenon called "Panopticon" (look it up). She also wrote about the increased amount of surveillance, whether by way of cameras in phones or governmental apparatus that we have not so blindly stumbled into and whether any of it makes a difference in stopping these types of abuses involving these children. It is here that I will voice this thought to Ms. Gay as well as the rest of the world to consider:

> Has it ever occurred to those who wonder that these incidences are now more than ever before being constantly shown in the media to reinforce the idea that those who are truly concerned are impotent as it relates to coming up with real solutions; and most importantly, being able to implement them?

Before you become the rabbit in someone else's rabbit hole it is very important for you to stop and understand that there truly are no coincidences. If you aren't making something happen, if it's happening, someone else did. If you didn't dig that rabbit hole, someone (or something) else did. The etymological definition of the word "Paradigm" means "to show side by side". Consider first, what you're being shown. Then know that you are, by your own volition, living in a paradigm of someone else's creation and paradigms, such as they are, have their own rules, texts, and subtexts. Remember I said earlier, if you can't know who you are, you have to be what they call you. Why? Because you don't know. You don't know what's truth or fiction and because of your ignorance you have no power to stop anything that's happening to you. You must have power because without power it is impossible to become a force. What power, you ask. In this instance, the power to choose. And not just to choose but to choose *wisely*. In order to do this you need two things:

Correct Knowledge

Yes Mr. and Mrs. (or Ms.) black America, this is what you're lacking. Of course, it always comes back to this. And why wouldn't it? How do I know you don't have correct knowledge? Simple. You have questions. Questions that if you had the correct knowledge you wouldn't have to ask. Beside this, look at the stage of black America. I would leave it at that, but I won't. Let me give you a couple of examples.

Ms. Gay speaks to the "presumption of guilt" as it relates to being black in America and in this, she is speaking in the general sense of being black in America. Sad as it is if black people would be brutally honest with themselves, they would realize the role they played in producing these presumptions. However, there are some presumptions that they had nothing to do with producing but find themselves subjected to on an alarming frequent basis. I happen to be aware that whenever a person (black or white) enters a courtroom as a "defendant" anywhere in America there are twelve presumptions they must overcome and yes one of them is the presumption of guilt. Can you, Mr. and Mrs. (or Ms.) black America name the other eleven? If you can, good. If you can't, why? And would it really matter if you would just find a way to keep your damn asses out of a courtroom? That way, you'll overcome something greater than the twelve presumptions and that is the necessity to overcome the twelve presumptions. Don't get me wrong, appearing in a courtroom is something that sometimes happens. Believe me, I am a witness to this. My suggestion:

> Never walk in then out of a courtroom without learning something that will keep you from ever having to walk in then out of a courtroom.

The other example of having correct knowledge being "Key" in forward movement is about just that: Keys.

Take a key ring with a thousand keys on it. Stand in front of a locked door. Now unlock the door.

Providing that the one key necessary to unlock this door is on this key ring, if you don't know which key is the "correct" key you may be standing in front of this door for quite a while. Such is the importance of having correct knowledge. The locked door is not the problem. You not knowing the correct key is. You have a thousand keys. Nine hundred and ninety-nine of them are the incorrect key for the door you are standing in front of. Only one key is the correct one. Such is the situation of you as "black" people. You are standing in front of a locked door. On the other side of the door is abundant life. On the side you are standing on is abundant destruction and death. Each black man and black woman along with their offspring are standing in front of a locked door with a thousand keys in their hand. Nine hundred and ninety-nine of them are incorrect keys. Only one of them is the correct key. And here is where I go back to the explanation of knowing who your true ancestors are. It is nothing (and I mean nothing) that you are going through that your ancient and intermediate ancestors did not go through. If that is the case (it is) then it is they with their wisdom that can provide you with the answer to which key unlocks which door. Each one of those keys unlocks a door. Each door is a problem situation. This whole example stands for the power of and in having correct knowledge. But even this is not enough because as desirous as it is knowledge, correct or otherwise, is only information (data) and in and of itself is insufficient. For example, you know which key the correct key is to open a specific door. You open it. Now what? How much of an *understanding* do you have of the environment you have just entered? Understanding is the other level of awareness you must have in order to prosper. Law governs all events and if you don't understand the laws that govern the events that can and do move and position you within your environment you will be lost. In order to prosper not only do you need an understanding of that which governs your environment you need to know and be able to utilize those laws in order to manipulate specific aspects of reality within your environment. In this I am speaking to the metaphysical context of your awareness. However, all movement relating to the metaphysical must first begin with movement on the physical. It is far easier to show a man he needs to first seek the kingdom of heaven when he has a full stomach than it is when he's hungry enough to eat a salamander. It is this type of "pie in the sky, by and by, when you die", as Reverend Ike would say, thinking that has kept black people from becoming as successful as they could be. The other thing that has kept them at the bottom of the societal ladder is their lack of understanding of the role that casualty plays in the existence of humanity. Every cause will most definitely have an effect. Every move a chess grandmaster makes is based on the moves that most likely will occur as a *result* of his/her initial move, all the way to fourth, fifth, or six moves ahead. Being mindful of the consequences of your actions is not just something that should be limited to chess players. If you take a serious, unbiased look at the plight of black America, a great amount of their lack of forward movement can be traced back to not doing this. You, as "black men and women, must realize that everything you do and everything you say causes a ripple in the waters of human existence. However, these "waters" are not of unlimited scope. They have boundaries and when the ripples that you have sent out over these waters reach those boundaries it is the nature of these ripples to return to the source from which they came. Hence, sayings like "You live by the sword you die by the sword" and "You reap what you sow" take on a seriousness that should never be taken for granted. Especially by a people who are stuck in something that has the brown color of mud but has a very sharp, unpleasant smell.

What Time Is It?

As I wrote the previous segment a thought occurred to me. It came in the form of a question. What aspect of existence ties all of this together? Just as quick the answer came. None of what I or anyone else recommends that you do nor anything you want to be successful in will ever come to fruition if you don't take this aspect of life gravely serious.

Practically everyone you know and don't know has a watch. Keeping up with what time it is is a worldwide concern. Clocks of one type or another are in almost everything. Because they are in computers, cars, phones, entertainment systems, etc., clocks symbolize a very important facet of the human existence: the need to know the time and to be on time. But this isn't about knowing the time, being on time, or clocks for that matter. Not in the context that most people, especially "black" people view this issue. And a crucial component of a successful life is the correct understanding of contextual perception. Such as is here. Read carefully.

Time, in and of itself is not of the essence. *Timing*, however, is. To be truthful, timing *is* everything. And everything *is* timing.

Do not be confused. Least of all about this. This is one of the most crucial aspects of life that you as "black" people have forgot that your ancestors taught you and as a result you as "black" people have doomed yourself to a lifetime of frustration. Practically everyone, whether you're "black" or "white" has experienced this, particularly when one has done something or said something that was correct (or at least to them it was) but whatever they did or said they did or said it at the incorrect time, which in some cases, is worse than doing or saying the incorrect thing at the incorrect time. A good sense of timing is something that is part training and part intuition. There are certain situations where common sense will dictate when and when not to move on a specific thing or when and when not to speak on a certain thing. The type, amount, and duration of your training will depend on how soon you can master the necessary task of sequencing your "inner clock". You know, that voice that you hear talking to you eventhough no one's within a mile of you. This is the voice that every time you disregard it you wind up as Satan's roommate. This voice also takes the form of a "sense". It is hard to describe this "sense", but you know it when you feel it. Disregard it at your peril. With that said, I'll sum up this section thus:

Somewhere within this coarse dialogue I wrote something about keys. I can, without doubt or contradiction tell you that you are being manipulated. By and through multiple sources. You must start and maintain the job of thinking for yourself. Believe me if you don't someone (or a bunch of someone's) will do it for you. In a sense, I'm presenting you with keys. Not necessarily to solve problems but to make you aware of the specifics of the problems you have as well as how you are responsible for their existence, which is notably the first step in solving them. I can also without doubt or contradiction tell you that there are no skeleton keys for you. There is only choice. The choices range from one to infinity. While it is true that every incorrect choice brings you closer to the correct choice, it also means the more time you will spend on the side of destruction and death. And while you may be able to duck and dodge destruction you sure as hell can't outmaneuver death and if you can't get to the key that unlocks the door to abundant life then abundant death is your calling and you will drag your children with you. My suggestion? Choose wisely. Or die miserably.

SECTION FIVE
A FOUNDATION YOU CAN WALK ON

Eventhough the underlying and overall concept of this entire chapter concerns itself with the underlying and overall development of your children, I could not begin the specifics of that until I first educated you and impressed upon you the importance not only of learning these things being discussed here but also the importance of you making sure your child *sees you living them.* You have to start being their major influence. You have to stop sending them mixed signals.

When you are trying to uplift a nation of people who at the time had no credible self-consciousness but were perpetuating an image of themselves that was created for them then it was somewhat okay to be "black and proud" and "young, gifted, and black" and espouse "black power" into every nook and cranny that it would fit into. This is a new era of time and you, personally and as a people must come to grips with a few facts:

1. Your ancestors could not have been lawfully nor legally held as slaves unless their political, legal and social identification was changed from what they were known as to that of Negroes, Blacks, and Coloreds. Doing this changed their status (class).
2. The fact that these three cowbells (Negro, Black, Colored) have absolutely nothing to do with skin color and everything to do with the description of being "the property of...".
3. The fact that every so called "conscious" description and definition associated with this term (black) has been concocted by the minds of misdirected, thus miseducated "black" people and disingenuous "white" people who attempt to apply this term in the metaphysical sense while keeping the context of the person in the physical sense of present time. A damn good reference to read about this is *The Myth Of Blackness* by Sheik Way-El.

I have faith that if "black" people thoroughly understood who and what they really are, they would understand the truth of the matter and it is this:

Your ancestors then and you now survived everything that was thrown, heaped, shoveled, dumped, and placed on their and your heads and in their and your paths and it had nothing to do with them or you being "black" or them or you identifying as such. They nor you didn't survive because they and you were black. They and you survived despite being termed black. Despite the musings of the pseudo-metaphysics, this being "black" did not, cannot, nor will not endue you with superhuman powers, contrary to popular belief. You were superhuman and endowed with the powers to become a force and in fact were a force long before you were known as black, and truth be told you were led to believe you were black in an effort to keep you from reaching back into the inner recesses of your minds and remembering who and what you really are. And now because of this you can't remember when *you* were faster than a speeding bullet, more powerful than a locomotive, able to leap tall buildings in a single bound, etc., etc., etc. If you can't remember that you had these attributes and how you manifested them then it will be impossible for you to see yourself defying the systemic thus institutional field of gravity as well as the self-imposed gravitational field of ignorance you find yourself in. This being the case, it will be impossible to teach your children about their true inheritance, which is their ancient ancestor's legacy to them. Knowledge such as this was supposed to be passed from generation to generation but if your head has been emptied what do you have left to pass? You can only pass on what you know, and you have done so. Based on my observations and a quick view of life in some of your communities ("hoods" as some of you call them) I am thoroughly convinced that a brain transplant has taken place and instead of having your ancestor's knowledge you have someone (or something) else's ancestral knowledge and are attempting to use it to run your life, which, as everybody and the entire solar system can see, is producing disastrous results.

How does it feel, living someone else's idea of a life? Frustrating, no? The reason it is frustrating is because buried deep, deep within you is the real you. Your true essence. As the lie you've been living increases in size and depth the fire that is your true self gets dimmer and dimmer and you get colder and colder until that fire is just a spark. And then the knowledge of it goes out and then you become an animated corpse; a husk with a face (black). A stateless zombie with a fictitious name and a fictitious identity living a fictitious life in a fictitious world. If you really want to know where your true self is right at this moment, all you have to do is see who is faster than a speeding bullet, stronger than a locomotive, able to leap to buildings in a single bound. It definitely ain't you. Nor your children although it is not too late for *some* of them. And speaking of your children, let's take a look at them.

Your Children - Your Single Biggest Asset Or Your
Single Biggest Liability

Hopefully you've researched what I've said because you got mad and wanted to prove me wrong. It doesn't matter. If you're honest with yourself and the research, you'll realize that raising your child to be "black" is more of a hinderance than a help because you are viewing blackness as some type of culture and in a sense it is. It is a pseudo culture made up of different assertions and presumptions, none of which have served to bring you out of your miserable state of poverty and decadence. And those who gave you this dog tag and the culture to go with it designed it that way. I told you at the beginning you've been manipulated. And you still are. As long as you continue to be your children will continue to make you wonder if they're your children because they have made the grown up determination that you are not their parents. When you finally decide to stop house sitting someone else's rabbit hole and find out who and what your ancestors are an entire system (way of doing things) will open before your eyes and not only will it show you how to rear your children it will also show you how to gain mastery over yourself and your environment. Your child's formulation begins with the following foundation. I called the "basics":

"Consider, you are a parent. The importance of the trust you have been endowed with; the being you have produced; it is your duty to support. Upon you depends on whether your child is a blessing or a curse to yourself or a useful or worthless member to the community.

Prepare them early with instruction and season their minds with the maximum of truth. Watch the bent of their inclinations, set them right in their youth and let no evil habit gain strength with their years. So shall they rise like a cedar on the mountain. Their heads shall be seen above the trees of the forest. The mind of your child should be like your own. Let it not want cultivation. The seed you soweth will be the seed that you shall reap."

In order to breed your children correctly you need to know a few things. That's right, I said "breed". One of the aspects of breeding is cultivation and certain characteristics which I will detail shortly must be cultivated within your child. But first you must research and understand the following concepts:

1. Teach	8. Justice	15. Ashamed	22. Wealth
2. Modesty	9. Sincerity	16. Benefits	23. Mind
3. Gratitude	10. Diligence	17. Love	24. Exalted
4. Charity	11. Benevolence	18. Health	25. Life

5. Obedience	12. Science	19. Fortune	26. Useful
6. Temperance	13. Religion	20. Honor	27. Death
7. Prudence	14. Bless	21. Reproach	28. Happy

And now, the characteristics. There are twelve of them. When I first encountered them, I referred to them as "Jacob's Ladder". My name is not Jacob, nor are any children I know. You, however, may replace the name of Jacob (unless your child's name really is Jacob) with your child's name. It just may keep your mindful of your objective, which hopefully is saving your children. In order to do this, you must do the following:

> Teach them obedience, and they shall bless you; teach them modesty, and they shall not be ashamed.
> Teach them gratitude, and they shall receive benefits; teach them charity, and they shall gain love.
> Teach them temperance, and they shall have health; teach them prudence and fortune shall attend them.
> Teach them justice, and they shall be honored by the world; teach them sincerity and their own heart shall not reproach them.
> Teach them diligence, and their wealth shall increase; teach them benevolence, and their minds shall be exalted.
> Teach them science, and their lives shall be useful; teach them religion, and their deaths shall be happy.

These are not my words. They are the time tested, honored words of the Ascended Masters which have been passed down from them to the generation of man. They, like nature, knows no color line. They (these principles) work for "white" children just as much as they'll work for "black" children. However, your children, Mr. and Mrs. (or Ms.) black America, especially your boys, need them more than any group or subgroup of people on the face of this earth. In cities across America, notably Chicago and Baltimore, it is young, "black" males between the ages of 16-28 that are single handedly driving up the murder rate and who are they murdering? Other black boys and young black men between the ages of 16-28. Add the occasional 9-year-old boy and 4- or 12-year-old girl and you have a good case for them being the most prolific genocidal maniacs of all time, anywhere topside planet dirt and spit. This must be dealt with. One way or the other. It's gotten to that point. For some it's too late. You will not be able to reach them. They will not let you reach them. Your face has no resemblance to that "real nigga" that they have come to know and love and call their own.

They will become a product of their own destruction and truth be told they must be destroyed. If only they would need the words of ascended masters like Noble Drew Ali, who transcribed the instructions I just passed on to you, they might, just might have hope. If not, the worst is yet to come. And before I leave the section, let me emphasize a truth that I've gone over but left this part out because I wanted to end this section on this note.

Dr. Lune A. Teek

SECTION SIX
The Hyphen –

There are a lot of you "black" folks who are uncomfortable with the use of the hyphen in describing your nationalistic ancestral identity. You say it doesn't matter, we're all Americans. Tsk, tsk, tsk. My are you naive. Through time and evolution, the brain of a gnat will get bigger. And so will yours. Eventually. Until then understand this.

Hyphens, whether they're in a sentence or in front of the name of a country are grammatical instruments that combine two different things or/ and ideas and makes them one thing/idea. The same goes for the hyphen in front of "American".

Unless your ancestors were given the name "Indian" by lost "pale skins" the only way that any government will recognize you is through that hyphen.

"LIAR! LIAR! LIAR!", some of you will scream. Before you break out the sackcloth and start throwing ashes around let me explain.

> "You are today, without doubt or contradiction what your ancient forefathers were."
>
> Timothy Drew Ali

This and other truths about you ("black" folks) are known by those who rule nations. In particularly those who rule these nations "behind the scenes". It was these people (the 2nd group) who by hook or/and by crook designed, developed, and deployed the policies, guidelines, and procedures that have become the laws that determine how an individual or group of individuals will be *recognized* by the government in which they live and the nations of the earth. Within this said government (United States) one *must* be a *recognized* member of a *recognized* nation of people either by ancestry (blood tie - jus sanguinis) or by birth on soil/land (law of soil – jus soli) other than this nation; this said nation being America. In short, if your ancestors weren't "Indians," you can't be a "Native-American". You can't, by the nature of what nationalistic reality is (nationality) be an "African-American". Africa is not a nation. It is a continent. Besides, if a "white" South African became a citizen of this country would you embrace his "African-Americanism"? (Shut up lying. Y'all are mad right now at white people because you say they're stealing "your" music, among other things). Let's examine this a little bit closer by examining the "Indian".

Once again, the people who are keenly aware of the origins of man and of mankind know good and damn well the people who inhabited this land before the "Great European Land Grab" were not "Indians". They also knew, as time went on and more enlightened "sensible" gatekeepers emerged that these people who were already here were more akin to you (yes you, "black" folks) than anyone else (meaning "them"), and these more enlightened, "sensible" gatekeepers decided that it would not be in their nor their progeny's best interest(s) if they let that little piece of apple pie sit in the Son (not a misprint or misspelling). So, they hid this truth from succeeding generations of both them and you. The elders knew, of course. Therefore "black" slaves hid and found solace in the "Indian" tribes from Florida all the way down to Belize and Brazil. As they slaughtered and/or colonized these "pure" tribes, the certainty of the ancient truth of "You are today without doubt or contradiction what your ancient forefathers were" was replaced with a "racial" classification construct that was designed to divide genotype similar groups of people by geographical designations; said designation is the declared "race" (Chinese, Japanese, Vietnamese, Koreans, India, etc. are "Asians; Pakistanis, Saudi Arabians, Iranians, Iraqis, etc. are Arabs, etc., etc., etc. What you and some of them don't know is you and all of them share the same ancient ancestorial blood-tie which technically makes you all one people). By doing this they could and did write them ("Indians") out of the bonds of American citizenship. This changed however, with the invention of something called the Bureau of Indian Affairs. Without going into too much detail about something you should already know, the BIA, as it's sometimes called, was to be an agency designed to be an office of assistance for and to the "Native American" in their quest to establish themselves and "assimilate into American society". It has been and still is in most ways a stumbling block. Sometimes literally. Interesting enough, there were "Indian" tribes who owned "black" slaves.

Be it all that said, the importance of what you need to know is this:

The days (and nights) of you or anyone else saying, "I got Indian blood in me," and climbing into a teepee are over. For good. The tribes and the U.S. government require that "Indian blood" of yours to be proven. The tribe itself must prove to the United States and the State(s) in which it resides their identity as a true, historically recognized tribe. Still don't understand? Still don't believe? Research the quest for tribal "federal" recognition status of the Lumbee Nation. Do you see a pattern. No? Okay, it's this:

In order to be truly recognized by this government as something other than a resident alien you must show an ancestry connection. This system is set up that way. Hence the hyphen. It is used within a nationality identification system:

Your National Descent Name -	*Your Birth Nation Name*
Irish (Ireland)	American = Irish-American
Scottish (Scotland)	American = Scottish-American
German (Germany)	American = German-American
Italian (Italy)	American = Italian-American
Russian (Russia)	American = Russian-American
Mexican (Mexico)	American = Mexican-American
Japanese (Japan)	American = Japanese-American
Chinese (China)	American = Chinese-American

And so on...

And here "black" people is where your problem(s) arise. Understand that the system is an undercover class structuring system. You have no "free" national descent name became the names used to identify you (Black, Negro, Colored) in this manor were given to slaves by slaveholders to identify (mark) property, which is what your ancestors were counted and identified as. I do believe Supreme Court Justice Daniels referred to them in the *Dred Scott* decision as "subjects of capture and purchase". I'm going to show you how bad a predicament this is for you.

If I asked you "what is your nationality?", some of you will say:
    "African American"
Some of you will say:
    "Black"
Some of you will say:
    "American"

If I instead of nationality, asked you "what is your race?", some of you will say:
    "African-American"
Some of you will say:
    "Black"
Some of you will absurdly say:
    "American"

Which one are you? Keep in mind nationality and racial identity are two separate issues. Trust and believe that this is a problem for you and if it remains so is you will be classified and recognized as a "second class citizen". Maybe this will begin to shed some light on the question most of you have asked:

"Why is it that people can come over here from other countries and do better than us?"

Know this and know it well:

Every question has an answer. Including this one. To find it, you might try starting with the hyphen.

Dr. Lune A. Teek

Section Seven
FOR THE "RETARDED" BLACK MALES
I JUST WROTE ABOUT
(AGES 15-35)

First, understand the context of the word I am using to describe you and your situation.

> Retarded-adj: Slow or limited in intellectual or emotional development or progress. (Webster's)

The root word is retard.

> Retard-vb: To slow up, esp. by preventing or hindering advance or accomplishment: impede (Webster's)

The word "retarded" is an adjective, which means it is a word that describes the condition of the subject matter it relates to. This makes it (the condition) an effect, or a result of a cause. In other words, the state of being retarded does not happen on its own. Something must cause it. The word retard is a verb (action-cause). The act of retarding (cause) must take place before one can be retarded (effect). If you would take a long, "hard", serious, brutal, honest look at the condition of your age group as a whole it is thoroughly impossible for you to come to any other conclusion that makes sense. And before you can fix something that you know is broken what's wrong with it must make sense. The question is, do you want to fix it? It is and can only be your choice. If assisting with the program of uplifting fallen humanity is something you can see yourself being a part of and you feel your condition in life can be better, there are some basic things you must do.

First, get rid of the "I don't give a fuck" attitude. *Ruff Neck* made M.C. Lyte a decent amount of change but the lifestyle will get you killed. You want to be a man or a thug? Remember. It's all about concepts. You can't be both. One has an esoteric nature to it while the other is the antithesis of common sense. Particularly for one whose ancestors ruled the world and the seven seas. But that part of your existence is unknown to you because you didn't give a fuck to know about it. But that's okay. A late start is better than being "The 'late' Mr. ______".

Think about this for a minute. If you have kids, take a look at them. Just look at them. Don't say or do shit. Just look at them. Now ask yourself, if you become "The 'late' Mr. _________," what are you leaving them? What knowledge have you given them? What memories will you leave them with? Will they even remember you? What will they remember you as? Will having your name and the memory of you as a part of their life be a blessing or a curse to them? There are several more questions I could come up with for you to consider but then I'd be doing your job.

The second thing you must realize is something I alluded to earlier:

You are being profiled.

It matters not whether you're in a gang. The fact is many gang members are individuals with melanin complexions within this age group. Be that as it may this is only one in a string of variables that play into this. The important thing is that you realize this. You don't have to understand it. You won't. Just know that you are. In order to mitigate this (it's not going to stop) you must change the way you think thus hopefully you will change the way you act. You are now going to take charge of your perceptions of life, regardless of the experiences (or lack thereof) you've had that shaped them. Specifically, if those perceptions are based on experiences of a negative nature that would tend to move you toward a left-handed path. Remember, something is retarding your forward advance and/or accomplishments. Misperceived conceptions are one of the things that will do that. They must be exorcised. To do this you must change the way you think about yourself, your environment, and those in your immediate circle who have not nor will consider the concept of renewing their minds, as well as those who you may be presently considering admission into your immediate circle. *You must either cut them off or cut them back.*

The third thing you must do is examine what you do. Nothing in the realm of justice proceeds without reason. What do you do and what is the reasoning behind it? Where did its motivation come from? Is it a positive or negative motivation? You may lie to others, but you cannot lie to yourself. If it is a negative motivation the acts manifested will bear fruit accordingly, and of course, you will be subject to the consequences. The same applies with positive motivations. The concept of that which you have sown is that which you shall reap applies here. With this in mind, let's review some things I wrote about earlier.

What or who motivates you to be "hard"? Do you really think it is natural for your "heart" to be in such a cold state? Is it natural for you to be a part of an environment that would create such a state within you? Were you aware of when this state occurred within you? What does your "self" say to you about it?

Dr. Lune A. Teek

There has to be a reckoning and I reckon your reckoning starts now. Yes, you Mr. black America between the ages of 15-30, must begin to realize that unless you make some drastic changes *you* will be the impetus that will destroy black America as you know it. And while I personally want this current mythological concept of "black" removed from the annuls of human history and the minds and hearts of the people who were branded with it I do not, under any circumstances seek their physical demise. What drastic changes, you may ask?

1. Get rid of the "hard". It's an image. It's not real and neither are you if you're seeking to portray it. Go back to the definition of "retarded." Something is hindering your emotional development. Without this development you become an uncaring, unfeeling clone, ready to be programmed. And yes, you have been programmed and your programmers literally have orgasms when you either take a "black" life or the "STATE OF __" takes yours. They, however, go into epileptic shock when you walk across a stage to get your college diploma. Give them the shits with their epileptic fits. Do something positive with your life. *Then help others do the same.*

2. If you're a "Real nigga"; stop. If you're trying to be a "Real nigga"; stop. If you're hanging out with a "Real nigga"; stop. Stop in the name of the law and because law governs all events the law that you're stopping in the name of is called the law of common sense. And then there's also the law of unintended consequence, aka; be careful what you wish for. Keep portraying this psychotic image of a "Real nigga" and eventually someone, somewhere will end up treating you like one. Now go through the annuls of history and see how real. Niggers/Niggas/Niggahs were treated. They were treated so nice that their "treatment" was put on United States post cards. No one in this age group who thinks of themselves as being a "real nigga" has the slightest clue as to how a real NIGGER was treated. Some of your Moor enlightened elders/ancestors have seen these post cards. Some have witnessed this "treatment" personally in other various forms and formats. You are the "fruit" of someone's loins and while your ways and actions to be sure are strange they can and will cause you to be an example of some tree's "Strange Fruit" (Research this song, who wrote it and the story behind it).

3. You are being profiled (Haven't I wrote this before?).
    And not by the police.
    You are being profiled by those who profile the police. Be that as it is, you must realize that a mandate based on the slow but very

progressive extermination of your life has been placed in motion and as with all mandates a set of objectives are being implemented. You must; for your own survival and the survival of your family and community begin to undo the ties that nail you to the cross of being in the crosshairs. Some of these ties were set by you. You fell into others by way of your ignorance of the trap. While I cannot tell you all the traps that are set for you (other authors have done a good job of this) I can tell you this: there are some very ingeniously subtle traps with your name on them. In order to see them you must "step outside of yourself". In short, you must employ a wisdom that is not a part of your everyday repartee. Stepping outside of yourself literally means stepping outside of the box. What box? Let me give you an example:

I am speaking to a particular age group. You are in this age group. What identifies you as such? I'll tell you. Your dress. Your walk. Your talk. Your mental state. The places you go. The music/musicians you like. The movies you watch. The places you live. How you live.

One of the things I have a hard time getting people to realize is that the only thing that is constant on this plane of existence is change. This phenomenon called "change" is often brought only by forces beyond our control or is a result of us not taking control. In your case, Mr. "black" man between the ages of 15-35, it is a combination of both. Remember if you can't govern yourself someone will surely come along and govern you. Such is the case here. How do you defeat that? Establish for yourself principles of action and govern yourself accordingly. Be incapable of change *in that which is right* and govern yourself accordingly. *This way, you become the captain and agent of change. Not it's slave.*

1. Your dress - Pull your damn pants up. Get a belt. Anytime you pay more money for a basketball shoe than you would for a dress shoe something is wrong. Anytime you would want to wear a basketball shoe more than you would a dress shoe something is wrong. Particularly if you can't play basketball.

2. Your walk - Tough guys don't need to walk "tough". Unless he was joking or proving a point, I'd give anyone one million dollars if someone can show me when Bruce Lee walked "tough". Confident, yes, "Tough" no. There is a difference.

3. Your talk - I mean, really. Do you really want to be a "nigga"? Do you really want me to call your mother a "bitch"?

4. Your mental state - An ignorant man is at the mercy of a fool. Do I really need to explain this? If so, you're ignorant. Too ignorant for your own or anyone else's good.
5. The places you go - Says a lot about you.
6. The music/musicians you like - Music soothes the savage beast. It can create one too.
7. The movies you watch - When Al Pacino died in *Scarface*, he (Al Pacino) resurrected from the dead to play other characters in other movies. If you die trying to be Al Pacino in *Scarface*, will you resurrect from the dead to play yourself? Probably not. Wanna see?
8. The places you live - What is a "hood"? While you're formulating your answer, know this: living in a "project" is NOT a badge of honor. Living in a slum community is NOT a badge of honor. Living in an area where you can't tell whether the gunshots are coming from the T.V. or across the street is NOT a badge of honor. If you think it is, you're stupid. Stop being stupid. Do you have an answer yet? Before you answer, how about telling me what happened to the "neighbor" that came before the "hood"? Have you ever stopped to think that one of the big differences between "white" communities and your community is that white people have "neighborhoods" while you still prefer to live in a "hood"? Think about it. Now do something about it. Don't worry about the answer. You can't come up with one that makes sense.

What I'm saying to you comes from the same place Smokey the Bear came from when he said, "Only you can prevent forest fires." A destructive mindset, which manifests itself by way of violence, neglect, and lack of constructive and productive standards are just as devastating to the "black" community ("hoods") as an out of control fire is to a forest. And yes, Mr. "black" man, only you can prevent this. Only you, Mr. "black" man is perpetuating it. Stop it. Stop it now! You're being manipulated. The next time you think of where you live as a "hood" think about the individuals who wore white ones on their head and know, like I wrote earlier, it's all about CONCEPTS. You're being manipulated into thinking being "hard", a "thug", and a "real nigga" is what you *must* be in order to survive. You were manipulated into thinking being book-smart was lame. Look around you. Nerds rule the world! You can't see that? What's wrong with you? You think a cop is going to pull the owner of Facebook out of his car a fill him full of holes? What does this guy have that you don't? Think about that the next time you update your Facebook page. You're being played for suckers. You're being played for punks. Walk with me while I show you this. These are the methods being used by your handlers in order to enact mind control. Pay attention:

1. Data mining
2. Focus groups
3. Profiling
4. Hypnotic Presentation
5. Code Words and Phrases
6. Audience Future Pacing
7. Neurolinguistic Programming

I trust that you will research each one of these so you will know not only what each one is and does but also what each looks like in whatever form it shows itself as and what forum it appears in. Only by doing this can you protect yourself and yours from it. Do it. Do it now! You can't say you're sucker free if you're the biggest Blow Pop in the bag.

For The "Black" Male "Professional"

You are being profiled.
What? You don't think so? You can't see?
Damn. How naïve of you.
No. How utterly stupid of you.

Do you actually think that the foot of opaque obstructionism and soft tyranny has been removed from your neck because you have somehow mustered up the funds and the credit rating to move in a predominately "white" neighborhood? Maybe you think that just because it takes a little longer ride in the elevator to get to your desk that you and that damned desk can't be thrown down the steps just as quick as a cat can lick its' ass.

Sure. You've got $5.00 in your pocket and $10.00 in the bank and for some strange reason you've forgotten that the color of your mind is not green. Besides, the $5.00 in your pocket is owned by the Federal Reserve while the $10.00 in the bank is owned by the bank; which by most accounts (pun intended) is owned by the Federal Reserve.

Oh yes, yes, yes. You're as sharp as a Ginsu triple bladed buzz saw as you're travelling to and fro through the streets of wherever you live U.S.A. in your brand new "just washed and waxed and had the tires and rims cleaned" Cadillac. Hopefully you haven't become so complacent therefore deranged enough to not believe that you can't be dragged from that same Cadillac and beat to death or at the very least to within an inch from it.

You are being profiled.

This is not a game. This is as real as it gets. And if you're not yet drunk on the wine of carnal things you should be asking why are you being profiled. A good question. Here's the answer.

You are being profiled because you somehow removed yourself from the bottom level of society without being snared and trapped by the snares and traps placed there by those who have an incentive to have a bottom level of society. In order to do that *you* had to have incentive and if you have incentive, you have ambition and if you have ambition, coupled with the ability to THINK eventually you will have power, and if you obtain power then maybe, just maybe, you might begin to realize that power is an illusion that's here today, gone tomorrow. Then you may begin to understand and undertake the necessary steps to become what you were always meant to be. Then you might begin the long, slow process to claim, and take control and then utilize the legacy that your Ancient forefathers and foremothers left for you. The legacy that was not insomuch stolen from you as it was given to "others" by you. It is being refined and utilized by these "others" as I write and you read. Once you have gained knowledge of self (higher) and gain a mastery over self (lower) you will then know that you are the FORCE which directs ALL power on this level of existence. Sadly, for some, this includes those "others". Sadly, for you, they (the "others") will use all methods at their disposal to keep this from happening. Including profiling you for your death. And if you happen to dodge this alternative ending for you, maybe you can save your "retarded" brothers and sons from that Satanic influenced and financed, make believe but very real lie called "the Streets".

WHY?...

... in most situations is far too often the last question asked. It reminds me of another wise saying/lesson taught for me by a little known, unassuming sage:

> "When thy bed is straw; thou sleepest in security; but
> when thou stretch thyself on roses, beware of the thorns."

Eventhough "why?" is the question one asks to become aware of the essence of understanding people, places, or things as well as situations, the answer(s) one gets are most often the least understood therefore the hardest to reconcile. "Black" mothers across this country are asking themselves, their friends, their families, their pastors, God him/herself, "why?". Why was my son/daughter killed? Way too many mothers. Way too many sons/

daughters. Way too many "whys?" without answers. At least ones that make sense. And you know what else doesn't make sense?

"Black" mothers and fathers have been struggling within themselves because they are at their wits end with fear and despair. They have no idea of what to say or teach their children on how to survive outside their homes. They are sick with worry that they'll see their children go outside their house and sometime later they will have to run somewhere only to see their son or daughter being photographed and measured, not for a graduation cap, gown, or picture, but for a chalk line at a crime scene. It seems as though a mother's admonishment of "Be careful" is not enough and at any rate way too late for way too many. Your job, Mr. "Black" man who has "waded through the muddy Jordan River" and made it to the other side, is to assist by being an agent of change. You need to be seen. You need to be heard. You need to be felt. And most of all, all of you need to be touched. And if what you see happening to your people does not touch you enough to move you to be a part of the mechanism that will change their current standing in the world then you are "in the way" and must be eliminated.

1. You must be seen - Do you know why Lebron James is more known than you? Because Lebron James is *seen* more than you. Do you know why Little Wayne is more known than you? Because Little Wayne is *seen* more than you. Do you know why the neighborhood dope man is more popular than you? Because the neighborhood dope man is *seen* more than you. And they're not just seen more than you, they're seen *makin' it* more than you. Oh, it's not that you're not makin' it. The difference is they're making their makin' it look better than your makin' it. *Optics are everything.* It's not all about the money. It's the perception one has of seeing themselves doing what it takes to make that money that moves people: The man who owns the team that Lebron James plays with makes more money than Lebron James. Sadly however, more black boys and young black men want to be a Lebron James than the owner of the team Lebron James plays for. And while there is an inspirational story behind the making of Lebron James, every relevant statistic known will bear out that it would be far easier for black boys and young black men to be the type and class of entrepreneur that the owner of this team is than it would be for them to have Lebron James' class and status in that environment. They want to be Lebron because Lebron is what/who they see. They do not see the owner of the team Lebron James plays for. What do they see Lebron do? They see him being the best there is. The same thing others saw with

Kobe, Shaq, Allen Iverson, Ervin "Magic" Johnson, Julius "Dr. J" Erwin, and of course, Michael Jordan. They saw all these men take charge and be in charge. *And they were/are playing a game.* And they were seen. The real "players" are not on the court. They OWN the court AND THE DAMN STADIUM THE COURT IS IN. The point here is that if you are a stockbroker, let these young men know the excitement of being that and then instill in them an excitement that would make them interested in this work. The same goes if you're a lawyer, doctor, architect, chemist, information technician, etc. And don't just get them excited, keep them that way. In other words, create your own rite of passage for them - mentor them. Instead of letting "the Street" be their mentor. You set the standard then be that standard. Remember, the most blessings come to the one who gives the most blessings. You've been blessed. Pay it back by paying it forward. There are a great number of organizations that you can give your time and talents to. Do that. It there is not one near you, create one. Trust me. The "black" life you save may be your own.

Section Eight
PERSPECTIVE

There are a few things that you don't know. Check that. There are a lot of things that you don't know. That is because you've been told enough of a lie about certain things (and people) to the point of acceptance of the lie. Once the lie is accepted that means you won't put any further thought into the idea that was a lie in the first place.

Columbus "discovered" America...

Benjamin Franklin "discovered" electricity...

George Washington "cut down the cherry tree"...

Abraham Lincoln "freed" the slaves...

Black, Negro, Colored, Africa, African-American, Hispanic, Indian, White, Asian, etc. are "races" of man...

You can find "justice" in the criminal justice system...

The "system" works...

etc.

etc.

etc.

Boy, were you taken for a bunch of milk toast cads. Saps even. You even believed that once you got "civil rights" you would "overcome". Okay. How's that workin' for ya? I run for my vomit bucket every time I hear a "black" person say. "We've come a long way but we've got long way to go."

A long way to go.

Where are you going?

How long is it going to take to get "there"?

How are you going to get "there"?

Where exactly is "there" located?

What are you going to do when you get "there"?

How long are you going to stay "there"?

What does "there" look like?

How will you know when you get "there"?

If I went, what would be the first thing that I would see in order to let me know that I've gotten "there"?

It's assertions like "we've got a long way to go" that tells someone like me that you don't have a clue of where you're going nor how to get there even if you did. As I alluded in an earlier section, you are *at least* a hundred years behind your salvation. Do you think your enemies will wait or stop until you catch up? Not hardly. Not even! Oh hell no. Sure you have a long way to go. You just don't know how long and what you have to do to get there. Let me show you. No. Let me educate you. After all, this journey of a thousand miles doesn't start with a step. It starts with you. Listen (no, read).

There's an old song that says, "A Change Is Gonna Come". When most people hear or think of that song, they relate to a change in their condition by way of a change in their environment, by way of a change occurring in other people ("white" people) or other entities (criminal justice system, political power, business, etc.). This is why "black" people are still marching and protesting in one way or another for the same things that they were marching and protesting for when this song first hit the charts. Black people are now as they were then looking for change in everyone or every place except the one place where the most dynamic change takes place: within themselves. Until this occurs, until you have knowledge and acknowledge who you truly are your condition as a people will remain the same. Why? Because you don't know how you got here (in this position) in the first place. Well, don't worry. That's what I'm here for. I'll tell you. Listen (read) closely.

Simply put, while you slept and fought amongst yourselves when you weren't sleeping, your enemy built an entire world around you. It would have been too impractical to kill you all (who's gonna dig a hole that big?) so they set up a system to contain you. The beauty of this system is it is set up so that

1. You don't know it's a system;
2. You don't know you're contained (It beats the crap out of digging a hole that big)

What you don't know might not hurt you physically, but it sure can make you go through a lot of emotional damage and mental stress. I'm going to start by saying this system has sets of protocols, as all systems do. All systems also have institutions through which the system manifests and expedites its protocols. Keep that little factoid in mind as you read. Every system operates within an environment. Some you can see, some you cannot. Some systems allow you to see some of this environment and at the same time makes others invisible to the naked eye. You, Mr. and Mrs. (or Mrs.) black America, are in such a system. The environment that you are in is one you cannot see with the naked eye, however you can see, feel, touch, hear, and smell its manifestations. The main manifestation produced by this environment is called "Second Class Citizen". How did you get there? Simple. You chose to be something that you're not. And you had no idea of the predicament that put you in. First, you must know and understand the truth. And the truth is this:

There is a such thing as the "Family Of Nations". These families of nations are bound, governed, recognized, and protected by a doctrine called the "Law Of Nations". While their constitutions and charters differ it is through the spirit of this doctrine that they are written and enforced. I can tell you without doubt or contradiction there is no negro, black, colored, nor African-American race attached to the Family Of Nations. I can tell you without doubt or contradiction there is no negro, black, colored, or African-American, nor Hispanic for that matter race attached to the human race. Strictly and technically speaking there is only one race: *the hum*

\an race. These other distinctions are of political and social origin and are used to denote political and social standing. Therefore, they are political and social constructs used specifically to denote political and social *class* distinctions. And here is where your caboose hit a dent in the track. A big dent. And your ignorance of the subject matter made it that much worse. The subject matter being who you are, and I can tell you who you truly are is the same as who you truly were before you agreed to be someone's "chip off the old auction block". You are today without doubt or contradiction what your ancient forefathers were. However, because you went to sleep and woke up in a new era of time a new environment was built right under your very own noses in your very own land. It was built by the bloodline of the very people you were at war with (when you weren't at war with yourselves) before you went to sleep. It is now time for you to wake up. You've heard the phrase "wake up" before. Some of you may have said it yourselves.

The reason why no one is going to wake up when you say it is because what you're saying wake up for has been proven ineffective. As I've already written, you cannot defeat an enemy that you have no understanding of and you do not know where to begin as it relates to doing that. In order to begin the process of *understanding* who or what has been keeping you in the basement of the house called progress you first need to *know* who or what has been keeping you in the basement of the house called progress. The answer to that, Mr. and Mrs. (or Ms.) black America, of course, is you. In order for you to stop being your own worst enemy you are going to have to discard a lot (No. Most) of what you thought you knew. This begins with a realization and then acceptance that most of what you were told and/ or taught about a myriad of things was fake. Yes, you were lied to. Badly. These lies are coloring (pun intended) your understanding of reality and your version of reality is blocking you from knowing, seeing, and being the truth. You are acting on these misguided perceptions. To your detriment. Let me give you an example.

Although this type of action has subsided at this point in the writing of this book (although I do expect that it will pick back up), there was a movement afoot to change, remove, tear down, destroy, etc. any building, statue, landmark, etc. that certain people ("black folks" and a few wayward guilt ridden "white" people) perceived as commemorating white people or events that were "racist". This phenomenon spread from city/town squares to college campuses. While the sentiment may or may not have been a noble one, ask yourselves a question or two. Don't worry, I'll ask you for you:

1. Some of these things are very old, which means they've been where they were for a long time. Why now do you want them gone?"
2. Did the removal, change, tearing down, or destroying of these ensigns make "racial" relations better? If so, how? If not, why?

To those who decided to march and protest against rebel flags, statues, and buildings:

Why stop at those? Why start at those? Why not "Keep it hot"? Don't play with it. Take it to the hilt. If you want to rid the world of "racist" inspired landmarks, start with the Lincoln Memorial.

Someone told you that Abraham Lincoln freed the slaves. Someone told you that Lincoln was a "friend" to black people. Someone lied to you. Badly. On both counts. Tell me this. Who was it who was purported to have uttered these words:

> "... Apprehension seems to exist among the people of the Southern States that by the accession of a Republic Administration their property and their peace and personal security are to be endangered.
>
> There has never been any reasonable cause for such apprehension. Indeed, the most ample evidence to the contrary has *all the while existed* and *has been open to their inspection. It is found in nearly all the published speeches of him who now addresses you.* I do but quote from one of those speeches when I declare that '*I have no purpose, directly or indirectly to interfere with the institution of slavery in the States where it exists.* I believe I have no lawful right to do so, and *I have no inclination to do so.*' Those who nominated and elected me did so *with full knowledge that I had made this and many similar declarations*, and have never recounted them..."
>
> (Emphasis the Author's)

Well, even if "they" lied to you about him at least he didn't lie about his statements referencing previous positions concerning issues that illustrated his true sentiments. Especially when it specifically came to how he truly felt about you. For instance:

1. "... I will say then, that *I am not, nor ever have been, in favor of bringing about in any way, the social and political equality of the white and black races...* I, as much as any other man *am in favor of having the superior position assigned to the white race...*"
2. "... My paramount objective in this struggle is to save the Union... if I could save the Union *without freeing any slaves* I would do it; if I could save it by freeing some and *leaving others alone*, I would also do that..."

And so he did. Honest Abe. If there was one thing that Abraham Lincoln was it was honest.

> The first example was from Lincoln's First Inaugural Address in 1861. The second example was from the Douglas-Lincoln debates in 1858. Douglas leveled a charge at Lincoln that he was for "Negro" equality. The third example was stated in 1862 when Lincoln was justifying his position as to why he was going to deprive certain slaveholders of their property. Lincoln also made statements seeming opposite of the above

The emphasis placed on certain phrases within these statements is mine. It's done for your benefit. Read them carefully. Research other statements by Lincoln. Definitely one of the best books I've read about Lincoln is Leonne Bennet's *Forced Into Glory*.

Now that you've read these quotes, read books and done other research, "What 'cha gonna do?" I'll tell you what. Let's march. Let's riot. No, let's just start an online petition demanding that the Lincoln Memorial be shut down then torn down. And after we tear down the Lincoln Memorial, let's hit the Washington Monument. Remember he cut down the cherry tree (Oh. I forgot. You don't know what the hell that *really* means because you fell for the lie they told you in school), and he had slaves. And if you're not too tired, let's go for the roundhouse and march on the Jefferson Memorial. You already know that story.

The point I'm making here is you can't always read a story backward and find a plot. The problem with that is it doesn't show you the big picture and if you don't have the big picture it means that you don't know something that is crucial to your understanding of "it". "It" being the truth of things. This is because you're reading the story in a manner in which it was never meant to be read—backward. In short, all of this marching, protesting, and tearing down and changing things will get you what? A new position created on a college campus called the "Office of Inclusiveness"? And that's going to further "the struggle" how? You're going to tear down that rebel flag. You're gonna show those racist "crackers" a thing or two, I hear ya. And I can tell you on good authority that you're not going to show "them" shit. And how is "showing them" going to stop one black boy or black girl from getting killed by a gun held by a black hand?

> "There is nothing wrong with being ignorant as we all are ignorant of certain things. It is, however, stupid to remain so."
>
> The Author

You, Mr. and Mrs. (or Ms.) black America are being manipulated via your ignorance. Your entire way of doing things perpetuates and in some ways facilitates the ease in which this happens. In other words, there are people who can spot you a mile away. And they're glad to see you coming. They know at least one of you will be around. Especially since they know there's one of you born every minute. Or so said P.T. Barnum.

You may think I'm having fun at your expense. And you would be right. I am. On the serious side, however, you have to stop being your own slave master. In order to do this, you have to start loving knowledge. You have to regenerate your need to learn. I'm going to give you another example of something I'll bet a lot of you don't know.

Did you know that in December of 1999 James Earl Ray was exonerated in the assination of Dr. Martin Luther King? (A "mock" trial)

Now if you're just going by this, you'll probably say that the jury was "racist". Nothing could be further from the truth. With that said, research what happened at this trial. You may or may not be surprised. If you don't remember or get anything from what you just read, remember and get this:

> It is not nor has it ever been about race. There is only one race: the human race. It always has and it always will be about *class*. Never forget that. Because there's only one race it is not a determinate of your class. Your class is determined within a "legal" (not "lawful") framework and systematically expedited through a series of institutions. The class hierarchy is identity based (white-black). Understand this if you understand nothing else. The terms "white" and "black" as it relates to human beings have absolutely NOTHING to do with skin complexion. It has everything to do with a class structure. You, "black" people, need to realize this and until you do you will be spinning

around in a circle. A good book for you to read is *A Prince Among Slaves* by Terry Alford. Here you will read a powerful story and if you're careful you may find out who you really are in the process, as well as the difference an identification tag like "Negro", "Black", or "Colored" makes as opposed to the identification of one who is classed as a human being. And a prince. Other books that would be helpful in your quest to come out of la-la land are:

Stolen Legacy George G. James

Sex and Race - Vol. I - J.A. Rodgers/Nature Has No Color Line - J.A. Rodgers

Ancient and Modern Britains - David Mac Ritchie - Vols. I & II

Five Negro Presidents - J.A. Rodgers

Six Black Presidents, Black Blood, White Masks - Auset Bakhufu

Othello's Children in The New World - José Pimenta-Bey

There are other books and authors I could give you, but these will clue you into what you should know. When it becomes apparent what ties them together you will then be able to do further research. I also, of course, could just tell you what you, as a people, are known as by this government to be your "lawful" recognition as well as how that identification alone will move you from second class citizen status. If I did that, however, I will be going against the premise of this book. It's about self help, remember? To see this movement at work, read *A Prince Among Slaves*. Oh, by the way!

You're probably finding it maddening as hell that I am constantly telling you that you're not "black" and at the same time constantly referring to you as "black". Question:

If I told you who you were would you believe *me*?

Maybe you would believe it if someone else wrote about it. Maybe you won't. It's okay. My discipline teaches me that the "Black" according to "Science" means death. There's absolutely nothing wrong with being dead. Evidently Mr. and Mrs. (or Ms.) "black" America, you seem to agree.

Part II

The Black Section

(And You Thought It Was Over)

SECTION ONE
THE LONG, SLOW CLIMB

Question: What did the man see when he reached the top of the
             mountain?

Answer: Everything and nothing.

Question: Who did the man see when he reached the top of the
             mountain?

Answer: Everyone and no one.

The Author

It is time, once again, to remind you Mr. and Mrs. (or Ms.) black America, of a significant truth. You have been and are being manipulated. This has been going on for a very, very long time. Oh, don't feel bad though. "White" people have been and are being manipulated too. It's just that the best manipulations were saved for you. Why?

If you paid attention to the previous section, you hopefully realized that you are not what you thought you were nor what everybody is calling you. Hopefully you realize that this is of grave importance. Hopefully you realize that I, personally am not going to tell you who you were before you decided to become eligible to become someone's property. Remember, this is *self-help*. Man (or woman) knows not by being told. If man (woman) must know, he or she must first be what he or she knows. Do you want me to teach your children, or do you want to get off your "black" asses and engage your children as you're supposed to? Once again, I ask, did you teach your son that it's okay to walk around the city with his pants halfway around his ass? No, you didn't. They learned this was cool while watching some clown on a rap video. These subliminal manipulations started with you and got you in a state of mental objectivity about the nonsense going on right under your noses. You had no idea that your son was being maneuvered into a position by which the way he wears his pants qualified him for criminal profile status. You and your children have to be saved and I'm here to save you. Well, sort of. If I can get you to think you can save yourself. Here's some suggestions. This is "teach a man how to fish" time. You may like these suggestions, you may not. Looking at the state of black America today, what have you got to lose? Remember the thousand keys? You only have but so long to get to the other side of that locked door. Here. Take the keys. Open the door. Let me show you...

... The Way

Let's turn to religion for a minute. You know, every people had a prophet come to them with a divine message. This message didn't necessarily sound like music from a Catholic mass, but it did serve a purpose. That purpose was to put people "back on track" because they had picked up some things and habits from people they had no business seeing while in places they had no business being. Such was and is the state of affairs of black people. The people you were seeing was everyone but the correct ones and you learned from these "folks". Thus, you picked up some very nasty habits that translated into you living a very nasty way of life which without doubt or contradiction will lead to your destruction. Here. I have a flashlight. As Michael Jackson said, "Let me show you the way to go. Follow me." Watch your step.

1.   Stop wanting to be entertained more than informed.

This is 99.9% percent of your problem. What must always follow lack of information? Ignorance, that's what. What must always follow ignorance? A slave mind. The difference between a master and his slave always has been and always will be what each one knows and the power to put that knowledge into practice. Freedom (True mastery of self) always has and always will begin and end between one's ears. My seventh and ninth grade English teacher gave me this important piece of wisdom that I've never forgotten. He told me this after I was "entertaining" the class. When class was over, he told me to stay over. After he dressed me down about me wasting my potential, he said these words:

"An ignorant man will always be at the mercy of a fool."
(Thank you Mr. Jon Miller)

Don't you think you've been at the mercy of fools long enough?

Learn to read the signs. There is a phenomenon happening on your television screens and across movie screens all over the country that you have no knowledge of whatsoever. This phenomenon is called Predictive Programming. Predictive Programming is television shows and movies that are fictional in the functional sense of being entertainment but in a dynamic sense they carry a hidden (and sometimes not so hidden) message/thesis. Shows like Scandal, House Of Cards, Tyrant, Blacklist, Homeland, etc. and movies like The Matrix, Star Wars, Specter, etc. are example of predictive programming. These shows and movies have a specific purpose.

There is a realism about these types of shows that defy imagination. An individual will notice this only if they are or have been made aware of the specified subject matter. Remember the show *24*? Yes, there is a real CTU in an undisclosed location and yes there is a real Jack Bauer. Just like there was and still is a 007. In order to understand the true context of The Matrix you have to be outside the Matrix. In order to understand the true context of the Wizard of Oz you have to be outside of Oz. Stop wanting to be entertained all the time and become informed. There are quite a few entities that want you that way. You don't think so? You want proof? Okay. I have a couple of questions for you.

Question: What was one of if not the first thing that was dropped from BET when Viacom bought it from Robert Johnson?

Answer: The News.

Question: What went next?

Answer: The Tavis Smiley Show.

Are you getting a picture here? Is it becoming clear? No wonder the slogan for BET is "We Got You". Now of course, this is my very, very humble opinion and legally I'm entitled to it. It doesn't have to be your own. But if it is, you just might be able to get at least one toe out of the Matrix called Oz.

2.   Stop marching. That's right. You heard me. Stop marching. If I see one more march I'll puke. The damn things don't work. They're band aids trying to cover a 44 Magnum hole. Stop it. This is not 1965. Do you want to be seen or do you want to be taken seriously? All this does is bring a lot of cameras, a lot of news people, a lot of con men (and women), and wears out a lot of shoes. You get absolutely no answers let alone no solutions. Another more important reason to stop this insane madness is because it gives those who set the agenda that you're marching against a chance to hijack it by sending paid agent provocateurs into the midst of you to sabotage it by doing dumb shit that has absolutely nothing to do with what you're marching for and the dumb shit they do will get all the press coverage, take away from the importance of the situation, and paint you, by association as a bunch of savages. The more time you spend defending yourselves from the actions of others means the less time you have to bring attention to your message and being taken seriously. These people are called "paid protestors" by those who know and/or set them in motion. I call them "chaos clowns" and they are paid plants designed specifically

to infiltrate crowds as well as infrastructures and can be individuals or bogus organizations funded by private individuals or in some cases governmental entities for the express purpose of expanding their agenda by exploiting yours. Stop marching. Stop it. You're moving someone else's agenda. You gave yours away as soon as you tied up your Nikes. Stop it. Stop it now.

3. Stop running from the truth. The truth is this:

No succeeding generation ever became successful unless it learned from the generation preceding it. With that said, it is no wonder that this generation of black youth, in general, isn't succeeding at anything but chaos, murder, and mayhem. And "older black generation", it's all your fault. What did the so called "black intellectuals" of the preceding generation teach the generation of today? What legacy did they leave for them to claim? I'll tell you. Nothing. Not a damn thing. Zip. Nada. Nothing. Don't agree? Prove me wrong. Where are your industries? Where are your manufacturers? Where are your information outlets. I talked about BET earlier. Why is it still called "Black Entertainment Television"? Why is "Black" Entertainment Television owned by a conglomeration that is owned by a "white" man? If you want a lesson on corporatocracy all you need to do is research Viacom and see just how many companies Viacom controls. After that find one, not two, not three, but one black owned conglomerate that is even in the same stratosphere with Viacom. You truly at this point have only one large scale black owned media outlet and that is Radio One and T.V. One, which is owned by Cathy Hughes. God bless her but, she can't hire everybody. Are you supporting her? If not, why? If you did support her and her sponsors T.V. and Radio One could be just as large as CBS and I Heart Radio. Then maybe Cathy Hughes might be able to hire everybody. The point is this:

The unemployment rate within the black community is directly proportional to the nonexistence of a viable black corporate infrastructure designed specifically to produce, mentor, and maintain black owned businesses, manufacturers, and suppliers with an emphasis on hiring black people. And this is your fault. Fix it. Now.

Sound radical? Sounds "racist"? If you're scared shit in my back pocket. If you're scared drop out of the human race and give your kids to me. Stop running. Turn around and face what's been killing you: Yourselves.

Tell me this. Why is it that two "white" men, namely Bill Gates and Jeff Bezos can buy every company listed on Black Enterprises 100 black business listings and still have change left over for a Coke and a smile? Stop running. And stop being scared to do the right thing. This country's economy cannot and will not see its best days until you see yours. Only you can make sure that happens. Speaking of that Black Enterprise list. Get a Forbes 100 list and put it beside a B.E. corporations list. Look at the worth of each corporation then total the worth of all corporations on each list. Then understand that corporations can't create themselves. People create them, nurture them, and maintain them. If white people and others along with you can create the type of wealth you see on that Forbes list, why the hell can't that translate over to the B.E. 100? Make it happen. Stop running. You're running out of time.

4.   There are far too many black boys and girls dying by violent means.

Whether it's police shootings, "black on black" shootings of whatever type, or abortions. This must stop and stop now. And I mean right now. Not tomorrow. Not next week. Not in a damn few minutes. Right now. The life expectancy of black children in Chicago is starting to look like the life expectancy of children in Ethiopia in the 1970's. I get heavily into the subject of police and police shootings in another chapter. Abortions are a subject I really, truly don't like to discuss, however for the sake of clarity, let me be clear. Except for instances of the endangerment of the life of the mother/child there is no need for a woman to have an abortion. Of course, there are the militant minded women and come along to get along type men who will scream "What about rape?", "What about incest?" "What about what about?" Relax. Stop it. Get a grip. I have an answer. What do you do with certain things you can no longer use, and you don't want to throw them away? You give them away, that's what you do. I know, you're mad, huffing and puffing like the little engine that won't. I told you in the beginning of this book that I'm not pulling any punches so still your brain and read. You've got to realize that everybody's agenda is not your agenda. Black women and black men have to stop being the cause of black death. There's even a name for it. It's called genocide. Abortion is a quick, easy, semi-painless way to put a quarter in the slot so you can play. Yes. In a very strange and twisted sense you are playing the same black on black crime syndicate game as the rest of the foolish. Either you are killing your children, your children are killing each other, or the police are finding ingenious ways to expedite a mandate. Speaking of the police and you. What's with this, "My son was just killed by the police. Yes Rev. Al, yes Rev. Jackson you can do the eulogy." Stop this craziness. What's wrong with the regular pastor at your church? It's the same church your 50 plus year old ass was baptized in and it was the same pastor who dunked your head in the pool. It's the same church you attempt to attend every other Sunday to listen to the same pastor, and by the way, the same pastor who married you (twice). The fact that you got or are attempting to get these people to speak means cameras and news. You know that. Why would you want that? What's your purpose? And don't say the exposure might stop the next black boy or black girl from being killed by police. It's not and it won't, and I have that on good authority. Stop this nonsense and leave these folks alone. The last thing you need if your son or daughter has been killed by police is sensationalism. Remember the mother in Baltimore who yoked her son off the street after she found out he was rioting? She got all the sensationalism she needed and didn't need Jesse nor Al to get it for her. All she did was be a mother. Wow! What a novel idea!

5. For suggestion #5 I am drawing from the theme of suggestion #3. Stop running. Yes Mr. and Mrs. (or Ms.) black America. Stop running from the inconvenient truth that while certainly not all but most of the cases where black boys and young black men had exchanges with police these exchanges were initiated due to behavior when or before being engaged. As anyone who has approached this subject matter with common sense would note and has noted there are people with badges, guns, and authority that should not have a badge, a gun, and most definitely not authority. These officials who use these ensigns for the express purpose of justification to commit murder by execution should be drawn, quartered, and each quarter should be burnt to a crisp. Of course, this is my very, very humble opinion. Be that as it may, these individuals make policing more dangerous and hectic for their counterparts than it has any right to be and I by way of this book make no excuses for these sons of bitches.

As for the squalid decisions made thus acts committed by a large segment of young black men that create the conditions necessary for police confrontation let me say this:

This is not a movie. This is not a game. "You have a target on your back" is not just some fucking glib saying anymore. And the target has moved from your back to center mass. You will die in these streets and for what? Maybe you, Mr. black man, can tell me and the world what type of honor you get from being shot down like a rabid dog in the middle, on the side, or in the ditch of this hallowed, holy, divine ground you call "the streets". How do you feel (If you could feel. Remember, you're dead.) lying in the middle, on the side, or in the ditch of this hallowed, holy, divine "street" after you've been "sacrificed" to the gods of stupidity? How does it feel to lay on the alter for six to ten hours while the high priests of the "CHURCH OF I'LL **TAKE**

YOUR LIFE **NIGGER**" move you this way and that way and that way so that they can complete their scoring adjustment system that shows:

Niggers-O US (U.S.) - Hey. Are you kidding?

There is a bigger problem at hand that needs to be addressed and dealt with. While you, Mr. and Mrs. (or Ms.) black America, are hollering, screaming, crying, protesting, looting, marching, and everything else you do when yet another of your sons are left lying in the middle of the "street", sightlessly watching the buzzards (human or bird) milling around overhead, the fact that your son was driving a stolen car; just robbed a store; just robbed a man, woman, child or some small animal; just beat up his girlfriend or wife and/or has 10 kilos of heroin in his sock totally gets lost. Then, when this is brought up cries from everywhere ranging from, "They didn't have to kill him" to, "He wasn't armed" rise up from anguished throats. While these and other lamentations may be true, they are entirely irrelevant after the fact. These things must be taken into consideration and taken seriously - before your sons and daughters become residents in a county morgue near you. Stop running and deal with it. Some things are not racially inspired. Some things are a race to see who can be the biggest fool inspired. This is one of those things.

6. I said earlier that this is not 1965. That was in reference to a particular context in which one has to see there must be a new way of doing things. Your enemy is not a lab rat. They are not, I repeat, are not running on a hamster wheel. Your enemy is more suitable to that of an octopus with tentacles that can and do reach anywhere and everywhere you are and are not. This is a new era of time and your thinking and acting must reflect that. You, Mr. and Mrs. (or Ms.) black America, with your "live for today fuck tomorrow" type of thinking has an enemy that has been laying plans to kill you for more than 2000 years. And although the concepts you were fighting for are the same the strategies you now use must fit the theater of war you are in as well as the change in the subject matter you are attempting to maintain and protect—namely your children. Make no mistake about it, you are in a war.

So what is the first thing you do when you find yourself in a war? You make sure you have a strategy that at least gives you a chance to win. But before I go to the next section, let me reiterate something just in case you didn't understand it the first time.

SECTION TWO
STOP PLAYING

I have made the distinct statement that black people should stop marching. This statement is distinct in that it is not a statement most black people want to hear let alone say. I gave my reasons and observation has proven them to be unassailable. But specifically speaking, my main rationale for this statement is that in these days and times for the issues that are of substance to this community the concept and practice of marching does not work. The powers that be don't give a shit about how many miles you walk or where you walk to nor what you do or say when you get there. As long as you are exercising your right to freely assemble and address grievances in a "peaceful" manor (they call this "peaceful protest") they'll let you blow off steam, have your say, get in a little exercise (Walking. Running if it gets out of hand and the police must get involved), and have a chance to be seen on T.V. And when you've done all that a few months later the same thing that got you marching in the first place happens all over again. Guess what happens then? You do the same old tired, useless, ill planned shit again. Same music. Same dance. It must occur to you at some point that if you are not getting the desired effect, you must change your response to the cause. Your opponent has the power to change the game as well as the rules at will. You have to stop playing checkers when you opponent is playing chess. If your strategy is not working you must be willing to abandon it. Marching is not working. Abandon it. Now.

SECTION THREE
FLEX IT BUT DON'T EXIT

You must be flexible enough to change when the rules of the game change. The rules of the game have changed.

1. I re-reiterate. You will get nothing done marching. A lot of people will not agree with this. So what? Who gives a shit? No matter what anyone says, stop marching. Stop it. Stop it now.

2. Force is applied pressure to or on a specific point. On a human level, force is a constant. You can either be force or be forced. It all depends upon what you know and understand and your ability to translate that into a workable strategy for change. We will discuss strategy in more depth in the next section.

3. You are facing a totally different animal now although it has the same spirit: Control.

    You may think it's Jim Crow (and you do). You may think it's racism (and you do). I can assure you without doubt or contradiction that it's neither. Those methods were used once upon a time in order to enact the same objective: Control.

    While there are bigoted individuals creating mischief and mayhem, they are not the main factors in this. The mainstream media is purposely highlighting certain incidences that can be construed as or in fact are bigotry in order to manipulate the general opinion of the general population and in doing this the general population is manipulated into seeing the small picture instead of the big one. And you, Mr. and Mrs. (or Ms.) black America are falling for it hook, line, and liquor bottle. And again, what's the first thing you do when you get chumped by the media? An easy answer. You break out the Nikes and start marching on that hamster wheel that's been set up specifically for you. They even put your name on it:

"BLACK" Hamster Wheel

    Trust me, they have one called "WHITE" Hamster Wheel too. It gets as much use as the "BLACK" one does. You even have some white hamsters that are fighting each other for a spot on the "Black" Hamster wheel. They're even carrying signs that say, "BLACK HAMSTER'S LIVES MATTER."

    A curious sight indeed.

Dr. Lune A. Teek

SECTION FOUR
A "BLACK" PRINT

Blueprint 2: a program of action.

(Webster's Dictionary)

Let's change the context here but stay on the same page. In short, let's look at what we're looking at.

A war you cannot win. You can, however, stage a revolution. In order to do this correctly you must first know what a revolution really is as well as what a revolution is not. Only when you're clear on this should you even consider to undertake any of what I am proposing. Research this carefully and thoroughly. Research different revolutions staged by different people throughout history.

> Revolution - 2a: a sudden, radical, or complete change; c: activity or movement designed to effect fundamental changes in the socioeconomic situation (as of a racial or cultural segment of the population).

(Webster's Dictionary)

Now that you're comfortable (or should be) with your definitions your first revolution will be with yourself. Are you revolution material (are you "built like that")? What are your strengths and weaknesses? Are you focused? More to the point, can you THINK? The ability to think quickly and clearly, to conceive congruent thought, place it in a context relevant to the situation, and create constructs powerful yet subtle enough to establish set marks or/and entire objectives is the only way you are going to survive let alone establish a design that can save your children. All this you must do while keeping a very cognizant eye on your enemies. It is with this aspect in mind that we will examine your strengths and weaknesses as it relates to your enemies. Everyone has them. You are no exception.

Do you, Mr. and Mrs. (or Ms.) black America, know who your enemies are? Oh, of course I don't mean you individually. Those enemies are inconsequential unless they're threatening you personally. I mean you as a people because these types of enemies don't see nor move against you as individuals. If they do, they do so because you have seen, done, or said too much. These are your Real enemies. I have a saying that I tell people who "think" they know something. I tell them this: "Talk is cheap. As a matter of fact, it doesn't cost anything. If someone isn't trying to kill you however, you

116

ain't saying nothing". Suffice it to say your enemies are more sophisticated, more detailed, and have a more far ranged agenda than can be seen by the unaided eye. So, if you don't know who your enemies are; if you can't call them by name nor recognize them by sight or sound then you cannot identify them. If you can't identify them you have no reference point. If you have no reference point you cannot begin to understand them. If you cannot understand them, how can you possibly defeat them?

You see, it's this type of sad sack incompetence within so called "revolutionary movements" that garners a lot of talk with no results other than to get themselves infiltrated and turned completely on their axis. They have no idea who their real enemies are nor how to sight them (physically nor psychically), so they let them walk through the front door. The next thing anyone knows their whole house has been rebuilt from the inside out and they're either unknowingly working for the CIA, going to jail, insane asylums, or their nearest neighborhood funeral parlor. Not the best places to stage a revolution to be sure. Now on to the next thing.

DEFINE YOUR OBJECTIVES

Then stick to them. No matter what. Your enemies have. For over 2000 years.

When I say "define your objectives" I'm taking for granted that you're gone down all the twists and turns of all the roads one must go down to determine, among other things, whether your objectives are realistic, obtainable, and most of all, in the best interest of all concerned. If these and other conditions have been met then by all means let nothing in heaven, hell, or earth stop nor deter you. Believe me, it can and often does happen. Let's take a look at one not so famous example.

Once upon a time, a little fellow by the name of Moses was told by the really, really big fellow ("God" to you heathens) to go and, "avenge the children of Israel of the Midianites". So, according to the story, he gathered one thousand men from each of the twelve tribes and went to war with the Midianites. And won. They killed all the kings and all the grown men of Midian, took all their property, and razed the city to the ground. They kept alive, however, all the women and children and returned to camp. Pretty much a breakfast fight.

Now, Moses didn't go along on this field trip (Upset stomach or something. I could have sworn I heard something that sounded like "diarrhea"), and when the captains came before him to give their report, he became very vexed and was greatly wroth. In short, he was pissed off. He asked the captains, "Have ye saved all the women alive?". He went on to explain why he asked this question and after this explanation he issued a simple set of commands. They went like this:

> "Now therefore kill every male among the little ones and kill every woman that hath known man by lying with him. But all the women children that hath not known a man by lying with him, keep alive for yourselves."

Of course, the captains were suprised by this and asked Moses for clarification to which he replied, "What's the problem? You can't hear? I didn't stutter. Get going! Move!!!" To which they scuttered out of there all the while thinking, "You know what? He *didn't* stutter. Son of a bitch! I could have sworn..."

Now, of course I took a few liberties with this story. Read it yourself. It's in the Bible. It can be found in Numbers 25:1-18; 31:1-54. You need to read all of this in order to understand why what went on did. This author's intention in including it here is to underline the importance of first clearly defining your objectives (which Moses did not do), then, having the discipline to carry them out. Regardless of what they come to look like. Oftentimes little things may get in the way. Thoughts can and do go awry when the optics for a set of objectives veers off to the left. You may or may not be suprised at how far a person can be diverted from their primary purpose by a little psychological manipulation. Here's a question for you. Consider it carefully.

If Moses had chosen you and you alone to kill all those women and children, could you have done it? Would you have done it? Could you/would you have done it without thought or reservation?

The answer you give will determine whether you believe in the objective as well as those who define and shape the objective. In the above story, the people had to believe in Moses to a point where they understood that whatever he commanded that they do

1. Came from God.
2. Was for the benefit of themselves.

They didn't have to see nor understand the objective. They just had to trust in those who shaped it. Be it little Moses, the "Big Guy", or both.

Understand that in order for what I am about to suggest to work there are going to have to be generals, captains, lieutenants, sergeants, and soldiers. And most of all there must be those who set, plan, shape, maneuver, and maintain the agenda, goals, and objectives. All of you are going to have to trust each other. None of you can do anything to break that trust. Failure of any kind by anyone will break that trust. Therefore, none of you can afford to fail. My suggestion, and this is to the planners, is that whatever role you place whomever in you better make damn sure he or she has mastered not only the role you place them in but themselves as well. There can be no mistakes allowed because your enemy damn well won't make any and is more than ready to make you pay for any of the ones you do. This is a serious undertaking I am suggesting and it has no time, energy nor patience with mediocrity, weakness, or excuses. The entities that are involved must be firmly bonded to the cause and its objectives. You cannot afford to be nor do otherwise.

PERSPECTIVE

One of the etymological definitions of this word means "to look through, see clearly". I am including the following quotes in this section in order to give you a clearer "perspective" of what's at stake.

1. "We of this mighty western republic have to grapple with the dangers that spring from popular self-government tried on a scale incomparably vaster than ever before in the history of mankind... it behooves us to remember that man can never escape being governed. Either they must govern themselves or they must submit to being governed by others. If from lawlessness or fickleness, from folly or self-indulgence, they refuse to govern themselves, then most assuredly in the end they will have to be governed from the outside. They can prevent the need of government from without by showing that they possess the power of government from within. A sovereign cannot make excuses for his failure, a sovereign must accept the responsibility for the exercise of the power that inheres in him, and where, as it is true in our Republic, the people are Sovern, then the people must show a sober understanding and a same and steadfast purpose if they are to preserve that orderly liberty upon which as a foundation every republic must rest"
   (FRANKLIN DELANO ROOSEVELT - JAMESTOWN EXPOSITION)

2. "An ignorant man will always be at the mercy of a fool." (Unknown)
3. "If you don't know who you are you have to be what they call you." (The Author)

4. "The ultimate ownership of all property is in the State; individual so-called "ownership" is only by virtue of Government, i.e., law amounting to mere user; and use must be in accordance with law and subordinate to the necessities of the State."

    (Senate Document #43: Senate Resolution No. 62, pg. 9 and par. 2; April 17, 1933; Senate Document #43, 73rd Congress, 1st Sesson)

You've read quotes #2 and #3 already. Quote #1 deserves your undivided attention. Not because it was the words of a former President, but because the state of being that it is warning about is the state of "black" America. You, as a people, must come to the realization that you are a sovereign nation of people, foreign to this national government, but at the same time a part of the parcel called "America". You won't recognize this until you know and understand who you, the Negro was before slavery. Quote #4 is of a paramount interest to you. Research this document if you can find it. If you continue reading this book you just might find a cure for this headache. You, Mr. and Mrs. (or Ms.) black America, have been deemed as not to be able to govern yourselves. Therefore, others are governing you. You can't see them, hear them, nor touch them. But they're there. And they've been there a long time.

Watching.

Moving.

Governing.

You.

SECTION FIVE
WHAT'S NEXT

One Lost Soul: Where are we?
The Other Lost Soul: I don't know.
One Lost Soul: How did we get here?
The Other Lost Soul: I don't know.
One Lost Soul: Which way do we go to get out?
The Other Lost Soul: I don't know.
One Lost Soul: Will we ever get out?
The Other Lost Soul:

The Author

So,

you've set your agenda(s) and goal(s) in order to manifest your objective(s). Now what's next? The impossible, that what. "What do you mean?", you may ask. The answer is simple and you Mr. and Mrs. (or Ms.) black America will, once I give you the complete answer, realize just how simple the answer is. What's next? You network.

No. No, No! I don't mean that fake-jacked bullshit you so called "professionals" play at doing. I mean a real live honest to damn God network, built from the dirt to the sky. You don't have that. You've never had that. You won't have that. Why? Because you, Mr. and Mrs. (or Ms.) black America, won't allow it. Why won't you allow it? Let's see.

1. You won't marshal the resources. This is no two-dollar, two bits undertaking here. You are trying to change your status from that of a refugee from a banana republic to that of "one of the people" and at the same time you're attempting to save your children from being shot down in "the street" like the dogs a lot of people think they are by some rabies infected brained cop or an idiot reject from the movie *The Gang Who Couldn't Shoot Straight* (which is more of a danger than the rabies brained cop). It's not that you can't marshal the resources. You can. Black people are one of if not the most prolific consumer spending blocks in this country. No, it's not that you can't. You won't. Here's why.

2. You refuse to recognize the difference between an issue and a problem. There is a difference. A big difference. Issues should be watched (monitored). Problems must be solved. You don't solve an issue. You don't watch a problem. Organizations with so-called "Black Agendas" are trying to solve issues they themselves see as

problems. This is largely due to misconceptions, misdirections, or just plain stupidity. And please don't attempt to excuse this lack of common sense by saying that issues can become problems. They sure can and will if you have no analysis or anyone with a smidgen of analytical training. How do you think your enemies know so much about you? Let me give you a view of this lack of understanding.

Behind every problem there is a set of issues and behind every issue there is a cause. You, black people, constantly confuse issues with problems because you either do not or will not deal with the root of your issues which is the *cause*. In short, you're attempting to solve problems while totally ignoring the cause(s) of the issue(s) that created the problem(s) in the first place. A total recipe for futility. And this is how your enemies set you up. They set you up by creating scenarios by which if you would just put a little thought into what you're seeing and/or experiencing you would realize that what you're seeing and/or experiencing is a dog and pony show. This is why analysis is so important. Look the word up. Study the definition. You are faced with something so huge, so large it's impossible to see anything without it. And yes, I know what it is because I've done the analysis. I understand how and why you're being manipulated to the point of thinking the sky is blue and how you'll put a person to the point of a sword or the barrel of a gun that tries to tell you otherwise. Particularly if they happen to look like you. And this is a cause, an issue, and a problem in and of itself. By the way, the sky is black. Not you.

3. This third reason why you, Mr. and Mrs. (or Ms.) black America will not network is because you will let ideological differences take precedence over the overall objective. Consider this for a moment. Or however long you wish to consider it. But consider it and see it as a problem you must.

What would be the result if every professional (and nonprofessional) black organization from black journalists to black attorneys; Fraternal/ Sorority organizations; all black churches; HBCOs; black business and professional chains; mentor organization/entertainment and media outlets, etc., somehow worked out all the logistics and became one massive resource and information (I like the word "intelligence" better) network in which issues that arise that may affect the black community and black people in general can be processed, analyzed accessed and effectively dealt with? It would be powerful, no? Yeah. Right. It ain't happening. Nope. Nada. Impossible.

Every one of the entities I just named has an agenda as well as a penchant for seeing themselves as Jesus Christ incarnate. Which of them do you think would subdue their delusions of grandeur for this particular cause? Very few if any and not enough in any case.

Aside from having the "Big 'I'" don't have time for "little 'U'" complex, too much internal information would have to be shared. Each organization would have to lay bare its financial strengths as well as their weaknesses. Some would have to merge to prevent redundancy. Others would have to merge strategically and/or tactically for the good of the overall objective eventhough they may have strong ideological differences over how certain things should be done. Picture the Nation Of Islam merging with the NAACP.

See what I mean?

Now mind you, I'm talking about not only an information (intelligence) resource, but also where one would go to find technical as well as minimum, intermediate, all the way up to maximum assistance regardless of the reason for the assistance. This network of professional and real-world knowledge and access would be national as well as worldwide, even having the infrastructure necessary to be able to reach inside the inner workings of every governmental agency in every country on the planet with the ability to remove and/or add information to databases within these said agencies. It would be bigger, stronger, and faster than the current "Octopus" simulacrum now in existence. Now answer this. Who's missing? Who's missing from this picture? I'll give you a hint: It's the only thing if you, Mr. and Mrs. (or Ms.) black America don't have in this mix it nor you don't have a snowballs chance in hell of succeeding. That's right. You guessed it (although I know you didn't). Stand back! Wait for it! Here it is!!! Don't Blink!!!

WHITE PEOPLE

Now if you had any thoughts in your mind that you could pull off the type of wizardry I'm contemplating without white people you're as delusional as I thought. If you thought that you should attempt to pull off the type of wizardry I'm contemplating without white people you're sick, plain crazy, and should be locked away in an insane asylum. You're not a lunatic. You're a looney tune.

Suprised? You shouldn't be. If you are then somebody doesn't know their NAACP history. The same thing happened just in reverse. American Jewish leaders had a cause, but they needed a vehicle. They found it in a certain creation of theirs called the Niagra Commission. Do the research. But that's neither here nor there for the purpose of this part of this discussion. This however is.

You must know that it is in white people's best interest that you get your shit together and through this type of format is the only way that can be done. Churches can't do it alone. The legal professional can't do it alone. Business can't do it alone. The media can't do it alone. HCBU's can't do it alone. The medical profession can't do it alone. The Nation of Islam can't do it alone and the NAACP can't do it period. The only way black people can save themselves is to save their children. By saving their children they save their future. By saving their future they save the country. There are white people out here who know this and will spare no expense in assisting you if you are deadly serious about an agenda that consists of upliftment and redemption in the truest sense of the word and that you have a plan in order to make this happen. Besides. You and these particular white people have something in common:

You have the same enemy.

Unlike you however, they know who and what that enemy is and have accepted that. The only thing they've been waiting for is for enough of you to wake up and catch up. Keep in mind, however, that every face that says they're with you isn't. Doesn't matter whether it's white face or black face.

4. There's a song that among other things asks the question, "Who's loving you?" It's a real nice song. Let's spin the record in another direction. I'd like to direct the question to "black agenda" organizations (NAACP, Black Lives Matter; etc.). But instead of asking "Who's loving you?", let me ask the question, "Who's *funding* you?" This will be a short section. Just remember this: Whoever is putting money in your pocket just might be attaching strings to your back. Make damn sure you know who's donating to you and

why. In the infrastructure I'm pushing this would mean having a financial information and intelligence tracking system in place that is second to none. Everyone from financial analysts to computer hackers would be put into place and play. It would be online, on time, real-time intelligence and analysis. Nothing, absolutely nothing would nor should happen until this was established. Why? Because if you're not careful, every dollar you stack could mean a string in your back. And eventhough your brain and heart may say stick to the objective the strings may say different. Remember that. You may not need to. This very thing is happening to you right now via certain "black agenda" groups.

5. Just in case you're wondering where are you supposed to get all these high-end geniuses that are supposed to be saving the world? Why, you grow them of course.

What do you mean, "You grow them" you may ask. Thanks for asking. I would normally say, "The answer is simple". But in this case the answer is not simple. At least not for you. The reason being is because you haven't developed the long-term consistency of objective necessary to do what I'm referencing. This falls under the heading of "long term human resource analysis/development". Your enemy is very good at this. As a matter of fact, they have become masters of this and along the way have raised it to the level of an art form. In case you, Mr. and Mrs. (or Ms.) black America are wondering what "long term human resource analysis/development" is, let me make it so plain that a baby can understand it. Which is what you are when it comes to this game:

> "Train up a child in the way he should go and when he
> is old, he will not depart from it." - Proverbs 22:6
>
> Holy Bible - KJV
> Church of LDS Version

And this is the secret. This is the key that has gained your enemies mastery over you for centuries. It is also the reason why you will never be able to do this. It's complicated.

You see, doing this requires an infrastructure to be set up in order to set up the infrastructure you need to set up. In short, a support system. But not just any old support system. Listen. I'm about to go out on a limb here. What I'm about to do goes totally against the grain as it relates to how I want this book to be. It is necessary though, that I go into this aspect of the development of your community. And while I may interject a bit of satire here and there don't get it twisted. What I'm about to tell you is a very serious secret. Not in so much as the procedure itself, but the fact that it is utilized by certain groups and organizations to obtain, maintain, and proliferate control in by which they consolidate power. It is an age old strategy that has been used by people from the Sumerians to the Russians and organizations from the Catholic Church to the Masons. It is a very powerful, very efficient system if done correctly and a drastically wasteful one if not. And yes, it starts with children. Doesn't it always?

Ordinarily, a child is trained so that it learns what it needs to in order to become independent and the parent, once they have taught the child what it needs in order to become independent will then send the child into the world to become independent. This, however, is not that type of instruction. There are several differences that define the concept of human resource analysis/development for the purpose of this instruction, and the main distinction is that you are not going to teach children to be independent. You are going to teach them how to be *interdependent.* Their whole existence is being groomed to serve the objective. *No thing or no one comes before nor is more important than the objective.* Not family, friends, country, *not even God* is more important than the objective (Imperative #1).

Now, I know this concept is new to some of you, but I want to assure you it is not a new concept. Let me explain what is going to take place. First let's examine what you're going to need. Well, some of what you need.

1. A child. (Preferably no younger than eleven nor older than thirteen. (Gender is irrelevant as each eventually will be trained to do certain things);
2. Behavioral and Social Psychologists (To determine the child's mental fitness and to monitor their behavioral and emotional patterns, all the while maintaining a state of readiness in order to stage an intervention if necessary. These findings are necessary in order to determine the suitability of this child to be able to take instruction and to fulfill later objectives.);
3. The Correct Parents. (It is obvious that the child will have parents. However, they may not be *the correct parents* for the child to have in order for it to reach full, maximum potential. In this case, an intervention team may have to be dispatched in order to extract the child from the parents or the parents from the child.)
4. An Extraction Team. (A team of no less than three individuals with the skills necessary to remove and/or replace unnecessary and/or unwanted people, places, and things that may hinder or derail

the child's progressive development or the overall objective. Also known as an Intervention Team (IT));

5. Strategic Human Resource Placement. (These are people (assets) that are strategically placed within the existing social, educational, business, legal, etc. structure whose sole purpose is to be the conduit for which the child gains entrance into the existing structure. They are to be placed in positions within the educational, legal, economic, medical, and social structure. They are to be assets placed within the entrances, intermediate, and exit stages of each. They should hold position of no less than mid to upper-level management. At this stage they are to be observers only. In case of emergency the extraction team will be dispatched. At no time will their identity be revealed to the child.

6. A Reinforcement Team. (No thing nor no one comes before or is more important than the objective. This is the first imperative and is the foundation of everything involved. This team is here to reinforce the imperative or loyalty *by any means necessary*. This team will work with the Extraction Team when and if necessary.);

7. Political and Media Operatives. (These assets are to operate independent from the inner structure but must be wedded to the First Imperative. They will function as gatekeepers and exterminators of any public and/or private information that may hinder the child's progressive development and/or the First Imperative.)

These are just seven (7) initiatives that need to be put in place *before* you can even begin a network on the scale of which I'm contemplating, which is one that will work. There are many more. Don't scoff. The correct, precise implementation of just these seven alone will take you a minimum of ten (10) years. Why so long? Simple. You must find people who can and will embrace, commit, and expedite their positions according to the First Imperative. The First Imperative is non-negotiable and is binding on all involved. It has no favorites and it brooks no argument. Extraction and Reinforcement Teams must perform their duties thoroughly and without bias. Either you will have loyalty to the network or you will have no network. The First Imperative is the Law and the law must live. Or else.

PERSPECTIVES OF PERCEPTIONS

I could go on with this, but I think, hope, and pray that you get the picture. You, as, a people, are at least 100 years behind your salvation and you will remain at least that far until you come to the realization that unless you do something akin to what has been proposed here you as a people will be reduced to a shadow of your former selves, which, truth be told, is a shadow of your current selves. I was born October 31, 1961. Black people in this country, in the aggregate were poor then and black people, in the aggregate in this country are poor now. Regardless of (and in my opinion because of) all the social programs, safety nets, wars on poverty, wars on drugs, wars on wars, etc., none of them, separately or together have lifted black people out of poverty. Government can't do it. No one else can, should, nor will do it but black people in conjunction with the *correct* white people. But it's not going to happen. At least not until black people in America stop being destructive minded, stop being envious and distrustful off each other; stop giving each other reasons to be distrustful of each other; understand they are smarter thereby more powerful than they give themselves credit for; and most of all, stop killing each other. Figuratively as well as literally.

PERSPECTIVES ON THE NETWORK

Look at your body. Consider that its nature baffles scientists to this day.

Your brain looks totally different than your feet. Your feet have a different function than your brain yet nevertheless, when both perform as they should you get something called walking, running, kicking, standing, etc. With that said, you had to learn how to do these things. When you started walking no one explained the complex nature of what you were doing and your parents didn't know how even if they wanted to and you could understand what the hell they were talking about. Complex as the process of walking, running, sitting, eating, talking, seeing, smelling, tasting and the host of other things humans and other living creature do, the point is that it takes different parts of the whole, working simultaneously in unison for any activity done by any part of the whole to be realized. The same concept applies to you Mr. and Mrs. (or Ms.) black America. You have a slew of networks. A network for this, a network for that, a network for everything but what should be networked. As a matter of fact, black America, you've got too damn many networks. You only need one. Your enemies only have one. They have a shitload of others just to have something to do or to throw twiddle minded folk off the track. Trust me. The one they have and use is highly resourceful and impregnable. You may be able to walk, run, or ride into the offshoots with a fair amount of allowed difficulty. The inner sanctum is something totally different. Speaking of different, the difference between what I've just explained and a lot of the networks that you as black people have is that your networks are incomplete at best (which makes them impotent) and at their worst they suffer from what I call a "lack of elastic vision". In short, you're trying to get "equal justice" in *America?* Your enemy is trying to take over the world and is about 2.6 seconds away from doing just that and you're focusing on "America"? I happen to know who's funding the largest black "networks in this country in the covert manner in which they normally fund organizations. All I'll EVER say about that is what I've already said:

WATCH OUT FOR STRINGS

Really black people. You're not ready for this. If you can build on what I've just explained to you, you might have a chance. If you can't, don't, or won't—may God have mercy on your souls because the Head of Satan will have its reckoning and you will once again know the sting of the Master's whip. Now read carefully. Slowly if necessary. But carefully.

What is needed to fulfill this network?

Whatever is needed will come from the network.

And this is the key.

The network will be a force Mr. and Mrs. (or Ms.) black America because for almost the first time in your modern existence it will not eat its own but give birth to its own. First you will plot out every position that is necessary within this network. From teachers to lawyers to doctors to real estate planners/developers/brokers/salespeople to tailors to janitors. Every position needs to be accounted for. Leave nothing to chance and take nothing for granted. Realize that at first you must develop this strategy and objective in every state in America (including Alaska). Other countries will come later.

Once you have the initial framework set, you are now ready to develop your resources — your children. Because of the nature of this network, the initial framework will of course consist of adults. They will be the trainers, facilitators, and instructors of these children. They will be training, facilitating and instructing them to be able to take their rightful place in society. And if you do it just right, the child won't even know. There will come a time when information pertinent to those responsibilities will be made known. That will come later. You will also train a set of these resources to be able to replace those in the framework. Within twenty years this network should be fully self-subsistent and self-regenerating. Mind you, I'm only referring to setting up your network. It's going to take you at least another twenty years before you see it bear fruit. It all depends on how thorough your objectives are. You, in all likelihood will see little if any of the works that you are attempting to fulfill. But then again, this is not for you. It's for your unborn generations. You're leaving them a legacy. It's what you lacked and is the evidence of why "black" America is in the state it's in. And why it's so "black".

LET'S TAKE IT FROM THE SIDE

A few things must first be said, I'm going to say them. You're going to hear. Of course you can't "hear" me, but you can read. These are my words. If you're how I know you are you won't like them. You will think them and I are too extreme. You have a right to think that. After all, this is a free country even though you are not free within it. Regardless of what you may think or feel none of that makes my words any less true and relevant to the subject matter. Because of this DO NOT, I repeat, DO NOT attempt to even consider what I am proposing unless you are serious about committing to its precepts. It will only end in failure.

A CHILD IS BORN

It's debatable whether a child is born with no state of mind. Here, we aren't taking any chances. For this intent and purpose, we're going to *give* this child a state of mind and we're going to nurture that state until it becomes a part and a partial of that child's existence all the way to adulthood. This is the first step. However, for one to give the light one must first have the light. As an expediter of this method, one cannot be ignorant. Regardless of the position one must be a master or at least an expert in their position. *Proficiency is not enough,* however professionalism is a must.

AND FINALLY, IN ALL SERIOUSNESS

You must be serious about this. Really serious. Deadly serious.

This is not a game. This is not a joke. And as I wrote earlier, if you are not going to view it and treat it as such do not attempt it. To be stark honest with you I hope you don't attempt it. Oh sure, you have a few criminal elements among you who "think" they have a network. They are not, however, self-subsistent. Your enemies are. In all actuality, they are the "real" gangsters. And yes. You must be just as smart, just as savvy, and just as ruthless as they are. But in order to do that, you must have your eyes opened. Just a tad. A good book to read in order to do just that is entitled *Operation Gladio* by Paul L Williams. A true story by the way. And it happened right under your nose. And probably still is. Keep that in mind when you read this book. Keep this in mind also. Remember the First Imperative? Watch what happens to those who violate it. It's how this game is played. If you can't play by the rules Mr. and Mrs. (or Ms.) black America, don't get on the field. At least not without a Kevlar. And if that is not enough for you to understand the First Imperative and the necessity of its implementation don't know what is.

And now on to the real reason behind why I wrote this book.

CHAPTER FIVE

You Have The Right to Remain Silent

Hush little baby don't you cry;
The policeman didn't mean to shoot
you in the eye...
(A black child's lullaby)

Section One

I'm going to tell you some things you don't know because those that do know won't tell you. It's not that they hate you or are racist or any of the ten thousand plus things agitated and angry people will mentally and verbally postulate. A determination has been made that solutions to a menacing problem can be obtained without having to make this information public. I, on the other hand, am aware of the futility and outright stupidity of this determination and the thinking that drives it. Am I calling the determiners stupid? No, I'm calling their thinking stupid.

There is an old saying that goes "Those who know don't talk and those who talk don't know." This oftentimes is a true saying. However, in some very rare and very necessary instances something unusual happens. A cat barks. A dog meows. A bird flies backward. A Jersey cow sings "Sweet Home Alabama." A three month old baby grows a full beard and recites the Gettysburg Address.

Regardless of what phenomenon occurs, it was necessary given the prevailing circumstance(s). This is one of those times in which the circumstances have created the necessity. Someone who knows is going to talk (in this case write). Hopefully you'll listen (in this case read and take heed). If you do, then you'll know. Therefore you will have been warned.

Even though this chapter is geared towards both black and white people it hopefully will make an impact on black people, who are at their wits end trying to figure out how to keep their children from becoming a statistic within a list that is definitely not a scholastic honor roll. Hopefully this bit of information will help you help them. Hopefully.

Section Two
"You have the right to remain silent"

Seven words.

And so begins a journey that for some marks the beginning of the end of life as they knew it. Some survive this sojourn but none come away from it unscathed. In truth, the moment one hears these words spoken to them, a death knell sounds and barring some act of God, the governor, the president, or a good attorney this individual enters the state of "civillus mortuus"- civil death. Or in the worst case scenario, eternal rest. Be they "black" or "white."

"You have the right to remain silent."

No you don't. Not anymore. But then again, you never did. Seems like a paradox, doesn't it? Probably is. But then again, life is full of 'em.

"You have the right to remain silent."

Have you ever considered these seven words? You probably haven't. If you've never had a reason for a police officer to begin this litany and direct it at you the television or movie screen is the closest you've gotten to this recital. However, if you've had an opportunity to have some love struck police officer sing this ode of Satan to you, you were probably so overwhelmed by the magnitude of it all that the words just rolled right by you. It is for you that I recite the first two sentences of this prose. These first two sentences are the most important. What comes after them is just mush.

"You have the right to remain silent.
If you give up the right to remain silent.
<u>Anything you say can and will be used</u>
<u>Against you in a court of law...</u>"

Notice what is emphasized. Notice it well. Make sure you put special emphasis on the words "can" and "will." Especially "will." This is not a misprint or mistake, and if you don't understand the connotation of it it will lead to your legal demise.

First off, this litany has been falsely labeled as "rights" (Miranda Rights). The technical term for these words as used by professionals in this field is called "Miranda Warning." And a warning it is indeed. However, if you are

Dr. Lune A. Teek

having these words read or recited to you the warning has come too late. It is with this and other sentiments in mind that I write the following:

Even though the context of this warning is just that - a warning, one still has the right to remain silent. There are those however, that never got the chance to hear these words. To them, silence, although a right, became a consequence. May they rest in peace. And silence.

Section Three
You are being watched and weighed

I used the term "professionals" earlier to imply the difference between those who work in the police and legal professions and you - the "civilian." The difference is as big as it is important and should never be overlooked. It is this:

They have been _trained_ to deal with you while you
have noY idea of how to deal with them.

I, however, am going to key you in on some things. Listen (or read) very carefully and keep up.

This section is entitled "You Are Being Watched And Weighed," and it is the first of a series of law enforcement tactics that I am going to explain to you. Because so much of the public perception about police versus civilian interactions are seen through the eyes of the civilian, he or she is only aware of what is going on in front of them. They oftentimes are totally unaware about what is happening beneath the surface of what they are seeing or experiencing. This is problematic when it comes to having an understanding of how an interaction between the two can go wrong. The problem(s) can become compounded when, as I alluded to, police officers are using tactics unknown to the civilian and the civilian is unaware of their use. The tactic I call being watched and weighed is a very important tactic ALL police officers are trained in. The laymen's terms for this would be observation (watched) and assessment (weighed). A response based on the result(s) of the assessment will be forthcoming. In short, based on "careful" and "critical" observation an assessment is made on how to deal with you given the situation and circumstance. We all too undeniably have witnessed that this is not the way the scenario plays itself out. I'll touch on this because it is ignorance on both sides that can and often does turn what can be described as a common sense approach all the way to the left. This is what _you_ must know.

No officer will ever arrive at a call scene "cold." Cold in this sense means arriving on a "hot" scene without the benefit of knowing something or at least having a sense of what's going on. Every patrol car has a radio and every radio can pick up the station dispatcher. By the way, "hot" in this sense means an active interaction between the police and suspects and/or perpetrators. Unless the call is for "all available units", based on the location of the call or incident, the dispatcher will dispatch a unit within the sector to that particular location. The dispatcher will then give the officer what I call "primary knowledge" of the incident they are going to confront. This knowledge will vary in depth and scope based upon how much information the dispatcher can get from the caller. So based on this, the officer heads up to the scene and it is here that issues can and often do develop and unless you (Civilian. In particular, "black civilian") take heed and understand what comes next, I guarantee what happens will be fatal for you. As you have already seen.

Why is this such a crucial juncture? Because the officer, once he or she has primary knowledge of an event has to mentally prepare for an intervention. What does this mean? Strictly put, it means that from the movement they get that call from dispatch, they have to mentally prepare themselves to TAKE CONTROL OF THE SITUATION BY ANY MEANS NECESSARY. I emphasize and capitalize this emphatically. Why? Police officers by the nature of the job and training must gain control of the call scene and anytime a police officer has made a determination that he or she cannot get nor maintain control of that call scene it is not going to end well for someone and police officers train long and hard to make sure that someone is not them.

When a police officer arrives on a scene he or she is trained to "weigh" all the participants and to assess possible actions by them. They are trained to match aggressive actions by participants with aggressive actions by themselves. They are trained to be able to assess a situation within a maximum time range of three seconds and even though an officer may not be a first responder to a call, this assessment training is crucial because he or she as a non first responder will more often than not arrive at a "hot" scene. This was the case in the 2014 shooting of a 17 year old in Chicago and the 2015 shooting in Cleveland of a child with a pellet gun. Whatever the situation is at the time of an officer's arrival his or her mindset by necessity must be prepared to be as fluid as the situation dictates. To be sure, a police officer has a different mindset if he or she is called to a bank robbery than they would have if they were called to get a cat out of a tree.

Section Four
How "Accidents" Happen

Police officers are trained to view most call situations in "worse case scenario" status for the duration of their contact with the situation and its participants until at such time he or she feels in control. And even then they are trained to be wary at all times because they are aware that the variables of any given situation are "fluid" (can change at any time). Anytime an officer arrives at a scene, they are in a defensive and offensive state of mind simultaneously which means that their state of mind is also fluid. Having this type of mental state on a consistent basis is tantamount to what one would have if he or she was in a war zone and to be honest, it is a theater of war, in particular with the growing numbers of police officers being shot and/or killed while just sitting in their patrol cars let alone while doing police business. With that said, one must understand that the police aren't called to come over and have milk and cookies. They are not going to be knocking on doors yelling "Trick or Treat." If a police officer has been summoned it is because something or someone has either gone, is going, or has the potential to go wrong and he or she is being called to fix it or them and fixing it or them may well call for something or someone to violently leave this plane of existence and as I've stated earlier it is always in that officer's mind that that someone might be them and they are trained to make sure that it's not.

Dr. Lune A. Teek

Section Five
Let me see your profile

The other half of being watched and weighed deals with the fact that based on certain concepts accepted and characteristics shown and/or practiced both black and white people have been and are being profiled not only by their local police departments but also by the Department of Homeland Security, which in and of itself brings with it a series of other problems. Case in point; do you know what a watchlist is? If you don't you need to find out what the Department of Homeland Security's watchlist is as well as who's on it. By the way, it may surprise some black people to know that white people are more profiled than they are. But for different reasons. Which is not at all surprising, especially to me.

Profiling is something that has been done since time immemorial and regardless of how loud you scream "I should be able to wear this," or "I should be able to wear that," or "I should be able to look this way," or "I should be able to look that way"; the truth of the matter is if you wear this or wear that and if you say this or say that, law enforcement has been mandated to make a determination, based on the above as to what your actions may or may not be, and if it fits an existing profile you will be dealt with according to a predetermined protocol. Period. End of story. For example:

A lot of young black males have adopted the practice of wearing "hoodies" (jackets or sweaters with a hood attached). Police have profiled the hoodie as a favorite article of clothing worn by certain gang members. Police and law enforcement in general view gangs as a threat to the peace and security of the community at large and, according to them, a certain number of crimes have or may have been committed by gang members in this type of dress. Ergo, if you are out at night (or day) wearing a hoodie, especially near a crime scene, you're subject to be stopped, frisked, or detained. Of course, other variables come into play (if you're a pregnant, middle aged white woman wearing Coke bottle glasses with a hoodie on you probably won't get stopped. At least not by the police), but it's those "other variables" that make profiling so insidious. Insidious yes. But effective just the same. At least in the eyes of law enforcement.

As it relates to racial profiling, that barn door has been left wide open and every last one of the horses have gone and they took their shit with them. They won't be coming back.

There was a time (I don't know when) when the statistic takers took a look at their statistics and according to said statistics determined that during a specific period of time, more violent crimes (murders, shootings, robberies, etc.) had been committed by black males within a certain age group. They then looked for similarities and characteristics, put them all together and bingo! That's all it took. Well, that and the "wrong" person or people getting shot, robbed, or killed. Then it became an issue. Thanks to those statistics and that "wrong" person practically all black males of certain ages are being profiled. Forever. No, forever and a day. Depending on where they live forever and a year. This word "forever" is important to note because once a profile starts it will not stop. Such is the nature of profiling. No matter how much you scream, holler, march, and sing "We Shall Overcome," the one thing you will not overcome is the profile. It won't stop. Police have been trained to deny this fact. They will deny it even if Jesus comes back wearing a hoodie. They will deny it and then put him under surveillance. Profiling is here to stay and racial profiling is a staple in that stable. It's what replaced the horses.

Take note: All profiles are not necessarily racial in nature. It may surprise you that veterans are on watch lists prepared by the government, for no other reason than they're veterans. This seems crazy if you're viewing this statement from across the room. But if you come a little closer, you'll see that the government, given all the shenanigans (Look up this word. The definition fits perfectly) it's involved in, has a vested interest in keeping a nervous but watchful eye on vets. Why? Because veterans are the only group of people in this country who are trained to kill and kill very effectively. It's what war-time veterans did for a living. The same way a stockbroker puts on a suit and tie to go to work and play the stock market, war-time veterans practically lived in their uniform and their job 24 hours a day, 7 days a week was very simple: kill. That's it, that's all. Kill. The more you kill the better your chances were of staying alive. So they had to be very effective and very efficient. Veterans who were in war-time theater along with special forces personnel, pound for pound are the deadliest individuals on the planet. And who do you think is responsible for that training and has put it to the most use? Yep. You guessed it. Good ole Uncle Sam. Bless his little heart.

Veterans aren't the only people profiled on watchlists that would surprise the average person. People who voted for certain candidates are on watchlists. People who view themselves as "sovereign" are on watchlists. You'd be surprised and amazed at whom the government views as a domestic thorn in its side. And you have President Barack H. Obama to thank for that. With the signing of the National Defense Authorization Act, or NDAA as it's sometimes referred to, this president took the Patriot Act and directed it squarely in the face and into the lap of the American Citizen (just for kicks, research what time it was when your president signed this bill into law).

Section Six
Potty Trained

You may have noticed that in previous sections I emphasized the words "train," "trained," and "training." I did this to emphasize a very important point and it is this:

Police officers are not "educated" in doing their jobs. They're trained in doing their jobs. There is a difference. A big difference.

Don't get me wrong through misunderstanding the statements. Police officers, by and large, are highly educated individuals. Some even have upper level degrees. This is not what I mean. What police officers go through as a process to prepare him or her to do their jobs is not so much **cerebral** as it is **instinctual.** In a given situation, police officers are not instructed to **think.** They are **trained** to act or react and these actions and reactions are often based on scenarios. This is of the utmost importance for you to know because if your actions, unbeknownst to you, start looking like a training scenario that police officer is going to stop seeing you, the person and start seeing you, the movie star. The problem here is that in training scenario films the star is more often than not the bad guy. And you know what happens to the bad guy. This is why you have so many police shootings. It has nothing whatsoever to do with "race." People, young black boys and black men in particular, do not understand that when they run, reach, resist, etc, they are playing out a scenario and the police officer responds in reaction mode. To be specific, police officers are trained in what is known as "situational response." The officer's action is a reaction to an action (or lack thereof) by you. That action (or lack thereof) has been relayed to that officer by way of a training video or a situational construct (exercise). He or she is going to respond based on scenario training. They have been **trained** in practically every situation scenario they could face. When your actions (or lack thereof) begin to look like the bad part of a training video **you stop being a human being and you become the training scenario come to life.** And you have no idea this is happening. Before you know it you're dead. Scenario over. LIfe over. But wait. There's more.

Now concerning police shootings and shoot outs. I don't know how many times I've heard people, from grieving mothers to armchair Johnny Cochranes say these words; "He didn't have to shoot him there"; "He didn't have to shoot him so many times"; "He could have shot him in the leg"; "It's not fair"; etc. Let me educate you on some things.

First of all, let me again say that I'm telling you things that the police and the legal profession will not tell you. Why? Because they are not obligated to. A lot of these issues fall under the purview of internal procedures and while I have not gone into great detail and depth concerning these issues (and I have done so on purpose); I have given you more than you had and more than you would have gotten. Suffice it to say I know what I'm talking about. Use the information accordingly. Then educate yourself in more detail.

With that said, police officers regardless of what you might have heard or think you know, are not **trained** to shoot to wound unless specifically ordered to do so. If a police officer fires a warning shot and hits you, your son, daughter, husband, wife, grandpa, grandma, uncle, aunt, cousin, or friend in the leg, arm, hand, or ass, after everything is over or/and you get out of the hospital, you or whomever got shot need to find that officer and thank him or her for showing you either mercy or how drunk they still were. Maybe they saw Jesus under that hoodie instead of your cousin.

Police officers are **trained** to shoot at and hit a bodily target area that they know as "center mass." Center mass is the area of your body from the bottom of your neck to your navel area. It is in this area that all your vital organs are housed. Shooting and hitting anything in this area with the type of rounds police officers use will cause severe trauma and/or massive hemorrhaging. This tactic (center mass shooting) is designed to do just that. It is designed to deliver the highest kill rate given the specified scenario as well as the greatest amount of mass exposed to the shooter. This is why this tactic is known as "deadly force" or "maximum force." This is why police officers are given (assigned) a protective vest and are **trained** in its use. Yes a head shot will give one an even greater kill rate but it is not the average officer's specified given scenario. The headshot is the specified prerogative of the marksman (sharpshooter, or as he or she is most widely known 'sniper' and is most likely delivered via rifle).

An officer is **trained** to lay you down as quickly and as efficiently as possible if he or she is given the need to do so. They are **trained** to apply whatever force that is applicable to the threat until at such time the threat is alleviated. It is in this grey area (watched and weighed) that the use of minimum force can change very quickly to maximum force.

We've gone over the use of deadly force concerning a police officer's firearm. Now let's deal with the use of force as it concerns the utilization of holds, which if done incorrectly can be just as deadly.

The holds police officers use basically fall into two categories:

1. Subdue
2. Submission

Holds designed to subdue a suspect are designed to contain them. Submission holds are designed to be used if the containment holds fail to make the suspect yield. Again this is a danger zone for both the officer and suspect. Especially the suspect. Submission holds are a last resort and are to be used first only if the situation warrants it. This is because submission holds are designed to put the suspect in extreme pain. This is important. Pay attention.

No officer is **trained** nor is allowed to use any hold that can be construed to be or actually is a "choke" hold. Any hold that can or is designed to cut off the flow of blood or oxygen to the brain is strictly forbidden by all police forces in this country. Not only can these holds cause death through shutting off blood and oxygen flow to the brain they can also cause death by strangulation and rupture of the larynx.

Now let's return to that word **trained** again. Just for a minute. Just long enough to point out something that by now should be obvious. In particular as it relates to the differences between you and the police.

As I've already stated the words **train**, **training**, **trained,** etc, are very important words in the context of this writing. It is important to you that these words are understood in the proper context because these words, in the context they're being used here imply beyond average skill. Therefore know and understand that you are not trained in the manner of a police officer. I know this is a bit redundant, but it is extremely necessary that I get you to see this, otherwise all of this is for naught. The term "suicide by cop," is beginning to be a very apt description of the actions of a lot of people. Young, black, boys and black men feel that because it was easy to kill Joe (age 9), Suzy (age 7), Harry (age 16), and Rashawn (age 23), it's probably just as easy to kill Officer Dan. As I've said, I will not be going into the specifics of police training. Suffice it to say that every police officer you see or don't see with a gun had to have a lot of training with it as well as shoot above a particular score before they were assigned one. They had to shoot from one knee. They had to shoot on both knees. They had to shoot lying down. They had to shoot standing up. They had to shoot on the run. They had to shoot standing still. They had to shoot still targets. They had to shoot moving targets. And that was after they learned practically everything there is to know about their weapons (some manuals call it a nomenclature). Oh. Did I mention "night fire?" For those of you who don't know what this is, it's when targets are placed at a particular distance and are fired upon. The thing here is it's at night at a range area with little or night light or inside with the lights out. The targets range from stationary to moving, far to close. The technical term (one of them) is also called "instinctive aim". Tracer rounds, which are ammunition with phosphorus tips, are normally used for this activity. It lets you know where you are shooting and it just plain looks good in the dark.

To put it in a nutshell, unless you catch a police officer totally off guard, your chances of coming out of an armed confrontation with one alive are slim to none.

What the public (you) needs to know and understand is that this is a new era of time and the concepts that deal with police- civilian interactions have changed and changed drastically. The three most important things you need to know and adjust to are these:

1. **Resistance is Futile**: There was a time when a person could question a police officer's methods are/or reason for his or her engagement with them. This has changed. Forever. Now police officers are trained to view the questioning of their methods and/ or authority as **resisting** their methods and/or commands. This is a highly important distinction as it switches the execution of a right of a citizen to that of a criminal act. And they will deal with you accordingly.

2. **Three strikes you're in (Deep Shit):** This aspect piggybacks the first. Please, please, please pay attention. This not only can it will save your life. Not taking it seriously will end it. You must understand that aspect #1 is now the law. It matters not what you think nor what you say, aspect #1 is the law. Deal with it so that you won't get dealt with.

A police officer stops you while walking down the street and wants to search you. According to **their law** (the constitution) you are allowed to question the reason for this search because:

1. The search is an invasion of your person and privacy;
2. The stop is a detainment and a check against your liberty interest;
3. The officer must have probably cause

So you question the officer as to why he or she is stopping you. The officer does not answer your question and instead tells you to put your hands behind your back. It is of the utmost importance for you to know that at this exact point a procedure/tactic has been initiated. The command "put your hands behind your back" began a process I choose to call "three strikes you're in." If you don't adhere to the first command (immediately) it will be followed by another command that is the first command repeated. The third command will be the same but will begin with the words "I am giving you a direct order," or something similar to that effect. It may be "this is your last time," or "I won't tell you again," or "This is your final warning." This "final warning," will be said in a more forceful tone and you will see him or her reach for something that will enforce the aforementioned command. Or worse. It is here that detainment turns into an arrest. An important point to note.

With this scenario, what this officer has done is put you on "lawful notice." He/she did this because training protocol dictates it. These three commands are symbolic of the following:

- 1st command- "you heard"
- 2nd command- "you understood"
- 3rd command- "you disobeyed"

Going through this protocol gives the officer legal standing to use force. The type of force will be determined by the situation. If the force used by the officer is excessive or exceeds lawful boundaries (the use of holds not sanctioned by training standards), they can be held liable. Once again, it is incumbent upon you to realize that what you think is happening versus what really is happening is as different as the Great Pumpkin is from Julius Caesar. Know that with the first command your life is being weighed in the balance. Questioning is resisting. Resisting will get you killed.

3. **How did it come to this?** You might ask. A good question Therefore, let's go to the third thing the public (you) should be aware of and that is the militarization of the domestic police officer. This is another thing police officers have been trained to deny. Some will however admit to this. While I could go deep into the acquiring of the military surplus hardware and other equipment by police departments, I won't. My focus here is to highlight the changing mentality of the police officer as he or she makes the transition from using domestic equipment to military "gear," and "hardware". It is here where the psychology of enforcement comes into play. A large part of this psychology is directed at you, the public, and as such it is a must that the officer can be trained to have the psyche to initiate and execute certain procedures. For example, a police officer has four ensigns (equipment) of deterrence:

    a. The uniform
    b. The stick
    c. The mace/taser
    d. The gun

Note the graduated level of each. When each graduation of deterrences comes an escalation of mental exertion needed to perform and this is because 'supposedly," the situation in which maximum deterrence is warranted requires it and it is here that the danger lurks.

Each officer was trained based upon "domestic" reference and their psyche tempered accordingly. Now take that same beat cop and put him or her in a jet black or camouflage uniform, take away their low cut oxfords and put them in a pair of jack boots. Blouse their pants, take away their service weapon and give them M-16s and M-60s and guess what happens: Nothing. And nothing will happen until something happens to their psyche and that has to be done by training. Military equipment was devised and designed to be handled and used by military personnel. There is a difference in the psychological training of a domestic police officer and that of a military security police officer and even though both require the proficient use of tactics it is the objectives that will determine the type of tactics utilized. Luckily for police departments (hence unlucky for you) most if not all of their training instructors have extensive military backgrounds and thus are very good at what they do. This is why understanding this section of this book is very important to you. If a particular mandate to operate in a certain manner has been given to your local police department you, as a civilian will never know. And this will in all likelihood make for an extremely terse and tense situation. Deadly even.

Mandates exist in every facet of life. Even you have them. You may not call them mandates but mandates they are nonetheless. Police departments are big on mandates. They wouldn't know how to operate without them. Your concern here is about a mandate that (subliminally in most cases) moves the officer from a domestic to a military mindset and that has changed his or her mental identification pattern. In other words, the domestic beat cop identifies you as "person," "people," "individual," "suspect," "perpetrator," etc. The officer that has gone "full metal jacket" has had a brain transplant. Instead of recognizing you as any of the above, you now have become "civilians," "targets," "domestics," "domestic threats," "security threats," "security risks," "collaterals," "bad actors," "state actors," "Assets," "Collaborators," etc. Once you juxtapose the definitions of these two sets of descriptive characteristics, you will see the psychological difference of reference that the officer must internalize in order to adhere to the mandate in which each set exists. Here is how this change looks in real time.

If your son is known by law enforcement to be a member of the Crips or Bloods affiliation, at one time he would be seen as a domestic municipal problem to be monitored and dealt with by your local police or sheriff department. Now, thanks to the National Defense Authorization Act (NDAA), your son, based on his membership within this group, which unbeknownst to many has been labeled as a Security Risk Group, is now labeled as a domestic threat. He is no longer seen by law enforcement as an "individual person" or "one of the people." The truth be told, he is technically no longer viewed as an American citizen. If he is in prison, and it becomes known by prison officials of his affiliation he will undergo a process known as "validation" and in effect will be stripped of his citizenship for the time he is under this scrutiny. He will be registered in all law enforcement databases as a member of a Security Risk Group and not only is a local police and sheriff department prerogative but a Department of Homeland Security monitored issue. As a member of a "security risk group" he is now a risk to the peace, security, and prosperity of the United States of America and as such is an "enemy of the state," and if he is an enemy of the state, he must by nature of the term be an enemy of the police. The issue here is that your local police or sheriff department didn't invent the term "Security Risk Group," nor any of its initiatives. Even most of the training of those involved in specific "task forces" is sponsored and directed by the Department of Homeland Security and/or the Department of Justice. Know this: Your local police and sheriff departments have been vested with the power to protect your locality. The Department of Homeland Security has been vested with the power to protect the United States of America and until your son has been declared a 'neutral' by the Governor and/or the President, he will be viewed as a possible "enemy combatant" and subject to engagement by any law enforcement agency as well as any military asset deemed necessary for his possible termination with extreme prejudice - the United States Marshals Task Force being the first ones tasked with that.

Section Seven
"United we stand, divided we fall"

Law enforcement, for as long as I have known it, moves and adheres to an age old adage:

United we stand, divided we fall.

And while this adage was used as a rallying cry for nationalistic unity its essence has not escaped the United States and the world in their never ending quest to do whatever is necessary in order to bring about the full establishment of a world wide police state. Do you think it's a joke? Do you think I'm joking? Do you think they're joking?

If you think law enforcement is not designing a network like what I've described then you're really behind the eight ball (and the 1 ball, the 2 ball, the 3 ball, and every other kind of ball that you could be behind). You cannot see this therefore you can't know this is happening. You are the subject matter of this surveillance state therefore you are too close to it. You can't see it, however, it can see you. After all, that's what it was designed to do. Let's take a look at some of the things that's taking a look at you. I'm going to list two. Research these carefully. Don't be fooled by the flowery language. There are thorns beneath the blossoms.

1. TheStrongCitiesNetwork.org (website)
2. Predictive Policing

The "Strong Cities Network," in reality is a strategy. It is being backed and funded by the Institute for Strategic Dialogue (InstituteforStrategicDialogue. org) which is an organization with some pretty heavy hitters within its ranks and you can best believe they are planning some pretty heavy things. All just for you.

Predictive Policing is something that you really need to understand. Actually it's being done (or was being done) now. You'll see this at work with such practices as "stop and frisk" and "Checkpoints/flashpoints." I can tell you that this system is fully automated in nature and works in the primary sense, by running specific variables, thus creating algorithms and a series of such that, according to the so-called "experts" will determine if you will commit a crime. This along with other futuristic strategies and tactics are already being used in certain cities and states and whether you want to believe it or not or whether you want to see it or not these strategies and tactics in the future will begin to look more militarily coordinated. And so will police officers. The military. The police. Together. What more could a facist possibly want?

Section Eight
Perspective

I have given you a bird's eye view of the concepts and practices of local law enforcement and how it operates upon you, the public. It was not conceived to be and therefore it is not an operations manual of the police departments across America. Nor was it intended to be read like one. I left out boring things like statistics, graphs, charts, etc. Why? Because none of those things will save your life when confronted by police. If you're black and are being pulled by a policeman in a traffic stop, it won't save your life to know that 68% of traffic stops by your particular police department are done against black people versus 32% against white people. What will save your life is being advised as to some of the tactics and strategies that may be used against you at said traffic stop. Being forewarned may forego you having a very, very terrible experience and in some ways a very, very unnecessary experience. If you feel you have the "right" to remain silent then by all means do so. However, don't start talking when the consequences begin. What do I mean? Simple. Anytime you are in a situation in which you are ignorant of the tactics and strategies that are being employed by the other party within that particular situation, barring the proverbial "garbage can getting lucky sometimes," you will always be on the losing end. And there are some losses that you cannot come back from. Example: your life. It's like playing chess with a grandmaster and you've only learned how the pieces are to be moved. It's like shooting a fish in a barrel. Pun definitely intended.

Case in point:

The vast majority of 'violent' interactions with police could be placed upon the at-large public perception of police officers as well as policing in general. It would be beyond foolish to think that there is a legal mandate that police harass and kill black people. It is not foolish to think that the wrong move at the wrong time during a police interaction will get one killed regardless whether they're 'black' or 'white.'

As this is the 'perspective' section, it bears noting that perspectives are based mostly on perception. It also bears noting that a particular perspective or a particular perception does not necessarily equal a truism. People do not come out of their mother's womb with a good or bad perception of police. LIke everything else in life, a person's perception(s) of police often stem from certain observations as viewed through the perspective of the observer. This is the reason why some segments of the general public's reactions to the "Not Guilty" verdicts in the trials of certain police officers have been as visceral as it has. While it may be said that the "Feds" will indict a ham sandwich; a good lawyer will make a jury find it "not guilty." Good lawyer or not, it's hard to have a positive perception of law enforcement when the media highlights those elf-brained clowns who choose to shoot children with B.B. guns and slam young girls on floors as if they were wrestling in the W.W.E.

It is for the above reasons and others that people have preconceived notions when it comes to police interactions. Believe and know that police shooting innocent, not so innocent, and down right dirt-dog guilty people, 'black' or 'white' didn't start yesterday. It is a tragedy and a travesty. One must beware, however. The police that you bash today may be the ones who may have to recover your stolen car, answer a break-in to your business or home, or - save your very life tomorrow.

Section Nine
"Don't think. Feel..."

... Is what Bruce Lee told his student in the movie *Enter the Dragon*. It seems as if Master Lee has come forth from the grave and given the same lecture to police officers in America. This will be a short section. There will not be a lot of explanation here. In short, take it for what it's worth as long as you take it.

What is happening in the streets of America between police officers and civilians is this:

Anytime a police officer **feels** their life or the life of someone else is in danger by an act that you may (or may not) have done or are doing they are going to shoot you.

External or internal invectives be damned. You're going down. Point blank. End of story. See you later, alligator. They'll sort the rest out later. At the point of execution (no pun intended), the fact that you're a son, father, mother, daughter, 'black,' 'white,' mentally unstable, finally getting your life together, etc ain't worth a damn. At that point, everything will come down to how you made that particular officer "'feel". Maybe someone (or someones) will eventually come up with a concrete determination of what constitutes a 'threat.' Until then, you have been advised.

Section Ten
STOP!! In the name of...of...of... oh, Whatever!

This section is about what one should do when one is stopped, detained, held, arrested, beat, sprayed, shot, etc, by the police. It is written with the intent and in the hopes of avoiding the last four when the first four are unavoidable.

Traffic Stops:

Arguably the most dangerous of interactional situations for civilians and officers. There is a lot of distance between you in your car/truck and the officer in his/her car/motorcycle. Unless you are driving a glass vehicle the police officer(whether on or off duty) cannot see what you're doing and any police officer that cannot see what you're doing at a traffic stop becomes a nervous police officer and that surely is no good for grown folks, children, and small animals. IF you belong to any of the above three, it is imperative that you understand this and keep it in your brain. It just might keep your brain in your head. Here's a few tips:

1. Don't be stupid - this is not a James Gagny movie. That "ya not gonna take me alive, coppa!!!" acting will not win you an Oscar. A bullet in the chest; yes. An oscar; no. Anytime your interaction with the police involves you being a suspect is the time when you need to use your brain more than your mouth. Read carefully and memorize this method. I call it the 3C's:

    a. Control
    b. Cordiality
    c. Cooperation

Former President George W. Bush once extolled "I am the decider!" I'm not going to get into the specifics of why he made that statement. Suffice it to say that in police/civilian interactions of this nature you will most often be the decider of how this interaction proceeds and closes and herein lies the 1st "C": Control. It is self control that I am speaking of. Here as well as in life, the only noun that you can truly control is self. How you respond to the questions that will be asked of you will determine the response you get. Even in unusual circumstances, if you maintain a calm demeanor, you may prevent a tense situation from escalating. This is extremely important. Why is it important? Because in these situations, the average police officer is just as afraid of you as you are of them. By having a calm demeanor I am not talking about sitting in your car with your back so ramrod straight that you'll have to wear a back brace for the next six years. Nor am I talking about having a look on your face like you're one of the zombies on "The Walking Dead". Why would they be afraid? Other than the obvious let me explain:

Section Eleven
Your License Plates

Somewhere on the bumper (back or front) of your car, you have what are known as license plates (tags). These metal objects have three features that make them important to law enforcement:

1.   The name of the state that the car is registered in
2.   Some alphabets;
3.   Some numbers

There probably are a small number of naive citizens who believe that all their license plate denotes is that you have insurance. This is definitely a wrong belief. Your license plate says a lot about you.

1.   Whatever information that's on your driver's license
2.   Traffic Violations (if any)
3.   Auto Accidents (if any)
4.   Criminal History (if any)
5.   Outstanding Warrants (if any)
6.   Other miscellaneous information

It is a well-known fact that before a police officer leaves his/her patrol car, they have run a records check on the license plate (number) on the car they have stopped or are about to stop. It is at this time that things can and often do start to drift to the left. Especially if numbers (4) and (5) happen to appear on this officer's computer screen or are heard from dispatch. If this does occur, trust me; this officer is not going to view you like the proverbial cat stuck in the tree.

It is a fact that 98% of people who have issues with items 2-5 are aware of them. It is also a fact that if items 2 and 5 have been issues long enough and they haven't been effectively dealt with, the police officer who stopped you now knows about them and is preparing to deal with them. It is here that your life and the lives of those who are with you are in the balance. What you say and do here will determine the outcome of this interaction. IF you lose control here; you can possibly lose your life. Once again, don't be stupid. A few things are in order. Read very carefully.

1.   (a) When I say the word "control," I am relating this word in the sense of the control one must have over themselves, ie; what they say or do. I AM NOT telling anyone involved in a police/civilian

interaction to attempt by any method to control the interactive environment. Remember what I stated earlier. It is a police officer's prerogative and job-related objective to control the situational environment that he/she encounters. Fulfillment of this objective is imperative. It is a must. Failure in this is not an option and whatever that needs to be done to fulfill this imperative will be done. By any means necessary.

(b) As I wrote earlier, if you have a violent criminal history or an outstanding warrant you are aware of this. If you did not know that by checking your license plate, the officer now knows this, you do now. It therefore places you in the category of idiot if you don't know or believe that because of this information, said police officer is not going to be wary of you. Especially with police shootings/killings on the uptick. How this officer is going to handle you depends on:

1. What your criminal history reveals;
2. What your outstanding warrants are;
3. The pitch, tone, and cadence of the first sentence you say;
4. What it is you say

Okay, let's cut to the chase. The most important thing that you (civilians) need to know is that the side of the road is no place to have a pissing contest with a police officer. Obey all commands. Make no sudden, unannounced moves. As a matter of fact, make no moves unless you're told to. When you do move, make only the move you're told to make. Give no information unless you are asked. When asked, answer as precisely and cordially as possible. Remember. There is a time and place to handle discrepancies, disputes, and distances of pee, and as I've stated earlier, the side of the road is not that place. Agreeability may save your life here. Hear?

I would be remiss if I did not state the following:

The feasibility of everything I just wrote revolves around these two things:

1. You are not some deranged, maniac psychopath hell-bent on suicide but afraid to pull the trigger yourself.
2. The police officer is not some deranged, maniac psychopath hell-bent on killing a motorist or two before the end of his shift.

Realize something, dear reader. While the above may seem at first glance satirical, trust and believe that if you dig deep enough into the statistics, I'm sure you will find more than one example of each.

2. Packin' heat? Stay off the street! There is an old saying: "If common sense was common then everybody would have it."

    Suffice it to say common sense is not common. There are people (men, mostly) who fall into the aforementioned categories (#4 - criminal history, #5 outstanding warrants) that feel as though they can defy gravity, rational thought, and gas from eating too many beans and decide they can drive around town with a gun. WIthout going into a long, drawn-out syllogism, if you're a convicted felon, don't get caught by the police driving, riding, or walking with a gun. Regardless of whether the laws against this change. Just don't.

    So you are a law abiding citizen who may be a licensed concealed carrier. If you tell the officer this, let the officer digest this information. If he/she asks to see your permit, S-L-O-W-L-Y get this permit (it should be with you everywhere you go), and hand it to the officer. Personally, I would only disclose this information if the situation warrants it. Doing so only makes the officer more nervous. Never, never, ever, ever in a billion, million years attempt to get your gun unless the officer asks you to, and never give a gun to a police officer, barrel-first.

3. Don't run- very simple. Don't run. I don't care if you're as guilty as Eve doing the nasty with a certain snake on Sunday- don't run. The only thing running will get you is tired, sweaty, and your ass beat half to death. And that's if you're lucky. Besides, you can't outrun a radio and you damn sure as hell can't outrun a snitch's big, fat mouth. Especially when Crime Stoppers is paying $5,000 to pry it open. Don't run. Just, don't run.

Non- Traffic Stops:

In these instances, some of the same 'common-sense' rules apply; with a couple of caveats.

1. This is not your grandma's police force. You can't just tell them to go away, and they simply go away. If the police have been called to your location- they're not leaving until they're satisfied with whatever they've been dispatched to determine is going on or not.

Be respectful and courteous during this time. Do not volunteer any information that is not asked for. Let them do their job.

2. If you are stopped by a police officer, whether the first or fiftieth time, control your mouth! If asked to show identification, do so. Nothing will get you slammed against the hood of a police car quicker than a smart mouth. Besides, lip-boxing with the police only makes this interaction longer. Why would you want that?

3. Realize that it's not always you. Due to the rise of a phenomenon called "see something-say something," civilians have been moved to call the police if they see something or someone that they perceive to be 'suspicious.' You must realize that this is one of the worst calls a police officer can get. Why? Because the nature of the call is not specific and is based on what the untrained caller thinks is suspicious activity. The officer's alert level is higher on these types of calls. It may be something. It may not be anything, but you are on your way home. Follow my instructions and you may make it there safely.

4. If you're 'dirty,' bite the bullet. It's better than the bullet biting you, which may happen if you try to run. Do not run!! A good stand is far better than a bad run. DO NOT RUN!!!

There are more things that I can list, but they're all 'common sense' things that you should know already. If you want to survive an interaction, you will remember these things and do them. If you feel you have a point to prove, you will do that. Just know that sometimes when one attempts to prove a point - they end up becoming a case-in-point. So for the love of God, Jesus, Job, and Mary don't end your life by becoming an unnecessary statistic. There are plenty other ways to make the 6 o'clock news. Here's a few more things to take with you.

1. As I stated earlier, do not volunteer any information to the police. Remember that "anything you say **can and will** be used against you in a court of law..." Answer all questions clearly, cordially, and truthfully. When stopped, whether walking or in your car, never, ever, in a billion, million years say 'yes,' when asked by a police officer, "do you know why I stopped you?" Unless you're doing 700 in a 35mph zone, you possibly have no idea why you were stopped. Here's the important thing. This question sets up probable cause, which, contrary to popular belief, is necessary for an officer to have in order to stop you. Remember that. Like I said, it's important.

2. If it is possible, have your license and registration in your wallet and have them ready to give to the officer when you're stopped. This will prevent you from having to reach into an area that is unseen by the officer. As stated, due to the rash of police shootings/killings, the officer's danger senses are just as heightened as yours. Unintended consequences happen when you're reaching into an unseen area.

3. If you are stopped while walking or at a scene, have your identification or proof of residence available. This means have it on you at all times. Contrary to popular belief, the police have the right to stop you at any time. They do need a reason (probably cause), however. If stopped- do not get upset. Do not yell, curse, or act belligerent. If you feel or know you've been disrespected or your 'rights' violated, note the officer's name, time of contact with you, names of other officers, etc, and file a report with the police department or have an attorney file it for you.

Section Twelve
You have the right to remain silent

I am going to end this chapter the same way I started it: seven words. You have the right to remain silent. Seven words. Not just seven words, but seven extremely powerful words. Powerful because they put total decision making in your hands. And it is this power; the power to decide; that makes you the creator of your own heaven, or your own hell. My advice to you: Give up the right to remain silent. Speak. But first, know what the hell you're talking about. Look.

As I stated earlier, I am not putting the entirety of my knowledge of this subject matter in this book. And yes, it is on purpose. The purpose of this book, and in particular this chapter, is to get you to think. Then follow through with a strategic plan. Surviving a police interaction is not as bad as you think. As long as you think. When you stop thinking is when things have a tendency to go left. Let me give you a bone to chew on. You might be doing this already. At least some of you might. If you're not, do so. Let's start with this!

Practice makes perfect and while this practice may not get rid of your faults, it may give you what you need to survive a police encounter. What I want you to do is role play.

Like I said, some of you may be doing this already. By the time this book gets published, this may be old hat. Even if it is, pick it up and put it on your head. You will need:

Scenario One:

- Someone to play a civilian
- Someone to play a cop

Scenario Two:

- Someone to play a bad guy
- Someone to play a victim
- Someone to play a cop

Scenario Three:

- Someone to play a driver
- Someone to play a passenger
- Someone to play a cop

<u>Scenario Four:</u>

- Someone to play a bad guy
- Some people to play hostages
- Some people to play cops

<u>Scenario Five:</u>

- Someone to play a homicidal/suicidal husband
- Someone to play an abused wife
- Someone to play a cop

These are five scenarios (obviously). You can come up with more. These are a start. Take the parameters of each scenario and develop the characters and situations. It would be best if a real police officer plays the role of the cop.

Please, take this exercise seriously. As I've stated earlier in this and other chapters of this book. THIS IS NOT A GAME.

If you think it is, ask some of the mothers and fathers, wifes and husbands, and other family members who have lost loved ones to police shootings. Finding and placing fault will not bring their loved ones back. I am sure that they would not want to see other lives lost. If it can happen to them, it can happen to you. Educate yourself. The life you save may be your own. And just to clear the air, let me state for the record:

This is not an "excuse the police, they know not what they do," type of chapter. Neither is it an "excuse the public, they know not what they do," type of chapter. It is a chapter designed for those who want to know why what is happening is happening. It is also a reminder that it will not stop unless information is disclosed, shared, and acted upon. As I've stated before, educate yourself, then educate others. Some of you have already formed workshops, held seminars, done national tours, and formed support groups. I'm asking you to do more. I'm asking you to train. No, I'm telling you that you must train. Remember. ALL POLICE OFFICERS TRAIN. You must train also. When faced with criminal or possible criminal situations, police officers are trained to take control of the situation. You, on the other hand, when faced with police interactions, will train to control yourself. Hopefully, I have given you enough information to start the process. But just in case you think I didn't...

This is a public service reminder:

Do not run from the police!
Do not run from the police!!
DO NOT RUN FROM THE POLICE!!!

Whether you're walking or driving, do not run from the police. I don't mean someone impersonating a police officer. I mean the real police. I am reiterating this because I know for a truth that not heeding this warning will exponentially increase your chance of being shot or killed by the police. Why? Because four things will happen to police officers when a suspect runs from them:

1. An adrenaline rush;
2. Exertion;
3. Anxiety (stress, fear);
4. An increased sense of your guilt

Look up the definition of the first three as they are in the order that they will occur to that officer if you run. The fourth, especially when piggybacked by the first three is what will get you shot if not killed. To the average police officer- if you run, then you're guilty. Hence the question, "why did you run?" That's if you're not dead. No need for questions.

As I've stated, police officers are not trained to give warning shots. They have to account for every bullet that they're issued. Therefore if you run and are trapped- DO NOT MOVE. DO NOT REACH. DO NOT TALK. DO NOT DO ANYTHING EXCEPT WHAT YOU ARE TOLD TO DO.

And yes- you will be roughed up. Depending on how long the chase was, beat up. Prepare for it. After all, you did run. What did you expect?

Once again, please, please take this stuff seriously. I know of which I speak because I have been militarily trained in law enforcement (Security Police Specialist, USAF). Even though my training extended itself to the protection of nuclear weapons, Basic Law Enforcement Training (BLET) was, and is, a prerequisite. I do not want to see you die and you will die if you don't heed these warnings. Lastly, understand this:

> This has little to nothing to do with race, racism, or bigotry. IF a 'white' man defies these warnings, he will be shot and/or killed too. Do not be fooled or fool yourself into thinking otherwise. IF you run from the police, your profile changes from a suspected criminal to a criminal suspect/fugitive. At that time, individual attributes, known or unknown, go out the window. As a now criminal

suspect/fugitive you must be stopped. At the end of every police chase is an adrenaline rushed, anxious, and possibly scared police officer. With a gun. Loaded at that. This is not a maybe or might-be. This is what will be. Because of this, your humanity has become non-existent. Because of this, you have allowed the police to become predators and you have become prey.

And it's all your fault.

Well, maybe not all. This is for 'black' people who are perplexed by the obvious. Since recent statistics state that young 'black,' males per capita are being killed by police more often than their 'white' counterparts, you are the focal point of this subsection. You must:

1. Stop talking about it and be about it - there has been a lot of talk about police shootings/killings within the 'black' community. There is still a lot of talk about this issue and this talk will continue, because the number of these shootings/killings will increase. How can I say this? Because you will not face-to-face confront yourselves and come to grips with what must be done, then do it. What must you do? Glad you asked.

2. Admitting is the first step- a strange people are those who will see a fire coming and will not move out of the way. A strange people it also is who will see wrong, know it is wrong, and will totally ignore it is wrong. I wrote about this earlier. The first thing that must happen within this 'black' community is that the parents of those who are the subject of the vast majority of police shootings/killings (black males between the age of 15-35) must come to grips with the fact that most (not all) of these interactions happen because someone did something and the police were called. And when this is the case, more often than not, it is not the reason that the police were called that got your son shot/killed, nor whether or not the officer was a bigot. It was his reaction to the police interaction. So how do you stop this?

   a. Realize and admit that this is a new era of time; the days of "Aw, he's just being a kid," are over. If you haven't noticed, 'black' kids/men are being killed by police from having pellet guns and selling loose cigarettes, to being in the 'wrong' area. You must be aware of the fact that people have started taking that "see something, say something," motto very seriously. These four words initially were conceptualized to make people become aware of possible moves by domestic or foreign terrorists. Your children and husbands are getting caught in this web.

b. With 2a stated, you, Mr. and Ms. 'Black' America, have to come to the realization that more often than not, the young black men that are getting shot/killed by police have either done or have been thought to have done something illegal, which of course will cause a police interaction. Not only do you have to come to grips with this troth, you have to start addressing it. You have to address it at home and abroad. You have to address it anytime the opportunity presents itself. In particular, when these issues arise. How does that look/sound? Anytime you hear, read, or see a situation where police have shot/killed a black man/woman- ask yourself, did this interaction occur because someone either did something or was suspected of doing something illegal. And before you say that it doesn't matter, let me assure you that it does and if you can still say that it doesn't after reading this chapter, then I didn't do my job or your brain isn't doing its job. The only way that you're going to curtail these instances from happening is to get to at least one if not the main root for this problem. And yes it is a problem. A big one. In order to solve it, you've got to take your head out of the sand (or your ass) and address this specific aspect head-on. You may not like or agree with me on this. Actually, I could care less. Truth does not change because we don't agree with it. It is what it is, and it will be what it will be until YOU change YOU. Now get to work.

CHAPTER SIX

The White Section...

"You should be so privileged..."

Dr. Lune A. Teek

SECTION ONE

HELP WANTED

One Lost Soul: Have You Lost Your Mind?
The Other Lost Soul: How would I know?!!

There's a "Help Wanted" sign on the door. It's been there for quite a while. A few people have gone in and inquired about the job. After hearing the requirements those few did like the rest. Thanks, but no thanks. I really am surprised that no one wants to take this job. It wasn't always like that. There was a time when there was a constant stream of people wanting to do this job. Every day at quitting time the boss had to turn people away, only to return in the morning to find the same constant stream of people with more faces added to the line. Yes, those were the days. Something changed, however. I think (I'm not sure) it happened. January 8, 2012. Something (I'm not quite sure) snapped. Suddenly the people stopped coming in long lines. Then the lines stopped completely. Now maybe five people at the most may come in a week. As someone who watched this from my shop window across the street this phenomenon really perplexed me. So, I went over to talk to the boss. He actually thought I came for the job. After I assure him that I didn't, he offered me coffee, which I thankfully accepted. I asked what happened to all the people who used to line up at the door everyday looking for a job. He looked at me with his sorrowful eyes and said, "Nobody wants to do the job." I asked why and what was the job. He said,

"It's a nasty, dirty job but somebody's got to do it.
Somebody's got to do the job of being white."

There was a lovable little frog who among other things would lament, "If ain't easy being green." Lately it looks like the same thing could be said about "white" people. Especially white males. I'm not going to go into that specific topic in this essay. Somebody else has to and should write that book. I am, however, going to highlight some things that put you and that frog in the same car seat.

I put the chapter "You Have The Right To Remain Silent" where I did to highlight specifics in the subject matter first then correlate them with how they effect "black" people as well as yourselves. I've dealt with black people. Now I'm going to deal with you. I'm now going to address the first set of you. You know. The set that other people say that they have to "watch out for". The ones that make the government sleep with one eye open. Yeah, those white folks. My kind of people.

You are being profiled.

This is particularly true if you are evangelist (The new name for Christians); belong to a "Tea Party" group or are subscribing to its philosophy; belong to a "Patriot", "Freeman", or "Sovereign" group; belong to a survivalist and/or militia group or subscribe to its philosophy; agree with or voted for Ron Paul; etc. Now that you've been told this, the natural question to ask is "why am I being profiled?" Good question. And while it may not be easy for you to answer it is for me. You're being profiled because -

You found out the truth.

And by God are "they" mad at you. Upset. Vexed. Pissed off, even.

Why?

Because you found out what it took countless man (and woman) hours, money, lies, deceit, covert and overt actions, misdirection, manipulations, and when these didn't work outright murder to hide and stay hidden. But despite (or in some cases because of) all that you still managed to dig through enough bullshit (and quite a bit of human shit too) to get to the one thing that certain "entities" piled all that shit upon in the first place.

The truth. And yes. Those "entities" are very, very, p.o.'ed at you and when say P.O.'ed I don't mean "Post Office", nor "potatoes and onions". There is only one person that these "entities" are more pissed off at than you and guess who that would be.

Me.

And those like me.

Why me?

Why those like me?

A simple answer for a simple question.

Because we listened.

We researched.

We listened some more.

We researched some more. In short,

We learned.

The more we learned the more we needed to learn.

And learn more we did.

Now the truth is out.

All the little secrets; the little monkeys kept trapped in a dark, dank cubbyhole secreted underneath folded tables and chairs that were locked away in a room with signs that read "Do Not Open"; "Do Not Enter"; "Under No Circumstance Is This Door To Be Opened"; "Contamination Hazard"; "Keep Out"; "Explosives"; "Poison"; "Halt! Go No Further"; "Trespassers Will Be Shot" (the only truthful sign). All these secrets have now come to light because we dared to not only open the door but to actually sit down with the little monkeys and have a decent conversation over coffee or tea (I never thought that little monkeys kept trapped in dark, dank, cubbyholes secreted underneath folded tables and chairs that were locked away in a room that had a door with all those disgusting signs nailed to it could be so cordial and well mannered.). It was an eye opening experience to say the least. However, regardless of (and maybe because of) the fact that the little monkeys acted as though they just graduated Magna Cum Laude with a doctorate from Miss Manners, by God "they" are still mad at you. Mad as hell. Mad as all get out. Mad as all get in. Dammit just plain mad. Mad at you. Mad at me.

Now, knowing the "machine" as I do, I know it takes a lot for them to get "rip roaring, 'better git going' mad. And that they are. How did they get that way? Let's examine that. The answer's simple.

You took me to school. You weren't supposed to do that. What did you teach me that made them so mad? Let's see...

1. It was *you* who taught me that the Constitution doesn't apply to me;
2. It was *you* who taught me that statues don't apply to me;
3. It was *you* who taught me that the United States is a corporation;
4. It was *you* who taught me what a birth certificate really does;
5. It was *you* who taught me what a birth certificate really is;
6. It was *you* who taught me what a birth certificate is really worth;
7. It was *you* who showed me the concept of "sovereignty";
8. It was *you* who told then showed me how the government has crafted the largest and most lucrative identity theft mechanism known to mankind;
9. It was *you* who taught me what the Federal Reserve really is;
10. It was *you* who taught me what the Federal Reserve really does;
11. It was *you* who taught me what the value of a dollar really is;
12. It was *you* who taught me who *really* owns that dollar;
13. It was *you* who taught me the difference between "driving" and "traveling";
14. It was *you* who taught me what a license really is;
15. It was *you* who taught me what a license really does;
16. It was *you* who taught me a court is something I never considered;
17. It was *you* who taught me a lawyer is something I never considered;
18. It was *you* who taught me what a flag (United States) with a yellow boarder is;
19. It was *you* who taught me what a judge really is;
20. It was *you* (along with another great man) who taught me the importance of tying history to future events

Need I go on? Trust me I can write a book on what I learned. I just might.

It is not because you have this knowledge that has classified you as a security "risk" group, nor is it the few documented screwballs who committed violent acts (which to this day I believe were agent provocateurs) that have pushed that status almost to its highest level. No, it's not any of that. It is because you are willing and have taught others (like me) this knowledge. In short, you are waking people up and getting them to *THINK*! And boy, boy, boy are they mad at you for that. You really weren't supposed to tell. You were supposed to keep this to yourselves. But you didn't. So now you've got to pay. You know what? Thank you.

SECTION TWO
THE "SALT" OF THE EARTH

Now let me get to the other group. You know, the nice, decent, hardworking "salt of the earth" "white" people. Whiter than white. White as the driven snow. Snow white (without those nasty dwarfs). Clorox white. White to the highest whitifity. Yea. You. I have a question for you. Consider it carefully.

Have you ever thought about why now, suddenly, you're being pressured into being politically correct? Why is it that suddenly all of you, regardless of station or status have been given a sign to hang around your necks with the words "WHITE PRIVILAGE" in big, bold neon letters? Why do you continue to wear it? I'll tell you why. You wear it because if you don't, you'll get another card to go around your neck with the word "RACIST" in the same hot pink, red and blue letters and you'd rather wear the "WHITE PRIVILAGE" card than the "RACIST" one. Oh yes. You'll wear the "WHITE PRIVILAGE" card even if you're dirt poor, on food stamps, and two minutes away from throwing a brick through a jailhouse window. Anything but that dread "R" word. You'd rather smack Jesus and kick Job in the ass than to be called a racist. Have you given thought to the fact that there is something behind this? Have you given thought to that fact that you are programmed to think and feel the way you do? Here's a question:

Why did you vote for Barak Obama? What did you know about his temperament? What did you know about his policies? What did you know about his philosophy? What did you know about his associations? Did he send a thrill up your leg? What did you know about Barak Obama? Did you vote for him because he was a Democrat? Hell so is Hillary Clinton. And she is as white as the board of health. And a woman to boot. So why did you vote for Barak Obama? Could it have been because you, along with millions of other uninformed "Black" people who did not and still do not know that there has already been a "Black Obama-like" president. (Barak Obama would be termed as a "Mulato".)

You, like them, wanted to see this country have a "Black" president. Okay. You've seen it. And you elected this particular one - twice. How'd that work for ya? It seems to me that you've got a case of what common sense folk call White Guilt. Well, today is your lucky day. I'm feeling very generous right about now and therefore I, yes, I, am going to work one (1) miracle and you, white people, have shown up just in a nick of time to receive this once in a lifetime gift. Today, here and now I am going to forgive you once and for all of that dreaded disease of White Guilt. Are you ready? Okay. Close your eyes. Relax. Breathe and believe. Repeat after me:

Dominos; Sugartose.
Stop the damn white guiltose.

There. You are now made whole. Go forth and sin no more.

What I am writing here is being done in an effort to provoke you to think. I could get very technical about who and what is making you think, feel, and behave this way. I chose satire so as not to scare you. You've been scared enough. If you think about these things, you might be able to understand that you're being manipulated. You're being conned into defending the indefensible by accepting the unacceptable. And how you're being manipulated is the most cruel, despicable, heartless, and animalistic method of all. It is the method of manipulation of the heart in order to get to the mind. In other words, if I can move you to "feel" that a certain thing/person/people (for example, "black" people) needs to be vindicated and/or validated (in this instance, for the evils of slavery, Jim Crow, segregation, etc.), you in all your glorious whiteness, will break all bounds, leap over any obstacle, do anything up to and including destroying those "white devils" who would dare treat your fellow "beings" in such an insensitive and heartless manner. The next thing you know you and your children are throwing off the cumbersome shackles of being "white" and picking up the bloodstained banner of "black". There was a time when mulato men and women were engaged in a practice called "passing for white". White guilt has gotten you (white people) so screwed up in the head now you're marching with more and bigger signs with "Black Lives Matter" on them than the black people who are marching with you. I never thought I'd see the day when groups of white people would try to "out-black" black people. And if that isn't enough, now you're trying to "out gay" gay people. And you're doing this without putting any thought into who or what is causing these eruptions. You really need to stop doing this. You're really screwing the country up. Besides. Who found you guilty and pronounced a sentence of a lifetime of being mushy minded? God, you say. Wow! Picture that. A white God with a white beard and white hair, waving around a white stick in which he hits white people on their white heads and asses and then sentences these white people to a lifetime of being white. Boy, it sucks being you. This country doesn't need "White" people being ashamed of who they are any more than it needs "black" people being ashamed of who they are. Nor does it need LGBT people who are shamed into being ashamed of who they are. If all the above mentioned folks continue to allow themselves to be manipulated into thinking that each of them, just as they are, don't deserve the love of others and to share love with others then the destruction that has been and is being planned for you will surely come to pass. Love, honor, and respect starts with the self and extends outward. Belief in anything opposite of that is to believe that "The nice little doggie won't bite."

Now you may think that I've veered away from the initial subject with this course of dialogue. Trust me, I haven't. For those whose work it is to design and expedite mandates like the one in place at this present time they had to be empowered, which can only be done via the vote. This is true for the designers, planners, expediters, and maintainers we, the people can see as well as the ones we don't. The difference is the ones we see are voted in through the ballot box. The ones we don't see are done through the vote of the assembled planners, expediters, etc. that we don't see. And probably never will.

With that said you, white people, are a very large voting bloc in this country. Pollsters divide you into different segments (men/women; men/women between the ages of...; independents/conservative, republicans, blue-collar; educated/uneducated; "blue dog" democrats; etc.). They don't do black people that way. They know that black people, except for a few brave souls who don't mind being called "Uncle Toms", vote in a single bloc. There will be a few hardened souls who will deny that they think and vote in a herdish manner. Overlook them. They know not what they do. They're in denial. Those whose job is to shape these mandates have also used different mandated methods in order to shape their minds into the acceptance of a reality that will keep them from achieving any status above mediocrity and they will fight to the death to protect this reality from all that pose a threat to it. They already know that black people, in demonstrative numbers, will vote democratic so whatever agenda is pushed from that side they will adhere to without question. You, on the other hand, are a different story. This is why I asked why you voted for Barak Obama. Did you think he could have become the president without you? What did you think when the remaining past presidents came to Barak Obama and the statement was made that they were all committed to making sure that he (Barak Obama) succeeded? Oh, you didn't notice that? You missed that meeting? Well, I did, and I didn't. Now comes the obvious question. Succeed at what? What or whose agenda is going to be pushed. Yours? Once again, how's that working for ya? I have a better question for you:

How do you know when someone's lying to you?

Stop and consider this question carefully. Think about the times when you've been lied to. How did you feel? Who was it? How long was it before you realized you were being lied to? Did you see it coming? Did it cause you a loss? Did you recover from it? How long did it take? What did it take?

I could have simply asked the one question of do you know when someone is lying to you. I asked the other questions because I know someone has and I wanted you to remember what it was like as well as to realize the fact that even after all that hurt and pain you still didn't then, nor have you now developed strategies that will let you know when someone is lying to you. When the trap snaps shut it's too late and the political aspect of this trap will close very, very soon unless you, yes you, white people, wake up. While I'd like to be tailoring this message to "black" people, I can't for reasons I've already iterated. I know and you'd better learn that until they stop seeing themselves as victims, stop internalizing the message of victimhood, and most of all, stop living like victims, the worst is yet to come. Believe me when I tell you that those who conceived, planned, maintain, and execute the said "mandates" have something very, very, very nasty in store for "victims".

So, white people. This part of your job is as simple as it is complex:

1. Thinking of, viewing, or treating "black" people as victims makes them so. Stop it. Stop thinking and acting like you must right every wrong that your "white" ancestors did. You can't count them all. They were legion. You're being conned and manipulated. Stop it. Now. You're doing the same thing with the LGBT community. Stop.

2. Stop putting people in power *over* you. The voting process is designed so that you can elect the people that you feel *can best represent your will*. I've heard politicians say, "I voted my conscience". Out of all the things an elected politician is *not* supposed to have one of those things is a conscience. This is the number one reason why Congress has the lowest approval ratings since the sun got hot. But you continue to vote these people into office. Listen. When you vote for people (as you must), do it with the full knowledge that the entire process is a dog and *pony show and they are not going to do what they promised you* they'd do. You don't believe me? Look at Washington, D.C. and get back with me. You'll find that black boys and young black men being shot in the streets which will lead to police getting shot; Vietnam Veterans; Korean Veterans, Golf War Veterans, or any other veterans of any other war being ostracized, abused, neglected and placed on "watch lists"; millions of families displaced due to home foreclosures and job closings; students drowning in student loan debt; etc. all started in the offices and "floor" of Capital Hill and other administrative fiefdoms situated along the masonically developed streets of this nation's capital. This is the easy part of your realization. Now get ready for the hard part:

Dr. Lune A. Teek

If you allow yourself to be viewed as a fool, you will be played as a fool.
Stop being foolish.
No politician in America is supposed to have a
"conscience". They're supposed to represent yours.

SECTION THREE
YOUR KIDS AND YOU

It's your fault.

It's all your fault.

You fell for the okidoki.

And as a result, you failed your children.

Do you know when the world stopped turning? No? Well, I do. The world stopped turning when a two-word concept came into being. It is impossible for me to believe that the creators of this concept could not conceive the harm it would cause. And while I am stopping short of placing the blame for all the world's present day ills on the shoulders of those who created this concept, I wish all the wishes that has ever been or ever be wished that they would have kept their thoughts to themselves, and their damn mouths shut.

Time Out.

Time Out.

Yeah. Time Out.

Two words that unleashed a reign of consequences the likes of which in all my years of life I've still yet to understand. And yes, you, white people, ushered in this cacophony of nonsense with open arms, dull mind, and of course, guilt lifting gratitude.

Time Out was crafted by, in my very humble opinion, the most psychotic minded, ill-natured, mean-spirited people topside planet htrae -"earth" spelled backwards, which is exactly what earth became when these diabolical people unleased this diabolical concept upon an already psychologically unbalanced group of people – white people to be exact.

Time Out was given to the earth populous as an alternative to corporal punishment, i.e., spanking (or for the more nuanced of us, "whuppin" your child's ass). At the time of its inception, most black people, to their credit, took one look at this and regaled it to the garbage, as should anyone with a lick of good sense should have done - along with the creators of this "walk-in child rearing utopian" idea. It, however, fell on the fertile *soil housed* within the infertile minds of white people. The weeds that sprang from these minds are choking common sense from a would-be sensible environment to this day. Let me explain.

SECTION FOUR
THE REAL DEATH OF COMMON SENSE

Example #1 - "I SAID 'NO', DAMMIT"

I can remember the first time that I heard and took notice of a child outright refusing his mother. It was in a K-Mart. The child and his mother were in the toy section. The child had pulled a toy off the shelf. It fell to the floor. The mother picked the toy up, put it back on the shelf, and turned back to looking at other toys. The child reached up, pulled the same toy off the shelf, and stood there looking at the toy on the floor. The child's mother comes back, picks the toy off the floor again, and tells the child to come over to where she was. The child, eyeing the toy again, said, "No!"

No.

No.

The boy said "No!".

This kid could not have been any more the eight years old. And yes, he was a little blond-haired, blue-eyed boy. The kind who, when he said "no" you knew it wasn't his first time saying "no" and that when he said "no" he meant "no". Not "maybe" or "hold on a minute", or "let's sit down and try to hash this thing out over a couple of peanut butter and jelly sandwiches". This was someone to whom "No" meant "No" and don't fuck with me no mo. And guess what? That's exactly what his mother did. After he pulled the toy off the shelf a third time, the mother's answer was to put the toy on a higher shelf.

What would *you* have done?

What do you do when your seven or eight year old tells you "no"? Mind you, this is *your* child.

Example #2- "I Divorce You!, I Divorce You!, I Divorce You!!!."

In certain Islamic traditions these words when pronounced by a woman's husband starts a process in which he can rid himself of her. Of course, in modern times there's more to the Islamic decree of divorce than this but everything whether it's Islamic in nature or otherwise starts with an intention, then an affirmation, then either action or inaction. Never before I heard, then read, then followed the news reports, did I ever think that I would see the day where a child would have an intention, then an affirmation, then follow those two things up with the act of divorcing its parents. Saw that day I did.

Now I not going to get into the specifics of this incident other than to say that it set a precedent. I dare (No. I double-ditch-dog dare) anyone 58 years or older who is reading this book to say that they could or can conceive of a child (when they were growing up) even considering such a thing as divorcing their parents. Hell, when this age group were kids they didn't have a complete conception of divorce let alone enough of one to conceive of applying the tactic to their parents. Some of you remember this case. I'll leave you to your memories.

These two examples illustrate a change in not only how parents view their children but more importantly how children view their parents. Time Out was designed, as I said earlier, to be an alternative to corporal punishment. Now I've heard most if not all the arguments against "spanking" children. Some sound decent. Some sound good. Some sound downright goofy. Let's be clear about some things.

Another phrase that I have used more than once is "This is a new era of time." Believe me. It is. And nothing could make this observation more evident than witnessing the mindset of the people that make up the "conscience of society" as well as those within the established institutions of same, as it relates to this subject. And this is where these "people" and I part company.

Time Out.

Time Out.

Give me a damn break.

If you've guessed I'm for corporal punishment you've guessed correctly. There's something to the concept of negative physical reinforcement. Time Out was primarily about negative *psychological* reinforcement. Correct (at least in my opinion) punishment occurs when both negative psychological and physical reinforcement occurs. Were you one of the kids who either touched a hot stove on your own or was burned by other means of contact? When's the last time you said, "Man am I bored. I guess I'll go sit on top of this red hot to the point of the pipes are about to pop stove."? I guarantee that if you got burned *period* when you were a kid if you live to be 50,000 years old you know that fire's hot. Now take a kid who's *about* to touch a hot stove but his mother comes in, fusses at him, then puts him in "Time Out". You tell me what's missing. I'll tell you. A healthy (if he doesn't get third degree burns - which he probably will) respect for stoves with fires in them. Now this is in no means telling you to sit your kid on top of a 10,000-degree stove (There are morons who will think that and dipshit morons who would do it) nor is it telling you to allow your child to cozy up to a red-hot stove. It does highlight the necessity of at least having a foundational knowledge at an early age of the surety of what I call the "severity of consequence". Let me explain what I mean.

It would seem as though the underlying rationale behind Time Out was that corporal punishment was too harsh (physical) for children and would psychologically harm them in the long term. They cited a lot of statistics from a lot of "studies" in order to attempt to prove this point. Personally, I have no problem with this. I also applaud it. I don't, however, believe for one second that this approach considered quite a few factors, none of which I for a second believe that the creators of this concept were not aware of.

If the only thing that a child is to expect from a specific behavior is to be given a stern reply and then told to go into an area or a space (the "corner") that they're already familiar with, or you take their favorite toy, or some other what I'd call benign form of "punishment", it would and does become easy for the child to adjust and adapt to these non-physical confrontations. In other words, there is no fire in the stove. Or at the least, the stove is warm. What made you, me, and anyone else with sense and nerve endings to not want to touch another hot stove is the unpleasant impression that it left. This is the severity of consequence.

The implementation of Time Out also was cultural. As I've noted, black parents by and large didn't adapt to this kind of parenting at all. They really didn't see the need of it. They understood that negative physical stimulation leaves a longer lasting impression on one than a nonphysical one. And to be fair, more than quite a few white parents didn't accept this what I'm sure some of them felt was a cotton candy like approach to disciplining children. More than enough did, however. Enough of them for it to be a cultural phenomenon. Those who are reading this book who are baby boomers are aware of this just as they are aware of whether their parents practiced it. I, for example, am one of millions of boomers, black and white, whose parents (mothers mostly) had to only give a certain look and everything in the world, especially our errant behavior, stopped. You didn't get that type of reaction by saying "Go to your room".

I remember the first time I heard a "man" call his mother a bitch. The total sentence was "I hate you, bitch!" And yes, it was a white guy.

Now it would be easy for me to make this up in order to prove a point. I'm not. I'm not making this up to prove a point. I'm including it here to make a point.

As I've said, I was born on October 31, 1961. As of the writing of this manuscript I am 54-year-old. There are people my age and above that I know who have never raised their voice at their mother let alone call her bitch. I've witnessed a mother slap her 34-year-old son (he really did deserve it.) and he sat his ass down on the couch and moped. The point that I'm making is this:

When mechanisms get put into place, for whatever reason, that on whatever level, upsets the balance of whatever a parent must do in order to enforce discipline be ready for the consequences. As I've so often stated, this is a new era of time. You want the truth, those who doubt *me?* Ask people in my age group and above, men especially, whether the "whippings" they got from their parents would be considered child abuse these days. More than likely they'll tell you yes. Then ask them when they were a child and their mother told them to do something they didn't want to do did they look her in the face and say "no". Then ask them have they ever called their mother a bitch. If you really want some animated answers to these three questions, ask black men in my age group. All you have to do then is ask them why they never did these things. And for the icing on the cake, ask them what their parents thought about "Time Out". Trust me. You're in for a lively "diss"-cussion.

Listen white people. I put this section here for a reason. You're slipping back into the la la land of parenting utopia where you feel that you can just let your child "breathe". Let them be free to make their own decisions. Let them make their own choices. HEY WHITE PEOPLE! WAKE THE FUCK UP! Your fucking children are choosing and deciding to fucking join ISIS! ISIS for Christ's sake! Yes, your 15 and 16 year old daughters are boarding a fricking plane to go somewhere they've never been to meet someone they've never met to serve (or should I say "*service*") in a man-made scenario in which they don't have a clue as to who the real players are and why they're playing in the first place. How do I know they don't know? Hell, because you don't even know! And you're grown! And if they aren't somewhere joining. ISIS they're on a college campus far away as they can get from you, hooked up with some left winged cause that will make damn sure the rest of us will "Feel The Bern". You know college isn't free. Why don't they? You know it never could be. Why don't they? You know life isn't free. Why don't they?

SECTION FIVE
WHAT YOU MUST DO

You've heard all this before. You just didn't do it. Therefore, this will be a short section! First thing's first:

You are your child's *parent*. You *are not* your child's friend.

Parent.

Friend.

Two very separate, distinct, different concepts. A lot of white parents have confused the two and they haven't stopped. They have these concepts confused because they are confused. A confused parent equals a confused child. Then something disturbing happens. Confused children will tend to bond to other confused children. Which can only lead to confusing, and in some cases that I will not cite here but history has recorded, deadly results. It's the way of the world. And why shouldn't it be? They are (*were* in some cases) the confused children of confused parents. Confused children born to confused parents can only breed a confused society. Therefore, the first thing you as white parents must do is

1.   Realize most of you are confused
2.   End the confusion.

What are you confused about? You may not agree with the answer but here it is nevertheless.

You are not only confused on how to raise your children you're also confused on whether or not you want to raise your children.

You may be thinking, "Wherein the hell did you get that idea from?"; "Where in the hell do you get off telling me this bullshit?"

Okay. I'll tell you.

I am basing the above statement on empirical observation. Let me explain. After that, make your own empirical observations.

The same reasoning that went into my explanation of why black parents have abdicated their position as parents is the rationale behind the above statements. Both of you have left the instruction and training of your children to videos and social media. The difference between how this parental incompetence manifests itself within the society at large is determined by the child's preference (video or social media) and how prolonged exposure to that preference is manifested by the child. Unlike black boys (some, not all), whose preference is prolonged exposure to rap videos in which the manifestation of this exposure leads to them wanting to have intimate conversations with a woman's ass cheeks while at the same time wanting to show the world their (figuratively and literally), your children's preference (some, not all) is video games. The more violently graphic and realistic the better. What's wrong with this? Nothing if you're a game manufacturer. There is a problem though. And it starts with a troubled mind belonging to a troubled child. And while the following situational scenario could be any child - black or white, recent and not too recent events have shown as that far too many white kids fit into this bloc.

Take some of the most violent video games. Turn them on, look at the screen. What would you see if you took away the background and got rid of the "bad guys/gals" and the bogie monsters? If you're following me in this example, all you would see is the weapon that is being used to kill them. Try it. Block out everything else. All you'll see is a knife, sword, ax, stick, or a gun. But that's the easy to get by part. Most of these games, at least some of the more popular ones will have the killing instrument situated in a manner to where it's

1. In your hands.
2. At your eye level.

Now, if you're playing this game, you are not aware of what is happening to you psychologically although you are aware that the game is more interesting this way. All because of this strategically placed (Yes. It's done on purpose and after a lot of expensive research) view your senses become more heightened and after a while, if you're not careful, you become the one *actually holding the gun.* If you take this to the extreme (which it already has), how big a leap is it from being a kid who's "just playin' a game", to someone who's being picked on at school, ignored by his/her mother and abused by his/her father, or just looking to be accepted, now thinking they're someone who is in control deciding "Today's the day when everyone shall pay!" This time instead of the weapons of a jacked-up video game he/she opts for an AR-15 or SW 9mm. Is this starting to look familiar white people?

Am I saying that game manufacturers are evil? No. Am I advocating that you stop your children from playing video games? Whatever gave you that idea? Am I saying you had better make damn sure you've got a good idea of what's going on in your kid's head before, while, and after he/she has played? You damn skippy I am. In order to do this, you're going to have to engage your child. Strickly put, you're going to have to engage your child's *mind.* This activity may be a little scary for you. If it gets to be a little too much for you, you can always take a Time Out.

Time Out.

Give me a fuckin' break.

SECTION SIX
RAP IT UP

Don't be afraid of the word. It won't bite you. And if it does, good.

Back in the 60's when the "cool" black guys wanted to talk to each other they said "Let's 'rap' about this" or "Let's 'rap' about that". In that lingo rap means talk. Here it means the same thing. If you want to "rap", however, you need to have something to rap about and you also need to know what you're rapping about.

You, White people, have been very vocal lately. The problem is that's all you've been doing. You've been "vocalizing". A bird can do the same thing. So can a dog, a cat, a bear, a horse, or a monkey. Am I calling you these five animals? No. I'm saying the worth of what you've been talking about is in the same range. The only time that a bear is telling you something of great importance is when he or she is telling you that you are in its territory, and you'd better get out before it beats your ass. A very important message indeed. In particular for you.

So, what should you be "rapping" about? How about this:

"Black lives matter. But so does mine."

"I put your ass in Congress, and I can take your ass out!"

"I'm not dirt. I'm not filth. You can't trap me with White guilt!"

"By the power vested in me, I'll shoot your ass." (2nd amendment)

I can come up with a lot of these but if I do that, I'll be doing the work for you and that's what's gotten you into the mess you're in now. Getting out is going to take you changing the way you think about yourself and life in general. In short,

> If you change the way you look at things.
> Things change the way they look.

I can't take credit for that piece of wisdom because I don't know who first came up with it. Whoever did, wherever you are, thank you. I know from experience that it works. It worked for me, and White people, it'll work for you. With that said, let me "rap" up this chapter.

SECTION SEVEN
WORDS TO LIVE BY

You Are Not The Sum Total Of What You See.

What you see has, by its very nature, limitations. Do not, under any circumstances allow yourself to be the sum of what you see. And never, ever allow yourself to be the sum total of what someone else sees. You've been doing a lot of that lately. A whole lot. Stop that. Stop it now. You're being used as the proverbial door mat for a host of people to wipe their lackluster developed emotions on. You've become more absorbent than a Bounty paper towel and nowhere near as strong. Stop it! Now! Last but not least –; learn to live *within* your children, not *through* your children.

THE LGBT SECTION

Disclaimer: I AM NOT AN ATTORNEY

The method contained in this chapter is for educational purposes only. It should be reviewed and researched by an Attorney of your choice (preferably one from the LGBT community) to determine its feasibility and your suitability for its use. Even if the strategies outlined in this section don't work, it is nice to dream.

Chapter Seven

If Wishes Were Rainbows

Stolen waters are sweet, and bread
eaten in secret is pleasant.
But he knoweth not that the dead are
there; and that her guests are in the
depths of hell.

Proverbs 9:17-18 (KJV)

My brother was gay.

Seriously.

I know, I know. When it comes to a topic such as this either everyone knows someone who's gay or they have a gay relative. It's like saying "most of my friends are black." My brother just happened to be homosexual. Was he this growing up? I don't know. I can't say. I wasn't in his head. However, if he were alive today, I'm quite sure he would get a big laugh out of and wouldn't want anything to do with something called "gay marriage", aka, civil unions. What the hell is that anyway? Gay marriage. Who came up with that name? Must have been a patient from the looney bin. Or was it? Let's examine this construct called "gay" marriage from another perspective. Mine. After all, this is how I see it, right? I mean, either you're married or not. Love, a much deeper form of marriage, begins in the heart and extends itself to the mind, then manifests itself outward. It's not "gay" nor "straight". Neither is marriage itself.

Here's a question: When did you (The LGBT community) start giving a shit about whether people accepted your "lifestyle" (meaning *you*)? On the surface this seems like an asinine question. Of course, there's the stereotyping and other dangers from dwarf brained idiots. But really, has a supreme court decision somehow zapped these what nots into a special place where the sun don't shine? Not hardly. As a matter of fact, it brought out more. Has the decision somehow calmed the waters between you and "evangelicals"? Are you kidding?

I am aware of the court case and the California proposition that started this Forest Fire as well as the brush fires that sparked from it. Suffice it to say I found it quite amusing. Oh, I knew the plaintiff would win (I upset quite a few people with that prediction). The political climate assured that. Speaking of political, did you like that change-up/knuckle ball/slider/curve ball pitch that Barak Obama threw when he was asked his views on gay marriage? He supposedly "evolved". What the hell does that mean? What is he? Some seven-eyed amoeba or something? Did you notice something else? Did you notice how after he "evolved" practically everybody, and their grandma Hattie suddenly "evolved" just like the seven-eyed amoebas that they all are. Even Hillary Clinton "evolved". Trust me. I can smell shit through a Glad Ziplock bag and all of that was the shittiest pile of shit that's ever been shit through a group of assholes since assholes came into existence. I guess it was okay though. It got the job done. I guess it feels good when someone "important" recognizes you. Eventhough and especially after these same people have denied your right to exist for so long. It almost makes you want to ask "why?". Or at least it should. The problem here is you didn't ask. It's just like playing chess and your opponent boldly puts their queen right in front of your piece. Even the grittiest of Grandmasters will back up and hold up. Why? Because eventhough they may not ask you you'd best believe they're asking themselves "why?". Chess is a funny game like that and so is life. Manipulation is such a large part of both. Let's get back to the question. Why haven't you asked "why?". I'm not saying ask the mom and pop who look at you like you're crazy when you walk by. I'm talking about the slew of big politicians in Washington D.C. and in your state legislatures who are standing on your shoulders so they can get a better view of power. You see, not only does "why" put people on record it puts their answer(s) to why on record also. You then get to determine whether they're human beings, shape shifters, or evolving amoeba. Now I'll get to the subject matter: "gay" marriage. Question:

Has it occurred to you that now that civil unions are recognized as "legal" you could have achieved the objectives of the original case without inviting the state to take a controlling interest in your relationship? And yes, you did let the government inside your relationship. "It" now has a controlling interest in it. How did you let "it" inside and at the same time give "it" a controlling interest?

Answer: You allowed "it" to issue you a marriage license.

Why did you do that?

Often when one wants something very much, one sometimes either forgets or takes for granted that there is an essence to that want. In doing that, one subjects themselves to the positives of that want for sure. However, because they neglected to consider the negatives and format a block against them, they also open themselves up to the consequences of not doing so. Depending on your viewpoint and your threshold for pain this is one of those times. And I really got a chance to see this. Most of you, when that verdict came down were screaming, hollering, clapping, and yapping. You couldn't wait to get to a Clerk of Court or Register Of Deeds office just to get the rope of government tied around your necks. Not to mention that debacle in Kentucky.

What was that all about?

What were/are you doing? Listen.

If you're a cook, sometimes, not all, but sometimes you have to be smarter than the pots and pans. Therefore.

SECTION TWO
LET ME EDUCATE YOU

A lesson in legal terminology is in order here. Bear with me. There's a point to this.

1. Marriage - The legal union of a man and a woman as husband and wife. Although the common law regarded marriage as a civil contract, it is more properly the civil status or relationship existing between a man and a woman who agree to and do live together as spouses. The essentials of a valid marriage are:
   1. Parties being capable of contracting marriage;
   2. Mutual consent and agreement;
   3. An actual contracting in the form prescribed by law

A contract if there ever was one. Take my word for it.

2. License - A revocable permission to commit some act that would otherwise be unlawful.
3. Contract - An agreement between two or more parties creating obligations that are enforceable or otherwise recognizable by law.
4. Registrar Of Deeds - A public official who records deeds, mortgage, and other instruments affecting real property.
5. Clerk Of Court - A court official responsible for filing papers, issuing process, and keeping records of court proceedings as generally specified by rule or statue.
6. Affidavit - A voluntary declaration of facts written down and sworn to by the declarant before an officer authorized to administer oaths.

Believe me when I tell you that I am aware of the reasons why you wanted this. Aside from the equity issues the issues of full spousal rights are poignant ones to say the least. However, as I said, there is a point to this. Here's the thing.

Could it be that after this verdict was given most of you placed more emphasis on the form behind being recognized than the recognition itself? In other words, some of you may have placed more emphasis on having a marriage license as an ensign representing legitimacy than the concept of the union itself. Even more to the point, some of you may have felt that obtaining a marriage license was really the key to legitimacy. If you would have thought about it, you could have concluded that it was the verdict and not the license that gave this union credibility. And yes, contrary to popular belief, the two *are* mutually exclusive eventhough you had to have the verdict in order to receive the license. Let's look at this from the technical aspect so you can see what I'm getting at. I will start with the following premise:

> Obtaining a marriage license turns what would normally be a two-party agreement into a three-party agreement: the parties being the bride, the groom, and the State, with the State having a controlling interest in it.

Don't agree? Fine. Your disagreement does not stop it from being so. In order to lessen your acute myopia, let's take a closer look at a couple of our legal definitions. First one up, marriage. Take notice of the emphasis.

> Marriage - The *legal* union of a *man* and *woman* as husband and wife. Although the *common law* regarded marriage as a civil contract, it's more properly the civil status or relationship existing between a man and a woman who agree to and do live together as spouses. The essentials of a valid marriage are, 1.) *Parties legally capable of contracting marriage*; 2.) Mutual consent and agreement; and 3.) *An actual contracting in the form prescribed by law.*

The first word that's emphasized in this definition is *legal*. For the sake of this topic and context instead of legal think "State Recognized". It not only sounds better but in this context it's more specific to the truth. Also understand that from a legal standpoint there is a difference in the terms "legal" and "lawful". The next two words, *man* and *woman* are at the core of all this gnawing and gashing of teeth, children and small animals.

If I hear the words, "Marriage is the union between a man and a woman" again I'll puke out my big toe. Of course it is. Every dunder-brained idiot knows that. Listen. In every relationship of the character in which we're referencing there is a man and a woman. Including homosexual and lesbian relationships. Someone relates to the male gender, and someone relates to the female gender, and this is what heterosexual men and women can't wrap their brain around. They *know* this but they can't understand the intangible concept of gender. Now, I'm referring to the average heterosexual civilian. Psychologists have figured out the fringes of this. Its why whenever this issue is being determined in children the first thing they do is break out the Barbie doll/G.I. Joe routine; "Which do you feel comfortable playing with?" To me, this is an extremely dangerous interrogative construct in which the determination of such a weighing subject is to be made. For example, if I were asked that question, I would say both and give the example of Barbie waiting for Joe to come home from deployment in Afghanistan wearing a matching bra and thong with six inch stilettoes (Fire Engine Red). Trust me. There are eight year olds who think this way. The reason I think this is dangerous is because if an eight-year-old does answer this question that way then other questions will follow that may not determine jack shit and depending on the direction these questions take it may get the child put on a terrorist watch list. But this is neither here nor there as it relates to the subject although it does say a lot about one's inability to grasp it. Suffice it to say that not everyone relates to the mental aspects of gender let alone the biological ones (Try tackling "intersexuality". I dare you.). It is most obvious from the definition given to the word "marriage" it is to be interpreted in a specific way and a concerted effort has been and still is under way to keep it that way. With that said, it is these two words, man and woman", referenced in the biological context that kept marriage from being a legal and lawful LGBT alternative.

The next emphasized phrase is "common law". A lengthy concept indeed. For the purposes of this discussion, let us say that according to the common law construct one did not need a "marriage license". All the couple needed to do was have proof of cohabitation as "man and wife" for a specified time. The biological interpretation relating to the opposite sex still applied. Okay. On to the next phrase, which is, "Parties capable of contracting marriage". In an effort to protect minors and the mentally challenged, this phrase became a part of contract law. Until the supreme court decision this phrase also disqualified you. Because of that sticky biological interpretation of "man" and "woman" you could not legally contract a marriage. You could have contracted anything or contracted with anyone or with anything on Earth, Jupiter, or Mars. You just couldn't marry it. Now you can, and this goes to the core of the topic of this chapter. I'll get to that in a minute. Let's look at the last emphasis point.

"An actual contracting in the form prescribed by law."

Please. Don't get it confused.

The question "which came first, the chicken or the egg?" has nothing to do with chickens nor eggs per se, rather it has everything to do with the importance of one over the other. The same holds true here. The law provides formats and prerequisites for certain types of contracts, i.e., must be in writing, must have witnesses, etc. The only thing, as I stated above, that was stopping you from performing *this* type of contract was you and your partner are not biological opposites. Now that the "law" has lifted that restriction, all you now need to do is let the state know of your intent to live as "man" and "wife". We'll get to that now. Just remember. You don't have to be a chicken to lay an egg.

Dr. Lune A. Teek

SECTION THREE
A LICENSE TO BILL

Earlier I alluded to the importance of certain things over other certain things and I was referring to my supposition that maybe you put way more emphasis on obtaining a marriage license as a means to have something that legitimizes your union. Well, brothers and sisters (regardless of your bio-make up), the license didn't and doesn't do that. That was done by way of the Supreme Court. "Gay" marriage is now "the law of the land". If you want a license, they must give it to you. However, if your intent is to live together as man and wife, without undue government influence, there just may be an alternative. Once again, this is for education purposes only. I am not an Attorney. You, however, don't have to be to study and know law. Study, learn, know, then be responsible for your own lives. With that said, let's look at some more important legal terms.

> License - A *revocable permission* to commit some act *that would otherwise be unlawful.*

By the way, these definitions are from Black's Law Dictionary. I just thought you should know that.

Look at the definition of this word. Even a rabid dodo bird's brain would detect all kinds of hazardous materials in this definition. I'm just pointing out the obvious ones. Starting with the words...

"...revocable permission..."

This sentiment appears at different times and is stated in different ways:
"The Lord giveth, the Lord taketh away..."
"I brought you into this world, I'll take your ass out..."
"Give me back my..."
and so on, and so on, and so on. The meaning, however pronounced is clear:
"What I gave you, I can take back."
And that, ladies and gentlemen (gender notwithstanding), presupposes (and rightly so) control. It moreover presupposes that you have no control over the revocation because you are not, of course, the revocator. You are the receiver of permission which by its very nature places you at a subordinate position. To test this theory, answer this question?
Who issued you this license? Ans: An agent of the State (government).

Whomever issued you your marriage license issued you license to marry. This regardless of what you've been told or think is permission. But then again, it could be any activity. It could be driving, fishing, cosmetology/barber, insurer, etc. In truth, the license doesn't add value to any activity that requires it, including and especially marriage. It does, however, give the state the power to regulate, tax, and literally choke the life out of it. Take driving as an example. Having a driver's license does not make one a good or better driver. Only knowledge and skill can do that. The driver is, however, stifled under the weight of having a plethora of rules and regulations, tolls, and other such revenue producing schemes, along with a statutory "requirement" to have said license. Violation of these blood and income sucking schemes are grounds for taking away the so called "privilege" of driving by "revoking" one's license and in some states the impounding of one's automobile. But this isn't about driving. It's about marriage. The state's grubby little paws inside yours can be just as devastating. Before I go further, I have to raise a very important issue.

SECTION FOUR
A VERY IMPORTANT ISSUE

There are a lot of issues that I will debate with anyone alive. There are a lot of issues that I will not debate at all. This is because either they are non-issues in my opinion or debating them is pointless. One issue that has been kicked around more times than Tom Brady's balls is whether marriage, "gay" or otherwise is a "God given right."

To me, this argument is pointless and a waste of time and energy. The LBGT community has wasted a lot of time and effort with this argument, which is why it never went anywhere. Why, you may ask? Because the subject matter (Marriage - gay or otherwise) stayed in the religious context. Religion, in and of itself and regardless of type, is belief based and belief is what man thinks perhaps is truth. I mean really, can you show me Jesus?" Nuff said.

It wasn't until it was taken out of the religious context and religiously maintained in the legal context did the issue move in your favor. A teachable moment indeed.

SECTION FIVE
A LICENSE TO BILL
(cont'd)

Now, let's get back to that insidious governmental safety pin called a license. Trust me. It's not safe for you but it is a safety net for the State. With that said, now that you've got the State in your affairs via the marriage license it automatically assumes what I call "prime standing" in your affairs. It assumes this position because a three-way contract has been established and because it is the issuer, facilitator, and enforcer of obligations connected with the "post existence" (divorce) of this contract the nature of its role(s) ensures this status. Of the three roles, the role of enforcer within the termination (divorce) phase of the marriage is where the effects of the State are felt the most. So, let's discuss this as this is the most important part of this writing.

One of the most traumatic experiences a person can go through is divorce. The word etymologically means "to divert". The word divert etymologically means "to turn in opposite directions". While the concept of marriage is to bring two people together in order to create a common union and the separation of that is (for some) a painful experience, it's made even more so when the two separated ends have to sit in front of a "perfect" stranger and have him or her decide who's going to get what. Yes, heterosexual couples have to do the same thing, but the difference is more often than not that "perfect" stranger you're in front of that is going to decide who gets what doesn't believe you should have been married in the first place (Hey. I'm just saying). Children being involved is an issue I don't need to cover as common sense should tell you that it further complicates matters.

Now this total stranger that most people call a judge gets sole discretion (along with something called "statues") to determine how your future will look. He's/She's doing this because you gave him/her the authority to do so and as I already stated the judge (and your Attorneys) are officers of the Court (State) and the State has prime standing while when it's over all you will be is left standing. How do you right this ship? How do you unstack the chips that have been stacked against you? Let's see.

SECTION SIX
STOP!!! IN THE NAME OF THE LAW!!!
PUT THE LICENSE DOWN!!!
NOW SLOWLY BACK AWAY FROM
THE STATE!!!

What does the law say marriage is? Yes, we're doing this again. It needs to be reinforced. Damn what the Church says. Damn what your parents say. Damn what your friends say. What does the law say? The law says marriage is a contract. I'm sure you can find more than a handful of court cites that say the same thing. The fact that a man and a woman, a man and a man, or a woman and a woman enter into this contract has now been made immaterial as to the "fitness" of the parties. With this fact being a truth, the only reason that anyone from the LGBT community should be at the Clerk of Court or Register of Deeds office is to get a file stamp for THEIR contract and Affidavit Of Intent.

> Affidavit - A voluntary declaration of facts written down and sworn to by the declarant before an officer authorized to administer oaths (A Notary). - Emphasis mine

Barring any illegal conditions with the contract and the affidavit, said conditions become legally recognized obligations between the parties and are legally enforceable by law. It is important to note that with this method one does not need to go to a Clerk of Court or Register Of Deeds however I STRONGLY advise it as this type of contract may need more than just a notary seal. Besides. A few things happen when you file your contracts with the Clerk or Register:

1. Filing here gives the public notice;
2. Filing here gives legal notice;
3. Filing here gives the document evidentiary authority status

What is another big plus for filing your documents? Well, for one thing it keeps them from filing theirs and that's the one sin that let my BFF Satan in (just kidding folks). It's the license (their document) that gives the State leverage. Why would you let a body (the State) that you know is hostile to your aims, goals, and person have leverage over any private relationship that you agree to? What's the purpose? As to what protects you, and your contract read the U.S. Constitution, Article 1, Section 10, which prohibits any State from passing a law that impairs the obligation(s) of Contracts. Article 4, Section 1 requires that States shall give full faith and credit to other States public acts, records, and judicial proceedings. An important thing to know is that contract law is based on two things. The first is the consent of the parties and the second is the intent of the parties. Consent and intent are not the same thing as one must be given before the other can be agreed to. A "meeting of the minds" must be reached in which the consent and intent of the parties is established. This is why an Affidavit of Consent and Intent (In fact, you can name it that) should be included with your contract.

SECTION SEVEN
YOUR CONTRACT

Contract - An agreement between two or more parties
creating obligations that are enforceable or
otherwise recognizable by law.

Your contract. Why do you need one? A simple but somewhat complicated answer. Let me explain. This is a new experience for you - marriage, that is. I've been through it. Eventhough the rules were written for heterosexuals, now that you have the title and the license (permission from, guess who?) the same also applies to you. Read closely.

Every state has marriage statues. My suggestion is that you get a copy of the marriage statues for your state and read them. Then you'll know what you're up against.

You need a contract because you (one "party") are forming a union (not a "relationship" - there is a difference in law) with someone else (the other "party") and based on the nature of this union obligations from you both are the consequence. There needs to be a record of

1. An agreement of your intention to form this union;
2. The nature of the union;
3. The roles both "parties" will assume in this union;
4. The responsibilities (obligations) of each party in this union;
5. Allowances for inclusion of additional parties (children) in this union and the delegation of responsibilities (obligations) to the initial parties for the care and maintenance of the additional parties;
6. The number of additional parties;
7. Prohibitions;
8. Sanctions for the violations of prohibitions;
9. Sanctions for the violations of obligations;
10. Division of assets, liabilities, additional parties (children) in the result of dissolution of the union;
11. Etc.

This can be pretty long and drawn out and, in my opinion, (as psychotic as it sometimes is) that is the way it should be. You're getting married, not shopping for a pair of yoga pants. Why should it be? Once again, simple. Once you file your contract and affidavit, what is in that contract and affidavit *is the law. Your law.* And *it supersedes state statue.* You don't think so? Can someone say, "Prenuptial Agreement"? Why are prenups so powerful? Article 1, Sec. 10 of the Constitution and Article 4, Section 1 of the Constitution. That's what they're based on. Your right to contract and the States' (all of them) obligation to recognize it. Your contract is no different. If it works for heterosexuals it has to work for you. The other reason why it should be more thorough and involved than your weekly grocery shopping list follows on the first reason. This now is *your* law. And trust me. If a Clerk of Court or Register Of Deeds stamps it and gives it a file number as long as you don't have anything illegal in it, it is enforceable in a court of law. In short, it is a legal document.

Dr. Lune A. Teek

SECTION EIGHT
WHAT THIS DOES FOR YOU

Another simple answer (I wish I had these "simple" answers when I got divorced) that at the same time is complicated. I will attempt to explain this without you throwing the book at the nearest garbage can and agreeing that the author is a Class 1, Grade A lunatic. Which I am.

In the event that you wish to dissolve (divorce) this union you're going to need to file a few things with the Clerk Of Court. If the dissolution (divorce) is amicable and everyone agrees with everything, all that is needed is a

1. Notice of Dissolution Of Marital Contract (to be signed by both parties);
2. Affidavit Of Dissolution Of Marital Contract (to be signed by both parties);
3. Order Of Dissolution Of Marital Contract (to be signed by both parties)

These three documents, which are made by you in sample copy form should have been in your original contract package that you initially filed with the Clerk or Registrar. Remember, filing things with these two puts whatever you file into the legal (their arena) and private (your arena) record. Your Clerk and your Registrar are highly important people in this respect. With that said, you will send the Clerk a cover letter referencing the nature of your request, the reference number of your original contract, and to record and file it. You will then send this same package to the Registrar Of Deeds with the same request. Once this is done and you have copies back from both with file numbers the dissolution has been filed and is complete. You will show these documents to change any transactions that are necessary. Now if your partner (or you) wants to get ducky with this, it gets messy. Just like any other messy divorce. But fear not, your contract saves you, or it kills you if you're trying to fight it. At any rate, this is what you should do.

First, you should remember that for every good piece of toast you have you'll have a bad piece. For every good dream you have you'll have a nightmare. For every good shit you have you'll have a bout with diarrhea. The same thing applies here. Having a contract in this situation gives you a lot of power. Especially if it is detailed and the details are specific. However, if you're the party that's contesting the terms, well, let's just say that month long continual diarrhea would be better for you. Get a lawyer. Both of you.

Unless something illegal is or has occurred or is a part of your initial contract it is extremely difficult to get out of one. Things like spousal abuse, infidelity, child abuse or endangerment can be grounds to void your union and these things should be included in your agreement. Remember though, what you put in your contract is law. What you don't put in your contract is wishful thinking and irrelevant to your cause if it shows itself to the advantage of the opposing party. For this reason I give you the same sentiment I'd give to a heterosexual couple. Know your partner and know what you both want. Give yourself a clause in your contract that allows you to add, change, or remove things within the contract. And always, always have a good lawyer on speed dial.

SECTION NINE
THE LOGIC BEHIND THIS
ARRANGEMENT

Just what is the logic behind having a contract union instead of a marriage license? How much power does it have? Good questions. You should pat yourself on the back for asking them. Let's start with understanding the role of a judge. Which is what you would be in front of if there is a controversy in the dissolution of this contract.

First understand that this is what a judge's purpose is: to settle controversy. So, what you or your partner (whichever one wants to terminate the contract) must do in order to get in front of a judge is file a complaint. This is in essence what is really happening when one files for divorce. You're now giving the Court jurisdiction to hear and settle the controversy. A judge adjudicates cases based on four things:

1. Statues:
2. Constitutional Law (U.S. or State);
3. Stare Decisis (Precedent);
4. Civil Law and/or Administrative Law

Each one of these issues in one way or another deals with contracts, whether it's adhesive, hidden or otherwise. When viewed this way one can say that ALL LAW IS CONTRACT. It's just a matter of who controls the contract and the terms.

If your issue has to come before a judge due to the nature of the contract (which is the nature of the relationship - marriage), the court must operate in civil jurisdiction. Nothing changes as it relates to how the judge must rule. In evidence in front of him or her is your Affidavits and Contract. The judge will most likely adhere to the contract agreement after a determination has been made that everything concerning the contract is legal; and more likely than not apply the terms of the agreement and decree an order that they be adhered to. Now to the other knuckle heads who might want to deny the power of your contract.

Let's say that the Social Security Administration doesn't want to pay you spousal support because you don't have a "State issued marriage license". That's fine. Sue the shit out of them. And when I say "sue" I mean sue their asses back to the stone age. Under what grounds? Violation of your constitutional right to contract and a host of other contract statues that they, not you, are bound by. Hopefully it won't come to that because you're going to send a copy of your contract to everyone that has an interest in having one, from the Secretary Of State of whatever State that you live in, to the Internal Revenue Services, to the Department Of Motor Vehicles, to the Social Security Administration. After ten days contact each office to confirm receipt of your contract and adherence to terms. As for their adherence to terms you don't need to contract with them. There adherence stems from administrative policy mandates that they must adhere to upon recognition of marital status. They may say that you don't have the authority to issue that type of contract and that marriage is a State prerogative. Boy, do I have tons of arguments for that one. At any rate, tell them to prove that assumptive assertion and point them back to the Constitution, otherwise give you your money or/and theirs.

SECTION TEN
WHY DID I WRITE THIS

Why did I write this to you? I'll tell you.

I wrote this because I have an acute knowledge of the tendency of people to see government as something other than themselves. I gringe when I hear someone say that they're trying to make the government work for them. It lets me know that government has become an external device that has, suddenly, become its own master. Because I am aware that nothing in and on this place of existence happens "suddenly", I know that government being what it has become is the result of a result. An effect of a cause. An effect caused by the gradual erosion of knowledge and common sense. Even that which is called "sudden death" is progressive. And the sudden death of that which one is supposed to know for one to govern oneself has been made most evident in recent times. As for "the government", the people who occupy these positions are *not* the government. The government (you) put them there, therefore they are not the government but the evidence that a government (you) exists. What I saw the LGBT community doing with respect to this issue moved me to write this section because I knew that they had lost sight of this. Eventhough you gained a hard-fought victory you put yourself right back into a position of being controlled by an entity that has assumed an authority that it could not reach on its own. In short but before I finish, let me give you an example of this. Go back to the second phrase I emphasized in the definition of the word "license":

"... that would otherwise be unlawful"

On one hand they argued that marriage (heterosexual of course) was an act "ordained by God" and a "God given right" and at the same time the State has deemed that without *its permission* (license) the act of marriage is unlawful. This sounds an awful lot like the State playing God. The State is telling you, literally, that you can't "legally" get married without its permission. Pretty powerful sentiment, no? I will leave you with this:

You fought long and hard in order to be free.
Stay that way.

CHAPTER EIGHT

Backward

What is birth,
but death in reverse.
What do you have then?
After death, all you have left,
You end as you begin.
The Author

This book has a Foreword. It stands to reason, therefore, that it has a backward. It's the way of the world. It's the way life is. It is the natural order of things. It is the way I, the author wanted it. And I get to choose.

But isn't that what this is all about? Choices? Isn't that what life is all about? Isn't that what "America" is all about?

Oh, but if it were only so easy for some.

As I stated in the Foreword this book took too long to publish. Not having a publishing deadline, while writing this type of book can get one in real trouble. I'm in that type of trouble and the only way I can get out of this type of trouble is to publish my way out. So, I must do what I must do. What type of trouble am I in? The worst type of trouble an author like me writing a book like this could be in:

Events take place which proves my thesis.

Ordinarily an author would be happy to be in this position. Such is not the case here. As I will explain.

As I was putting the finishing touches on the rewrite of this book, a man was shot and killed in a convenience store parking lot in Baton Rouge, Louisiana. The very next day, another man was shot and killed at a traffic stop in Minneapolis, Minnesota. These two men who were killed had some things in common in that they both were "black", were killed by police officers, and their encounters were recorded. Allegedly, as a retaliation for these two killings, a man opens fire at police who were monitoring a protest march in Dallas, Texas. Five officers were killed, several others were injured. One innocent bystander was injured by shrapnel. Five people killed. The shooter, a "black" man, was blown up by an explosive carrying robot.

As I watched these incidents unfold, I went back to Chapter Five. Chapter Five is titled "You Have The Right To Remain Silent". I went back over my notes, other rewrites, and the entire finished chapter. I put all of these in a folder. I had that folder with me everytime I would hear someone interviewed about these incidents. Not once did I hear anyone mention anything in Chapter Five. Some came close. None were specific. After an entire week of listening to people in and outside the system give interviews and speeches I got very, very upset. Then I got angry. Then I got mad. I got mad because eventhough you as a civilian didn't know it, I knew that I was seeing that "determination" being put into play. That determination being the one I wrote about in the beginning of Chapter Five:

> "... A determination has been made that the solutions to a menacing problem can be obtained without having to make this information public. I, on the other hand, am aware of the futility and outright stupidity of this determination and the thinking that drives it. Am I calling the determiners stupid? No. I'm just calling their thinking stupid."

Chapter Five - "You Have The Right To Remain Silent."

I am now calling the determiners stupid. That's right. I said it.

You're Stupid. And as a public service (and because you've made that same damn determination again which is why I'm pissed off) I am calling you out.

DETERMINER NO. 1
ALL CHIEFS OF POLICE

Do I want you to tell all your secrets? No.

Do I want you to fall on the sword wielded by the stupid? No.

What I want is very simple. I want you to be the Police Department.

No, No, No! Not what you're fooling the people with. What you're supposed to be.

See, there was a time when police departments were localized and they dealt with local problems. Their mandates were local in nature. That is not the case anymore. Most, if not all of you have sold your souls and are walking hand in hand with something in which none of you fully understand. You are getting mandates from the Department Of Homeland Security as well as the United States Department Of Justice. You can and may deny this. I have no problem with that. Do what you like.

These mandates you have received deal with perceived threats of "extreme violence," as well as groups and individuals that are perceived to be or are a part of a movement of "violent extremism". You have been given a list of such groups/organizations and individuals and their profiles. You have been "trained" via literature, audio/video, lecture, and training scenario on how to approach and interact with said groups. You have been told that either these people are a threat to the government, a threat to society, or are within a specific age group in which the probability of them being or reacting violently within the parameters of society is high. Therefore, if you as a police officer has an encounter with them and they show *the least* bit of resistance you are to mark them as a hostile and deal with them accordingly.

I'm not too far off, am I?

Of course I'm not. As I said earlier, resistance is futile. Resistance will get you killed.

I know what I'm writing about. And whom.

How much do you really, truly know about the people and/or groups you've been profiling? How much study/research have you done on your own, using *your own brain*. Not your law enforcement brain. Yours. The brain you had before you joined the police force.

Do you still have that brain? Can you channel that brain?

If you can't, here lies your problem. Here lies *THE* problem.

Listen, Mr./Mrs./Ms. Police Chief. YOU are the head, the face, the conscience/conscious of your force. You reflect them just like they reflect you (more so the latter). When you end your shift brief instead of saying "Protect yourselves" (which is self-evident) do you say go Protect and Serve"? Whether you know or believe it or not you (yes, you) are the first and last line of defense from an objective being put in place that will place the United States in anarchy and possibly bring it to the brink of civil war and instead of the police keeping the peace they will be active combatants. And do not be the fool and fool yourself into thinking that just because you're the police you've got a winner. You can't keep up with a criminal mind with a blank check and access to the black market. The objective now is to not only get the individual civilian to fear what you might do but to get *you* scared of what the individual civilian might do. Seems to be working pretty well. And all of this for what end.

The ultimate objective.

Absolute control.

You have no idea, Mr./Mrs./Ms. Police Chief, that you are a knight being moved on a grand chess board by those who are playing *13 level, multi-dimensional chess*. Yes.

You are being manipulated.

You are being psychologically pulled into the realm of the federal and military law enforcement structure. Your *training* agendas and methods are slowly but surely being refined to fit federal and military agenda and profiles. You are slowly but surely training your officers to not necessarily *police* areas but to *occupy* them (those who read this who have had certain specific military training will understand the nuances of this). Those who watched the individual who killed the police officers in Dallas, Texas get blown up had no idea that they were seeing a *military* style take out of an insurgent. Well, most didn't know. I was among those that did. I was a Security Police Specialist in the United States Air Force. My job was to guard nuclear weapons and nuclear weapon systems.

Listen. I've already covered this in Chapter Five. This has to stop and it has to stop now. I'm not saying this because police officers are shooting "black" men. Hell. It should tell you something that the Justice Department will not cite their own statistics showing that more "white" men are shot and killed by policemen than "black" men per capita. The Attorney General will go on National television and say everything but that. And guess who gets thrown under the bus (and then shot and/or killed) in the end. You guessed it. Your officers.

I'm going to end this conversation with you like this. This is between you and me and that cat sleeping over there in the corner.

Both you and I know this ain't gonna stop. Six or seven months from now this will blow over, people will go back to being and doing what they were being and doing and BAM!!! It's gonna happen again. They'll be crying, wailing, gnawing and gashing of teeth. Marching, praying, television shows, etc. White people carrying "Black Lives Matter" signs. Hillary Clinton saying, "white people need to understand", etc., etc., etc. Every damn thing you're seeing and hearing now. All because a determination was made that this problem could be solved by not divulging this information to the public. And if the public reads this book the public had better ask. But to no avail. Because you, Mr./Mrs./Ms. Police Chief will deny it. You'll call me and this information a lie. You'd rather slap Jesus' teeth down his throat than to admit any of this to the public.

But that's okay. I understand. Jesus might not though. After all, it's his teeth that's on the line. Regardless of all of what I just wrote, many police chiefs in this country are absolute professionals who care about their officers and the public. Be this as it may, I'm asking you to do more. I've given you an outline of a program at the end of Chapter Five. Use it. Some of you are. More of you need to. And by the way, get the public involved. They need this. In truth, they need you.

Dr. Lune A. Teek

SECTION TWO
TO THE ULTIMATE DETERMINER:

YOU

Let me explain something to you, and by God or whatever deity you pray to you had better take notice and take heed.

I started writing this book on the night of October 31, 2015. This section of this book is a rewrite. It is now January 25, 2017.

As with the earlier sections of this book, you may agree or disagree with its content. You may think its condescending, preachy, or patronizing. I get that. I welcome all views. My intent is to hopefully draw enough interest in the subject matter from you so that if you won't destroy the rock that's been placed on your brain at least you might move it around a little.

A lot has taken place since I started writing this book. A lot was taking place before I started it. The interests I headline in this book (you.) have progressed in a lot of areas. Some of you have regressed. And I mean badly. As this is the "Backward" chapter, I am going to reiterate certain subjects. I am also going to touch some current ones.

To "Black people."

It seems as though everyone is traveling "East" except you.

Why?

Why are you still so determined to go "North" when it is evident that it is there that all the "dead" are buried? Oh, I forgot.

You're black

And "black" according to science means death. So you're going home.

Black according to science means death and as long as you cannot or will not resurrect the true descendant nature of your forefathers and foremothers you will be, in the eyes and sentiments of free men and women everywhere, a walking, talking, shitting and eating corpse wherever you may be found on this planet.

You really have no choice. You must die. You must be dead.

Why?

Because you have no lifeline. Let me explain this lest you deny the truth of the statement. Again:

Your *ancient* ancestors are the holders and distributors of that rarified oxygen that I choose to call "specified knowledge, understanding, and wisdom". Because most of you don't know how to access this information or don't think it's important to do so you will be relegated to "back of the bus" status. Why? Because even if you did know how to get to the front of the bus you don't know how to stay there. So even if you get to the front of the bus, while looking out of the window you'll see a horse talking to its own shit, leave your seat to attempt to listen to the conversation, loose yourself in the conversation, and forget why you're on the bus in the first place. By then you will think that you should never have been there. And by going in that circle (which you have been since I can remember) you will never realize that it's you who *owns* the bus.

And yes, that is a problem.

It's called "the problem of not knowing your place in the affairs of men".

It will remain a problem until you learn the truth about who your *ancient* forefathers and foremothers were, and of course, become imitators of them.

It will remain a problem until you stop reading Exodus 20:12 and actually do it. You must *truly* understand what Exodus 20:12 is telling you to do. Most of you don't and most of your pastors don't have a clue. Otherwise, they would clue you in to its importance. But then again, they just might not. For they know if they did you might learn something that would make them useless and obsolete. And because this is a problem for them it becomes a problem for you. Lucky for you that I like you. Why?

Because I am going to explain Exodus 20:12 to you.

The truth of it.

Not *my* truth.

THE truth.

If anyone tries to give you another explanation or alters this one by any degree get away from them.

Run.

Quickly.

And don't look back.

Dr. Lune A. Teek

SECTION THREE
EXODUS 20:12
(YOUR BEST FRIEND)

"Honor thy father and mother, that thy
days may be long upon the land which
the LORD thy God giveth thee."

Exodus 20:12 (KJV)

We can do this without getting fancy-smancy and pulling out the Greek-Aramaic dictionary if we remember one thing:

Context, like optics, is everything. Especially in English. Joined at the hip with context, is nuance.

Nuance: 1: a subtle distinction or variation. 2: a subtle quality.
(Webster's Dictionary)

Subtle: 1a: DELICATE, ELUSIVE; b: difficult to understand or distinguish. 2a: PERCEPTIVE, REFINED; b: having or marked by keen insight and ability to penetrate deeply and thoroughly.
(Webster's Dictionary)

Subtle.
This verse was written via #1 (a and b), so in order to understand it you must be #2 (a and b).

The terms "father" and "mother" in this context are not referring to your immediate birth father and mother. You can only understand the nuance of this by following the storyline before Exodus 20:12. You must be subtle (2a and b) enough to get the point. The terms "father" and "mother" here are meant to be representative of the terms "forefathers" and "foremothers", or more succinctly put, your ancestors.

Now let's look at the term "honor".

Skip all the definitions of this word as presented within your Webster's. They don't apply to the exact context of this verse. Here again, is where you must be subtle (2a and b) enough to apply logic. Those who are good at crossword puzzles are skilled at this. What's another word for what we do when we honor our fallen heroes?

Commemorate - 1: to call to remembrance (Webster's Dictionary)

Notice the synonym of this word.

Keep - 1: to take notice of by appropriate conduct: FULFILL as a: to be faithful to. b: to act fittingly in relation to. c: to conform to in habits or conduct. d: to stay in accord with; 2: PRESERVE, MAINTAIN: as a: to watch over and defend; 3: 6a: to stay or continue in. 72c: to persist in a practice.

Get the picture? Remember. Context, like optics, is everything.

Simply put, Mr. and Mrs. (or Ms.) black America, a large (very large) part of the reason why you have the conditions you have is that you have no reference point to pull from in order to acquire the knowledge, understanding, and wisdom necessary to solve your problems. In order to realize the importance of this statement and the ones I have written that are similar in nature to it, you must first remember Ecclesiastes 1:9-11. And once you've read that, how about reading Chapter 3:15:

> "That which is has already been, and what is to be
> has already been; and God requires an account of what
> is past..."

If God requires an account of what is past surely you need to whip out your note pad. Your ancestors had and solved the same issues you have. Learn from them. How? Listen. Stop limiting yourself. A few things to think about are in order here.

Look. You've got to hear this at some point from someone so it might as well be me. First things first. Boycott Black History Month (Hey! Don't look at the book like it's a water moccasin, I told you I am a Class 1, Grade A lunatic. One however, that you'd do well to listen to). Dr. Carter G. Woodson had a decent idea when he introduced Black History Week to you. And I'm not saying abandon it entirely. It (and you) however, need an update. It has gotten to the point to where the subject matters related within the perimeters of this phenomenon have the look and feel of an unrelated and unrelatable trivial pursuit game. I'm not saying that the accomplishments and actions of the men and women within these stories are trivial. I am saying that the only thing that little "black" boys and little "black" girls will learn during the entire month of February is what? A bunch of disjointed facts about a group of people which illustrates what? Who is responsible for the overall presentation of these factoids? Or are "black" people supposed to pull these little pieces of folded paper from out of a fishbowl and then do what? Why is it that the vast majority of Black History facts are related to events civil war onward?

While these questions may seem irrelevant, childish, or even stupid and this syllogism downright retarded, humor me for a second.

What were "black" people doing during the Crusades? Where were "black" people and what were they doing during the advent of Christianity? During the formation building, and apex of the Roman Empire, did "black" people have an empire and where was it? When the stones were erected in the earth that would someday be called "Stonehenge", where were "black" people and what were they doing? Did it ever occur to you, "black" people, that the United States of America was the United States of America before 1787 and that it had a constitution before this date and had presidents that served under said Constitution? Who were these men? Is this one of the factoids on one of those folded pieces of paper in that fishbowl?

When the first hole was dug in which the first brick was placed for the Great Wall of China to be erected, where were "black" people and what were they up to? When the Dead Sea Scrolls were found, where would we find "black" people and what would we find them doing? When the cornerstone for the Alhambra was laid where were "black" people? What about the cornerstone for the Vatican?

There are answers to these questions. There are people who know the answers to these questions (Hint: I will never ask you a question I don't know the answer to). The issue here is do you know. And did you get the answers by reaching into a fishbowl? Listen. I get that there's a nice, warm, fuzzy feeling one gets by having an entire month dedicated to them. However, it means absolutely jack shit to feel nice, warm, and fuzzy the entire month of February then go back to being the same old tired, worn out second class citizen March 1st. It's not enough to say that you come from a lineage of kings and queens. You've got to know it. Then prove it. As I was once informed, "Sovereignty begins and ends between your ears".

Someone is pointing you in a specific direction.

In a circle.

A Hamster wheel.

For "black" hamsters.

By being on this hamster wheel it means you will never find your way back to your ancient ancestors and the knowledge they used to solve the problems of their day, which in truth, are the same problems of this day. Remember Ecclesiastes 3:15

> "That which is has already been, and what is to be has
> already been, and God requires an account of what is past"

A wise man once said,

> "In order to change the condition of a people you must first change their literature." Noble Drew Ali

Who your ancestors are is detailed in practically every encyclopedia and dictionary that you have ever picked up and read. The problem is that you have been misdirected and redirected to other people, places, and things. You have been taught about the accomplishments of ancient peoples and you had no idea that they were either your ancestors or connected to your ancestors because they did not have the names nor did they call themselves blacks, negroes, colored folks or any of these other disfigurements of identification you have latched on to. And that, my friends, handicaps you severely. You have contributed to or have been the cause of many of the most known and spectacular events in known existence and because you have been tricked into believing that you are a totally different people from the ancients who achieved this greatness most of you neglect to see yourselves as their modern day equivalents. Remember:

> "You are today, without doubt or contradiction what your ancient forefathers were."

"According to all true and divine records of the human race there is no negro, black, or colored race attached to the human family."

There is only one race: the human race; subdivided into two groups:

Asiatic and European

There, I said it.

No amount of doubting by you nor hollering and screaming "liar" by others is going to change this truth. Trust me. If I tell you a cat is a pig then stick little Button's ass in front of a trough. She'll know what to do.

Stop limiting yourself. The chronological amalgamation of your history most assuredly takes longer than a month and will span the entire globe. Your mission should you decide to accept it, is to learn it, bring it forward, internalize it, then live it. Right now you're doing mock-ups of knowledge that has and is being spoon fed to you for the express purpose of not allowing you to know that:

1. You are genetically and therefore ancestrally connected to every dark hued and brown man, woman, and child on this planet. You

were given the title "African-American" in an effort to blind you from the truth that the aboriginals from China to Australia, and from Mexico to India are your blood brothers, sisters, mothers and fathers;

2. You were given the title of "African-American" in an effort to obfuscate the true identity of that empire that arose from Africa to take over much of Europe. Yes, I'm talking about that same group of people from which grew the Atlantic slave trade. Yes, your intermediate ancestors, who, by the way, had adopted Islam (not Christianity) as their religion;

3. You were given the title "African-American" in an effort to hide the above two truths (and others), and by doing so has engaged in a grand clandestine scheme to hide the fact that by engaging in some assiduous study and research of the first two truths listed above (and others) said study and research will lead to you learning that at one time or another your ancestors (ancient and intermediate) were ruling one part of the world or the other for well over 1196 years (give or take a few);

4. You were given the title "African-American" in an effort to keep the masses of you from ever finding out, thus uttering the federally recognized name of your intermediate ancestors because by you knowing this recognized name you are free to put it in front of the hyphen of "-American". Because this name is what it is (a worldwide recognized "nation" of people) it is recognized as a "Nationality". It is the worldwide, historically recognized name of an empire that spanned the Northwestern and Southwestern shores of what is now known as Africa, the inhabitants of which are historically recognized as the descendants and direct individuals that were made up of the compelled participants of the Atlantic slave trade – your intermediate ancestors, and regardless to where in Africa your ancestor's tribe was found you still can use this name and be federally recognized as having a nationality;

5. You were given the title of "African-American" in an effort to supplant the knowledge that even the "founding fathers" of this country knew who your intermediate ancestors were. They made many treaties with the "leader" (He is called something else. You find out.) of your intermediate ancestors. At least one of those treaties is in existence and is fully functional as of this day.

Listen. If by some effort of yours you find out the truth about yourself and your nationality let no one tell you otherwise and that you are not eligible to claim title to that. Generally, you will not need to prove it. Those who are in power, particularly those who are in power in government already know this. Technically, you still don't have to prove it. History itself is your witness. Call it to the witness stand. And this brings us full circle – Exodus 20:12.

So, with all the knowledge, understanding, and wisdom of your forefathers and foremothers at your disposal surely you can stop at least one lame brained clown in Chicago from killing another precious little four-year-old girl or boy "by mistake", thus assisting in the killing of your entire bloodline – "for purpose."

Look. There was a time when you could look backward in the past and sing that old negro spiritual "How I Got Over". That time is long gone. The time when history was something that you got melancholy over; something that was made up of other people's accomplishments that made you "feel good about yourself" is over. History for you, in this new era, must be a brand new paradigm. To you, history must now represent a strategy that is an integral part of an overall objective and the learning of your history, *as a whole,* a key tactic in the achievement of same. There are aspects of your history that if you brought them forward and correctly proclaimed them you would be immediately recognized by the government in which you live and it would instantly change your legal and political status. This, in turn, depending upon your efforts, would change your economic and social status. Which in turn would change your present condition as well as your status in the world. However, there is at least one more thing that you need to come to grips with. Remember, the truth will make you free and I am here to either take the shackles off your brain or take them and bust you upside the head. Of course, which one of these that becomes your reality will be totally up to you. I am your most humble servant. With that said, I might as well stop "wading in the water" and go on ahead and drown. As I said earlier, somebody's got to tell you this and it might as well be me.

There are a great many of you who have been postulating this supposed truth that you have a "right" to vote. Many of you vehemently put forth this assertion. Stop it. Stop it now. By continuing this supposition of nonsense, you are supplying comic relief to those who put the cheese on the hamster wheel that you're currently treading on. They're rolling in the aisle in fact. Let me acquaint you with a truth. Not an opinion, but a truth.

There is NO such thing as a "right" to vote.
Especially for "black" people.

Someone has soiled themselves after reading this. I'll take a ten-minute break so you can change underwear. Don't forget to wash.

Okay. You're back. Now let me educate you.

Once again, the act of voting is not a right of the citizenry, 15th Amendment notwithstanding. As a matter of fact, the 15th amendment does not give anyone the "right" to vote. All it does is prohibit the government from discriminating against anyone based on sex, race, religion, origin, etc. States (which technically voting is a prerogative of) are free to set other parameters as they see fit if those parameters do not fall into the 15th amendment prohibitions.

Voting is a *privilege*. Do you "hear" me "black" people? Voting is a privilege. It is the result of something. The act of voting is the result of the country having a particular type of political system that is Constitutionally structured that allows the citizenry to choose (vote for) their respective representatives. It is nothing more. Nothing less. Because it is a by-product of the Constitution, this act can and would change if by some stretch of fate the political system changes. That would take a re-write of the Constitution but hell, there are those who believe that the Constitution has been aborted anyway. But I digress.

The point that I am making is that because you have taken the power of this privilege for granted those who know that you are going to vote for them are taking you for granted. This was so eloquently said by Donald Trump, who most of you see as a bigot. Whatever *you* think he is in one statement he summed up your relationship with the Democratic Party for the last 50 years. I'm not going to repeat the statement. You know it already. If you don't ask somebody. At any rate, he told you more truth in that one statement than any democratic presidential candidate that you have voted for other than JFK in the last 50 years (and you see what telling the truth did for JFK. Like I said, if someone isn't trying to kill you you ain't saying nothing).

While voting is a privilege it is also a power. As with all forms of decision making, cause and effect come into play. Elections have consequences and this act brings those consequences into existence. Do you know what your friendly neighborhood candidate's *true* vision is versus what they are telling you? No. You don't. That's why your environmental, social, legal, and economic condition as a people has not changed in the last 50 years and in some of these instances it has gotten worse. How do you change this scenario? Simple. Go back to the chapter where I discuss networking. You must have a network. Study it carefully. In the development of this network, you, yourselves must develop a sense of the importance of information. And not just any information. The *correct* information is essential. You must develop and master the analytical skills necessary to transform information into intelligence. Trust me. There is a difference. You must know when to use it and understand how to use it. And lastly, you must not be afraid to use it. Regardless of the methods you must employ.

"What do you mean?", you're probably saying.

You heard (read) me. Read between the lines.

Understand?

The concept I just described is called "leverage" and it is one in a host of strategies you must use to achieve objectives. What does this have to do with voting?

If you have to ask that question then you are asinine. Instead of answering it let me give you an example that answers it.

The legislature of North Carolina enacted a law called "HB-2" (House Bill #2). For the sake of brevity I'm not going to get into the specifics of this law. Unless you've been under a rock you know about it already. Suffice it to say it was a controversial law to say the least.

The people who were against this law (liberals) tried everything to get this law done away with. And when I say everything I mean everything. The legislators (republicans) weren't budging. Until one thing happened. And here is where the concept of leverage comes in.

Once again, for the sake of brevity as well as sanity (mine) I will not go into the specifics of what happened here. I will tell you this.

The people who voted for the legislators who enacted HB2 and fought to keep it enacted were pretty happy with their handiwork. They felt that their interests were being respected and upheld. At least until a nasty little bug called the NCAA crawled into the soil called North Carolina. They had already been there but they were content to be content as long as they were well fed (money and influence) via the athletic programs embedded within the North Carolina school system. When it appeared that HB2 was an afront to the LGBT community (In truth it wasn't. It was just framed that way.), the NCAA bit the State of North Carolina. Hard. Where it hurt them the most. Right in the pocket it keeps its wallet. They threatened to pull all conference tournament games (The really "big" ones) indefinitely or at least until they repealed this law. Then they gave them a deadline.

It was touch and go for a moment. Then it became more touching than going. Then those doing the most touching got scared and wanted to go. As the clock ticked toward the witching hour purposed by the magicians of the NCAA the going got tough and the tough...well... turned to mush. Magicians tend to do that sort of thing to people every now and then.

In the end, just in a nick of time, HB2 was repealed. Once again in the good old Tarheel State money talked and conservative voters walked. Or did they? I'll let you, reader, research what "HB" (House Bill) replaced HB2.

Suffice it to say that not everyone on either side was happy with the results. Read it for yourselves. It's HB142.

The point I am making to you, Mr. and Mrs. (or Ms.) "black" America is the question(s) I am asking you:

> Are you as a people organized enough to be organized enough to have an organized structure that is organized enough to be organized enough to produce the type of leverage that the NCAA produced in order to achieve an objective? If not, why? If so, why have you not utilized it to better your standing and in turn better your condition as a people?

It is my contention that you, black people, get all upset, hot, sticky, and bothered with white people about a contrived concept called "White Privilege" because you, as a people, have failed miserably at the above. You have failed miserably at the above mainly because of two reasons:

1. There is no unity among you as it relates to *this* type of agenda;
2. You do not know how to conceive, formulate, and maintain *this* type of agenda

Harriet Tubman's "Underground Railroad" is the closest thing you've had to this type of agenda. You haven't had it since.

Once again, what does this have to do with voting? Read closely. Remember:

> Power is an illusion. It is here today, gone tomorrow. It is and always will be force that directs the power.

When you vote, you are *expressing* your will. You have *manifested* nothing. When you have formulated the apparatus that you can use in order to make sure that "*your* will be done" then that/those individual/individuals that you voted into office become the power that you, the force controls. Until you really, truly become a "Special Interest" you're of no interest at all. You're just "special". Stop being "special".

SECTION FOUR
JUST IN CASE YOU FORGOT

You are not blacks.
You are not negroes.
You are not coloreds.
You are not African-Americans.
Etc.
These are not your "race".
These are not your "nationality".
Can a "man" be Negro, Black, Colored"?
No.
Why?
Because "man" was made in the image and likeness of God.
Let me introduce you to a few definitions. Follow my lead. I may drive you crazy, but I won't steer you wrong. Mr. Webster; if you please...

Phyl-or Phylo-	comb form [L, fr. Gk, fr. phylē, phylon: akin to GK. phyein to bring forth - more at BE]: tribe: race: phylum <phylogeny>
Phylesis -	the course of evolutionary or phylogenetic development.
Phylogenetic - 1:	Of or relating to phylogeny. 2: Based on natural evolutionary relationships. 3: Acquired in the course of phylogenetic development: RACIAL
Phylogeny - 1:	The racial history of a kind of organism. 2: The evolution of a genetically related group of organisms as distinguished from the development of the individual organism. 3: The history or course of the development of something (as a word or custom).
Phylum - a:	direct line of descent within a group. b: A group that constitutes or has the unity of a phylum. 2: A group of languages related more remotely than those of a family or stock.
Stock - 5a:	The original (as a man, race, or language) from which others derive: SOURCE b(1): The descendants of one individual: FAMILY, LINEAGE (2): A compound organism - compare CLONE C: An infraspecific group usu, having unity of descent.

Race - 2a:	A family, tribe, people, or nation belonging to the same stock. b: A class or kind of people united by community of interests, habits, or characteristics. 3a: An actually or potentially interbreeding group within a species: also: A taxonomic category (as a subspecies) representing such a group. b: BREED. C: A division of mankind possessing traits that are transmissible by descent and sufficient to characterize as a distinct human type.
Taxon - 2:	The name applied to a taxonomic group in a formal system of nomenclature.
Taxonomy - 1:	The study of the general principles of scientific classification: SYSTEMATICS. 2. CLASSI-FICATION specif: orderly classification of plants and animals according to their presumed natural relationships

There, Mr. and Mrs. (or Ms.) black America. This is what the start of your research should have looked like. In doing this I've done ⅓ of the work for you. By all means do not limit yourselves to these definitions pulled from Webster's. So, what is this this "racial" issue all about? Why does it dominate existence in America?

Those of us who know and understand the truth behind this issue are aware of the answer to this question. Moreover, we know and understand it from a different perspective than the average. Yes, this country (and the world for that matter) is divided. It is divided, however, by and through a lie. A lie called "race." A context that once viewed from the lens of cold, hard logic is as insidious as it is insane. While the concept exists, the context applied to it is as deadly as a rattlesnake.

Think about it reader. If you accept the premise of the context of race, *as it has been given to you*, how can you not be divided? Look at what you are allowing yourselves to be called:

Black

White

Supposed opposites of a spectrum that all of you know but none of you have seen thus experienced: the spectrum of humanity and the oneness of that spectrum. Those of us who understand this oneness understand the meaning of this statement:

There is only one race: the human race.

Regardless of the geographical dichotomy that exists this statement holds true. These pseudo-identifications and the stereotypes that came (and in some cases are still coming) with them are responsible for more murder and mayhem than any other cause known to man. And until you, reader, recognize that there is no such thing as the nature of a *black* man nor the nature of a *white* man these divisions will continue to exist as well as become deadlier. There is only *one* nature that metaphysically is shared by man and that is *human* nature. Everything else is a myth manufactured within the minds of men (and women) who were showing the diabolical part of that human nature.

SECTION FIVE
IS THIS "BLACK" ENOUGH FOR YA?

The late, great R&B recording artist Billy Paul ("Me and Mrs. Jones," etc.) recorded a song that asks the question "Am I Black Enough For Ya?". While listening to Mr. Paul count various aspirations via "moving on up", I could not help but ask myself if "black" people, as a whole (or in the aggregate) realized all of these aspirations would they be "black enough" to, as a whole (or in the aggregate), move their social and economic standard of living, not necessarily past, but equal to that of "white people"? And if not, what would it take? Hence, the over and under lying impetus for this book. Let's step back for a moment. Fade to black.

Let me show you the importance of questioning what you've been given to wrap yourselves up in. If you do this correctly, you may find that the blanket you've been given may be infested with fleas, syphilis, or worse; lies.

First, review the definition of the words I just gave you. They all have a common theme. If you view them close enough, you'll be able to detect that theme.

Now, read from the words "Phylesis" to "Phylum" and key in on the word "Stock" within the definition of the word "Phylum". Go to the definition of the word "Stock". Center yourself on definition 5a:

> "The original (as a man, race, or language) from which others derive: SOURCE"
> Remember:
> "According to all *True* and *Divine* records of the human race there is no negro, black, or colored race attached to the human family..."
>
> Timothy Drew Ali (Emphasis mine)

Now go to definition b(1): of this word:

> "The descendants of one individual:
> FAMILY, LINEAGE"

Remember:

> "You are today, *without doubt or contradiction* what your ancient forefathers were..."
>
> Timothy Drew Ali (Emphasis mine)

Okay, now that you've done that go and find *all* of the "True" and "Divine" records of human existence that you can lay your hands, feet, eyes, arms, or anything else you come up with on and scroll back to the beginning of that existence and find that one original that the rest of humanity came from. Scroll forward and find that one individual from which a family descended from. Did the term (name) "black" appear in any of these "True" and "Divine" records when describing this individual? What about the term (name) "White"? In order to test this one need go no farther than the most read and revered record of human existence ever to have been written: the "good" book.

> "This is the book of the generations of Adam. In the day that God created man, in the likeness of God made he him; Male and female created he them; and blessed them, *and called their name Adam*, in the day when they were created..."
>
> Genesis 5:1-2 (Emphasis mine)

Whether or not the hue of the males and females that "HE" created were "black" or "white" is debatable and will continue to be debated by fools who will try to put forth an unknowable supposition. What is not debatable is that, at least in this particular "True" and "Divine" record, "HE" didn't call "their" name black. Nor white for that matter. So where did you get that "racial" distinction from?

Look at the definition of race. By-pass the first two as they only confirm what you've just read. Key in on the last part of the third definition:

> "3(a)...also: A taxonomic category..."

Taxonomic.

What the hell's that?

Taxonomy - 1: The study of the general principles of scientific classification: SYSTEMATICS. 8: CLASSIFICATION specf: orderly classification of plants and animals according to their presumed natural relationships.

There's a lot going on with this. Let me explain. You may think I'm wrong but let me explain anyway.

Dr. Lune A. Teek

Let me start off by saying that manipulation is a science. It has a method involved with it. Its principles are psychologically relationshiped based and those relationships are contextually *presumed*. If the manipulator is successful, then the manipulatee will *assume* their role in the presumptive relationship. The relationship is contextually presumed because every con must have a maker and a mark (A mover and a sucker). Each must be good at what they do in order for the con to be successful. A mover must be good at moving the game along (the second a "game" stagnates it's over.). Why do you think a card shark never stops talking in a "game" of Three Card Monty?). A sucker must be good at being a sucker. Some suckers are better suckers than others. A good maker (mover) can spot a good mark (sucker) a mile away. A fantastic mover can spot a fantastic sucker a hundred miles away. You, "black" people, have been fantastically good suckers.

> Taxonomic - 1: The study of the general principles of scientific classification: SYSTEMATICS.

I asked you a question earlier in this book. The significance of this question should become apparent to you now.

> "Who told you that you were "black?"

I asked you another question after that:

> "Did you give them permission to call you 'black', 'negro', 'colored'...?".

Once again...

> Taxonomic - 1: The study of the general principles of scientific classification: SYSTEMATICS. 2: CLASSIFICATION specf: Orderly classification of plants and animals according to their presumed natural relationships.

Let me make this even clearer to you.

> Status - "A person's *legal condition* insofar as it is imposed *by law without the person's consent*; as opposed to a condition that a person has *acquired by agreement*" (Black's Law Dictionary, 7th Ed. - Emphasis mine)

Q. What was your "legal condition" when you were first called "colored"; then "negro" on these shores of "America"?

A. Slaves.

Q. Who was the first to call you "colored"; then "negro"?

A. Your slave master.

Q. Will you define the word "colored"?

A. Colored means anything that has been painted, stained, varnished or dyed.

Q. What of yours was legally painted over, stained over, varnished over, and dyed?

A. Your national descendent identity, be it tribal or otherwise as well as your divine creed.

Q. What is a man without a national descendent identity nor a divine creed?

A. He is ⅗ ths of a "free man".

Q. Will you explain this concept of "⅗ ths?

A. In the legal and social "sciences" (physical as well as metaphysical) a man has five aspects. He is made up of the

    1.) Physical

    2.) Soul

    3.) Spirit

And as such he has a

    4.) Descendent Identity (Modern name - Nationality)

    5.) Divine Creed (Modern name - Belief System)

Those who created the "catch and non-release" system called slavery understood that no one can change a man's descendant nature (physical, soul, spirit) unless his power extends beyond the Great Universal Creator. Change it, no. Create an environment where it won't be recognized – Yes. So, a "legal" environment called "institutional slavery" was crafted and a system titled "involuntary servitude" was designed to facilitate the objectives of the institution. Because it is not now nor was it then lawful for one human to enslave another "involuntarily", this "institution" (the institution of slavery) was constantly under attack. As it broke under the constant assault, systems and methods in which a man was able to proclaim and declare his descendant identity became open to the former slave. Too much time had elapsed and too many generations had passed for some of these unfortunate men and women and because of this they had lost the knowledge of their former selves and their true homeland. It is under this cloud that the former slaves bonded and branded themselves and their future progeny with the only identity that they knew; that of "negro"/and or "colored". In doing this, they were not identified nor recognized by their true descendent identity and by not knowing this they could not identify, recognize, nor practice their true divine creed. And because they knew not who they were nor how to proclaim who they were even if they did, they gave themselves and their progeny to a government that would determine and change their identity at will. After all, what was a "negro" to a slave master? Property. Property has no rights because it has no liberty interest and for a right to be enforced liberty interests must first be established. The "black"/ "negro" man or woman, because of this lack of movement from the identity of property has then and always will have their humanity challenged until they remove themselves from the identity of something that will always get them dropped off at their master's doorstep. So, what must you have in order to be the "master of the house" instead of the "house nigger"?

1. Body
2. Soul
3. Spirit
4. Descendent Identity (National Origin)
5. Divine Creed (Belief/Faith system)

It must be understood by you that entrance into "the family of nations" is not predicated upon the contextual definition of "race" that you have grafted to your mental conception of yourselves and others. In fact, that context has been given to those who accept it as a mechanism to keep them out.

And it's working.

Perfectly.

Is America divided? Of course it is. Not by race, however, but by ideology. The concept of race is not an ideology. It is a fact. The context of race that has gripped the minds of the American populace is an ideology. A sick, twisted ideology designed by sick, twisted people in order to achieve a sick, twisted objective.

And it's working.

Perfectly.

SECTION FOUR
WHITE PEOPLE
(REPRISE)

You surprised me.
Really, you did.
I never thought you'd do it.
At least not this quickly.
But, you did. And I'm proud of you.
Well, at least some of you.

Some of you got the message that this book expounded on before you read it. Some of you are still involved in an assault on common sense. You're attempting to save a concept called "America" and you have no idea what this concept really means. You have no *clear* idea of what's troubling "America" nor who's troubling "America". This will ensure your continued existence on the "WHITE HAMSTER WHEEL". For years to come.

For those of you who suddenly remembered, "Hey! I'm White", with one flip of a switch in a voting booth you have saved "America". Or so you thought. There's nothing wrong with having good intentions. However, you know what they say the road to hell is paved with, right? Welcome to the wonderful world of ass-fault spreading.

I am, however, proud that you've stopped being politically correct and understood the necessity of voting for a like-minded leader of the "free" world. You also grew a set of ball's big enough to find a bat and knock back those who had grown enough of a set of balls that allowed them to call you racist. Boy did you have to grow a set in order to do that. But grow them you did and I'm proud of you. However, a set of balls isn't the only thing you need to grow. A deep sense (awareness) of the truth of things is an essential accessory to have when you have a big set of balls. Not only will having this awareness keep you from trying to take a bull by the horns that will prove impossible for you to control but it will also keep your balls from being trampled on by said bull.

I've made a lot of statements in this book by way of quotes. If you view these quotes closely, you'll see that they develop into a common theme. Here's a couple of things for you to consider. Consider them closely.

> "You can have economics without politics, but you can't have politics without economics."
> "An ignorant man is at the mercy of a fool."
> "You will either force or be forced."
> "Freedom is the manifestation of a particular state of mind."

There's a method to the madness here. You must know that there is gold at the end of the rainbow. The rainbow, damn it, does not end at 1600 Pennsylvania Avenue. It goes through there, but it doesn't end there. This I can tell you without doubt or contradiction.

Where does it end, you might ask. Good question. Easy answer.

It ends wherever you are whenever you fulfill your objective(s), providing that you have them. If you don't, well, there's always work at the "WHITE HAMSTER WHEEL"

And now it's time for a dose of reality.

SECTION FIVE
TEAR 'EM DOWN
(REPRISE)

August 12, 2017
A day that will go down in the annals of history.
This is the day when "America" made a complete ass of itself.
The day when assholes reigned supreme.
And all of them stank.
It is also a day when a brave woman died.
Needlessly.
Senselessly.

I wrote the "Perspectives" portion of "The 'Black' Section" in the Spring of 2016. This is important. I stated in the first chapter that this book was written in a two-year time span. And so it was. In the "Perspectives" section I wrote about the movement that was afoot that had/has the objective of Civil War memorabilia removal as its sole function. I wrote about statements from Abraham Lincoln. I asked the same questions that Donald Trump (and others *after* him) asked. All of this before Donald Trump walked down that escalator and into the office of President of the United States.

The first words of the second paragraph of the "Foreword" of this book is "This book took entirely too long to publish/ write". I've never written nor uttered no truer words.

In everyone's life there are times when they "sense" things. The thought, I am sure, has occurred to most people that as it relates to race, race relations, and racial issues in general, that something(s) is wrong. They can't put a finger, foot, or toe on it, but something's not right. And they are absolutely 100% correct. How is it that a "Black" man, who had the same eyes, ears, nose, and throat that a "White" man has be thought of as different from said "White" man?" How can a "White" man, who has the same eyes, ears, nose, and throat that a "Black" man has be thought of as different than said "Black" man. Bigots on both sides claim that the other is cursed and they both point to Biblical scripture as proof.

Fools!

Idiots!

Simpletons!

Nowhere in the Bible can.you find such nonsense. You are being used as useful idiots by mental magicians who are playing mind games with your brains because, fuck, you sure as hell, aren't using them.

People have died because of your idiocy.
People will die because of your idiocy.

The "black" will say that the "white" is the devil.
The white will say that the "black" is a monkey.
The both of you look, well - rather stupid.
Hey, "Black" man.
Hey, "Black" woman.
Do you actually think that "tearing down" compacted dirt edifices that you have been walking, running, and driving by; eating lunch in front of; watching the birds shit on; etc. is going to make "America" a better place?
Really?
Hey "White" man.
Hey "White" woman.
How many times have you passed these same lumps of dirt and spit with your children in tow? Did you stop and give them a history lesson? How much do you yourself knew about the history behind these gray rocks? Not just some history but the entirety of it. If you don't know, why? If you do, why haven't you put on your "Teacher's Cap"?

It's very easy to blame Donald Trump because he called out the foolishness that I told you would happen whenever you put on a pair of Nikes and marched. Besides, in order for you to continue these shenanigans you must have a scapegoat. Donald Trump seems very convenient. Especially when he's making it so easy.

It is also very easy for President Trump to say, "We all bleed the same blood." He is not the first or only person to say this. Very few people are aware of how deeply this statement is rooted in esoteric truth. On the basic level, however, it would be wise for our President as well as others who believe this sentiment to know and understand that no one sees blood until it's shed and by then it's too late. Blood that is out of sight is blood that is out of mind. It may improve your sight and your mental faculties if you would change your perception of what you view as truth. Know that if you change the way you look at things (and people) things (and people) will change the way they look.

Earlier in this book I asked the question will tearing down Confederate statues stop one black boy (or man) or one black girl (or woman) from getting killed by a gun that was held by a black hand. This question presupposes that the black men and women who suddenly want these statues gone really give a rat's ass about those boys and girls (and women and men) who are dying by guns being held by black hands. Look at this:

$$(12 \times 2) \div 2 - 1 =$$

Remember that?

Remember how some of you thought that this was the dumbest, lamest example anyone could give to attempt to prove a point? Do you remember why I chose that specific example? Let me do this one more time for the really, really "smart" people who think they have all the "answers".

The formula entitled "Order Of Operations" requires one to solve whatever operation is in parenthesis FIRST. It will be impossible to solve the problem otherwise because the essence of understanding Order Of Operations involves knowing and adhering to priorities. Which operation do you do first (The one in parenthesis, of course)? Do you know how to do this operation? If you don't, you can't (or shouldn't) go to the next step.

Once again, "black" man, "black" woman, which "operation" do you do first? Tear down a statue of a dead man riding a dead horse or attempt to keep a dead brained fool from ending a live life? There are a lot of black boys and black girls who, as of the writing of this book, have died by violent means. The hand that held the gun was the same hue as theirs's. Did the individual that killed them have Robert E. Lee on their mind? Were they a Nazi? A Klan member? Were they even a fucking Republican? I think not.

Oh, by the way.

Hey, "White people!"

Stop with this "I want to be on the front line fighting to end racism" garbage. This is not what you're doing so stop it. Stop it damn now. All you're doing is trying to let the most people that you can see that you're not a "racist". You want to prove that you're not a racist? Stop calling "black" people "black" and find out what their *true* legally and lawfully recognized identity is and call them that. If they don't know explain it to them. And while you're at it stop calling yourself "white". Look at something that's white. Does that look like you? I think not.

> "White means purity and purity means God and God
> means the ruler of the land."

Are you pure?

Are you God?

Are you the ruler of the land?

I think not. Regardless of the thinking of some of you.

Stop this.

Now!

In case you didn't understand the above, let me say (write) it so that you will. Once again, "White" people, this is not about race. It never has been. It is not now. This is about class. Understand that you are not "white" because of the pigment (or lack thereof) of your skin nor is this a gateway in by which you receive some perceived "privilege". You're "white" because a system was put in place (by some of your more diabolically intentioned ancestors) that was designed to peg you as such. The same way that "black" people's great ancestors didn't have a system that labled them as "black", your great ancestors didn't have such garbage that labled you as "white". You were either English, Irish, Spanish, German, Norsemen, Gauls, Visigoths, French, Greek, Roman, Spartan, etc., etc., etc. You were called a lot of things but you can bet your pink asses you were weren't called "white". This is a relatively new system produced by your relatively new relatives. You are today without doubt or contradiction what your ancient forefathers were.

There is only one race

The Human race.

Subdivided into two groups.

Asiatic and European.

Remembering and adhering to this will save you a lot of heartache and strife.

It may even save your life

Charlottesville, Virginia didn't have to happen.

But it did.

Read the book.

Change your mind

And heal.

SECTION SIX
IT ENDS WHERE IT BEGINS
IT BEGINS WHERE IT ENDS

I earlier wrote that the rainbow does not end at 1600 Pennsylvania Avenue. I meant that. While there is a seat of power at this address it is not the ultimate seat "in the East". One would do well to note that...

> ... true power lies behind the throne, because the throne is always connected to a network...

Always has been.
Always will be.
Always.
Once again, you must have a deep awareness of the truth of things. When I saw Henry Kissinger with Donald Trump, I was immediately made aware of the truth of things. When I knew one of Sarah Palin's chief advisors was Henry Kissinger, I was immediately made aware of the truth of things. Of course, this is not meant to imply anything disparaging about Henry Kissinger. I'm sure he is a fine man and has served the network well. 'Nuff said.

SECTION SEVEN
BEING MADE AWARE OF THE TRUTH
OF THINGS

This will be a short section. By now you should have mastered this information. By golly if not, this section will not be the only short reckoning in your life.

You would be correct in understanding that it would be correct to have a correct understanding of things. The *correct* understanding, yes. A *politically* correct understanding, no. Because truth needs no support, any attempt to bend it in order to make it "softer and fluffier" makes the bender look as foolish as the grotesque monstrosity that they reshaped the truth into. At least in the minds of those who know that "what it is is what it is".

Whatever happened to "Say what you mean and mean what you say"? Suffice it to say this works both ways. Never, ever, in a million-billion years accept watered down, stepped on, concentrated, siphoned through a strainer information as truth. If you have the slightest doubt that someone is not telling you "everything" as "everything" really is, investigate it with every resource you can put your eyes, ears, nose, and/or throat on. And put your hands, feet, and ass to work while you're at it. You've been played and made a fool of for a very long time and you still are. The only chance you have of turning this tide is to stop being taken in by slick talking politicians who promise you the sun, moon, and stars while only having the same thing that Pig Pen got for Halloween:

A damn rock.

Now don't get me wrong. There's nothing wrong with rocks. Some of my best friends are rocks. Some of my hottest nights were with rocks. Friends, dates, yes. Trick or treat, no.

Think about this for a moment. Go back and watch "It's The Great Pumpkin Charlie Brown". Key in and focus on Pig Pen and his situation. Understand that the phenomena of Pig Pen getting a rock happened *every time* the gang went to a house. Coincidence? You decide.

Think about it.

What is a rock?

Compacted dirt.

What was Pig Pen?

Compacted dirt (and proud of it).

The "truth" of things.

People treated Pig Pen the way they perceived that he perceived himself.

Compacted dirt.

Did he perceive himself that way?

Study Pig Pen.

Sometimes optics are everything. They definitely are the gateway to physical perception.

I'm not going to get too deep into politics. That's the next book. I am, however, going to tell you that if you don't stop believing that without *close* supervision of those that you vote into office you will be perceived as Pig Pen and you will get...... A rock.

A damned rock at that.

SECTION EIGHT
THE END

If, as I stated in the beginning chapter of this book, I have done what I set out to do by writing this book hopefully I made you at least begin to question the context of what has been a very perplexing problem for a great many people. Recent events dictate that the misunderstanding of the context of this construct called race has caused this same great many people to commit all sorts of mischief and mayhem, including murder. Gobbels spoke very vehemently about "The Big Lie" and yes, when it comes to race and how people, not only in America, but worldwide understand its meaning the truth of "The Big Lie" is very evident.

Consider:

> Black - The absence of light (Extreme end of the spectrum - subject to frequency)
> White - The absence of *hue* (Extreme end of the spectrum - subject to frequency)

If you hold to the literal concepts of these two alone, you are lacking the two things necessary for fundamental human existence. It is hue that protects you from over exposure to light. On an elementary level, it is light that keeps you from bumping into things that growl in the dark. The truth of the matter is that as it relates to your metaphysical self (higher - self), which is your true nature, there is no such thing as black or white. If you only would not forget that you have a higher - self you could move beyond the limitations of "black" and "white" as set down by the creators of the context behind this monstrosity of a construct.

> There is only ONE race.
> The HUMAN race.

> Therefore –
> There is no such thing as an interracial relationship.
> There is no such thing as interracial marriage.
> There is no such thing as an interracial child.
> All are members of the human family;
> Part and partial of the human race.

Yes. I am writing this section of this book after the Charlottesville, Virginia riots. And because of what I saw concerning this incident and incidents like it it is proof positive of the importance of the contents of this book.

I stated earlier that to every question there is an answer. I also stated that I would ask no question that I couldn't answer – correctly.

The truth of the first assertion is of a certainty. The truth of the second assertion is neither here nor there as it relates to your personal experiences concerning the subject matter discussed in this book. I mean, just how much anxiety have you experienced because of "race"? How much physical and/or mental confrontations/abuses have you experienced because of "race"? How much of the above have you placed on others? It may help to know that the best strategies on how to combat a problem, real or perceived, can be best developed and deployed when one has the truest insight on said problems existence – past, present, and future. "Race" just happens to be one such problem whose existence – past, present, and future, that most of humanity doesn't have *true* insight on. And that, in and of itself is a problem.

Have you really stopped to think
"black" man/woman
"white" man/woman
of the absurdity of marching, screaming, fighting, dying, etc., in order to achieve "social justice" by way of "racial equity" while at the same time perceiving and thus calling yourselves two contrasting concepts?

> "Black" people calling "white" people "white".
> "White" people calling "black" people "black".

Total opposites.

> Is "black" white?
> Is "white" black?

Know, understand, and accept the above question/statement for what it is. Any attempt to justify the above actions will make the attempt and the attempter look very, very foolish.

> There is only ONE race:
> The HUMAN race.

The term "humanity" encapsulates ALL people. It embraces ALL people. Regardless of phenotype.
Can you say that about "black"?
Can you say that about "white"?

Can you say "HUMAN" Lives Matter?

Would you say that?

If not, why?

Remember the above warning.

"White" people please. For the love of God or what or whoever you hold sacred; stop calling "black" people "black". Find out who they really are and help them honor that.

"Black" people please. For the love of God or what or whoever you hold sacred; stop calling "white" people "white". Find out who they really are and help them honor that.

If you believe as I do, there is one thing that binds all human beings and that is the capacity to love *without pre-existing conditions.*

A gift from our Creator.

It is a sad state of affairs, however, that we often exhibit this love only when catastrophic catastrophes occur.

The Klan member who is on the roof of his house with his wife and children and is three feet away from water totally submerging him and his family cares not if the boat that is approaching is being driven by a

"black" man; a

"Jew"; or a

"Trans-Sexual"

At least I would hope not.

Love, such as it is is light and when it is present it obliterates all darkness. Notice what I wrote here.

"Love is *light...*

Not "white".

...and when it is present it obliterates all *darkness.*"

Not *blackness.*

What this references is that what love is and what love does often transcends the boundaries of limited thought. So how does one manifest love?

Very simple answer.

Stop being human and become human.

PROBLEMS REVISED

Earlier I stated that you (Americans) are doing a piss poor job of problem solving. The evidence of this is so overwhelming it's comical. But no one's laughing. At least no one that you can see. Sadly, it's the same things over, and over, and over again. It's gotten to the point that some of you will see the problems coming and you won't even move the hell out of the way let alone try to stop them. And then there are those who scream, shout, cry, and roll on the ground trying to tell you what's coming and how to avoid it and what do you call them? What do you tell them?

"He's a conspiracy kook. Hey, shut up conspiracy kook!!!".

At some point you have to listen to somebody. Case in point:

In the 60's, 70's, and 80's how many people have written and/or performed songs iterating the problems of the country? Think about it.

Edwin Starr told you about War.

The Temptations told you about a ball of confusion.

Freda Payne told the country to bring the boys home.

Marvin Gaye ("Picket Lines. And Picket Signs. Don't
Punish me – With brutality.")

What's changed? Not a damned thing.

And don't forget about the four dead in Ohio.

So here we are talking about "race". A subject so ambiguous that at present no one can logically answer the question of what makes them a "race".

Hey "black man". What makes you "black"? *Who* made you "black"? Please don't say God.

Hey "white man". What makes you "white"? *Who* made you "white"? Please don't say God.

Hey Mr. Mexican. What makes you "Hispanic"? What makes you a language (Latin)?

Shall I ask the "Indian" what makes him "Native American" when he was here before either one of those Italian guys?

When did being just a plain ol' human become so passé?

Hey "black folks". Try this experiment.

The next time that you have a conversation describing someone or even if you are referring to someone who is "white", describe them or refer to them without saying that they're "white" (Oh, by the way. Just because I like "you people" let me pass along this little factoid. There is NO such thing as a Caucasian. I just thought I'd pass that along as a public service.). See how well you do.

Dr. Lune A. Teek

The point that I have been attempting to make through this book is that it is not "race" that is dividing the people of America. It is the ignorance of the truth of this subject and the people acting on this ignorance that is dividing America. As I have stated earlier it is impossible for "black" people and "white" people to say that they both are equal when the very premise of being "black" people and "white" people dictate they are opposites.

How the hell hard is this to understand?

"Oh, you're oversimplifying this. You don't understand."

To those of you who have the above sentiment I have the following:

Why would you kill a gnat with a sledgehammer, then pick up said gnat with a front-end loader?

Trying to equalize "black" people and "white" people is the ultimate paradox that without doubt or contradiction will remain a paradox until they both stop being something that makes their identity/existence paradoxical.

Hey. Here's an idea.

Try "Humanity".

That's it.

Nothing else.

Nothing at all.

Nothing.

Nada.

Zip.

Kaput.

Fini to.

Nien.

Stop.

Anyone who tries to add or take away from the above gets, as my dear, old, sainted grandmother would say, "the piss fire slapped out them."

AND NOW, THE LAST WORD

Regardless to how silly, stupid or downright pointless this book may seem or actually is to some, it does address a serious issue with a serious premise.

It is not about race.

It is all about class.

Always has been.

Always will be.

However, there is one thing that bridges the gap that "race" as well as "class" by their very natures must form. That one thing is - LOVE.

Let me explain.

242

The "true" context of race does not have a structured hierarchical format but does allow for a specific context of dichotomy.

> Dichotomy - 3a: Forking; esp.: repeated bifurcation.
> b: a system of branching in which the main axis forks repeatedly into two branches. c: branching of *an ancestrial line* into two *equal* diverging branches.
> (Webster's Dictionary - Emphasis mine)

There is only *one* race.
The human race.
Subdivided into *two* groups.
Asiatic and European.
Research "Asiatic Languages" and see what you get. Research "European Languages" and see what you get. Research the people who speak these languages.

In short, what people have been mistaking for race in reality is class and as long as they keep referencing themselves by names that define different stages/ranks/degrees of a diabolically crafted social, political, and legal hierarchical format it will be impossible for them to be about thus bring about the one thing that the physician needs to "heal thyself":

Love.

In your research of those who speak Asiatic languages understand that within their own spheres of reality and existence they are civilized people just as those who speak European languages. Neither is better than the other. Both look for and deserve the same thing:

Love.

The ancestors of these are the ancestors of yours. The problems you have today are the problems your ancestors overcame. The knowledge of those ancestors are the solutions to today's problems. Let me use one of those ancestrial problem - solution models for an example. Once upon a time...

... there was this guy named "Jesus" (Some dispute this name. They say that the letter "J" was not invented at the time this guy lived. For the sake of brevity, your sanity, and the storyline, just roll with it.). He looked around his town and saw how badly people were treating each other. He saw this as a problem.

Now this Jesus guy was well known for thinking outside the box; plus the fact that he would do really cool stuff that most of the people of the town took to calling "miracles". So, one day while he was seeing someone really getting the crappy end of the stick, then getting hit over the head with said crap ended stick, Jesus said these words to his crew (Excuse me, "disciples"):

> "Do unto others as you would have
> others do unto you."

In all actuality, the sum of man's (and woman's) problems could be eliminated immediately if the sum of man (and woman) would adhere to this one sentence. How? Because this one sentence, if adhered to, forces one to see others as themselves. Not as they see themselves, but *as* themselves. Here's an example:

It's easy for someone to hit someone else on the head with a hammer. Just draw back and, PING!!!! Didn't feel a thing, right? Consider this, however. What would happen if everything that you did to someone had the same effect on you? Now, go back to the hammer. How many times can you hit yourself on the head with a hammer? How hard?

Trust and believe. If you knew you would feel the same pain someone would feel if you hit them on the head with a hammer you would have a Nerf ball in your hand instead of a hammer. And you'd be very careful with it too.

The truth of the matter is that every problem in existence (including bigotry) has a solution. Remember, there is nothing new under the sun, nor on top of it. All humanity must do is love itself enough to do the work that it takes to apply the correct solutions to correctly identified problems.

If you truly believe that God so loved the world (you) that He gave His only begotten Son (Jesus), then you should know the truth as to why He did this. Simply put, Jesus came to man (and woman) to explain, then show them how to solve their own problems and to not create new ones in the process. Somehow, not surprisingly, all the "Amens" and the "Hallelujahs" people were throwing all over the place drowned out this aspect of the Father and the Son's objective. Find it, pick it up, dust it off, and put it into practice. And if you do it just right, who knows? Someone might mistake you for Jesus.

God so loved you that He gave you life. It's yours. Think about this. You are alive now because someone thousands of years ago lived then died. Within you is the sum total of wisdom left by those who lived thousands of years before you. Therefore, if you think about it, your life is worth more to others than it is to yourself. And in this mystery lies the essence of life;

The essence of existence;
The essence of Love;
The essence of The Cross.

Forgive me for getting all religious on you. I really didn't mean to, but there is a time and place for everything and this was as good a time as any.

I cannot say when this book will reach your hands or in fact, it ever will. Sad as it truly is, whenever or if it does, we will still be torturing each other with the same issues that we are allowing to divide us. This is because we will refuse to see the obvious because we will refuse to do the obvious:

"...Be ye not of this world.
but be ye transformed by
the renewing of your mind."

When I use the term "we", I am not speaking of we as a nation called America. I am speaking of we as a planetary species called "humanity". It is of no account if "black" people and "white" people can live in harmony in America but not in France, Spain, or Italy. It does no good if dark hued "black" people and lighter hued "black" people in America can see themselves as one and be viewed by the government as one but dark hued "black" people and lighter hued "black" people in Brazil cannot.

You have a lot of work to do. First and foremost, on yourselves, Even that cannot begin until you adhere to the above quote reportedly stated by the Apostle Paul a few centuries ago.

"... be ye transformed by the renewing
of your mind."

Anyone can renew their mind at any time about anything. All it takes is for one to want to do so and the will to manifest that want into reality. After that, the rest is simple.

THE LAST SECTION

So now it's on you. I've done my part. I've given you what you need to begin to make a serious start on changing the world and achieving that elusive state of mind and being that everyone calls "Peace". Trust and believe, it is not unobtainable. How long it takes, like everything else, depends totally on you. If you think your condition can be better, make it so. If you think that the condition of the world can be better, make it so. I've done the hard part. Now you must do your part. You now know the truth about what is dividing America as well as what's not. The time to do something about it is now. I'm depending on you.

I'm depending on you because I believe in you.

If I didn't, I wouldn't have written this book.